Boris Groys
Particular Cases

# Boris Groys

# Particular Cases

Sternberg Press

# Contents

# Methodological Introduction

When a theorist writes about individual artists and artworks, the reader's first expectation is usually that the theorist is applying his or her general theory of art to certain particular cases. As the reader of the texts collected here will see, that is not my approach. The reason is simple enough: I do not have any general theory of art to apply. Yes, I have written about art for some time, and yes, I write theoretical texts. But that does not mean that I have any theory of art. Rather, my writing moves from one particular case to other particular cases. In this sense my writing follows the trajectory of English law rather than that of French law. I do not arrive at particular judgments from some general principles but, rather, keep in mind my earlier judgments when I have to make a new one. Thus, I try to remain faithful to my former writing—and not to a general theory.

The judgments made here are not value judgments. The reason for this is also simple: I cannot be critical—I like everything I see. So I avoid negative judgments, but I also avoid positive judgments because those could produce the wrong impression that I like something more than I like everything else. That is why I do not write about topics like the aesthetic impact of a particular artwork, its chances on the art market, or the career of the artist who produced this work. I think that other people have better judgment concerning these and many other related things. Instead, I try to follow an impulse that a particular artwork gives me. Certain artworks and artists push my imagination and thinking in a particular direction—and I try to follow, to keep going further and further in this direction, to see how strong the initial impulse was and how far it brings me. It is not a method of hermeneutics; I do not try to approach the artwork and its "content" or "message." Rather, I try to go away from the artwork and look at the world by the gaze that is not quite my own gaze anymore because it was modified, changed by the encounter with this particular artwork. I try to understand art as a mind-changing, gaze-changing practice—as if contemporary artists, being secular through and through, can still produce metanoia in the soul of the spectator.

Of course, not every artwork offers the possibility to be seen this way. However, the selection of texts collected in this book is not dictated by my choice alone. Each piece of writing—and, especially, art writing—is reactive more than active: one is asked to write about a certain artist and one does it if one feels capable of doing it. But the central role of the accident in cultural production—be it art making or writing—would be a good topic for another book.

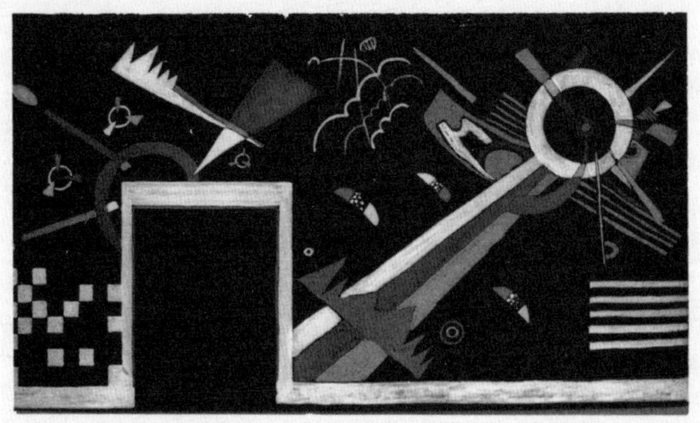

Wassily Kandinsky, sketch for a mural for the Juryfreie
Kunstschau, Berlin, 1922

1
Wassily Kandinsky
Art as Rhetoric

In light of recent discussions about art as knowledge production and the ways art should or could be taught, it seems fitting to look back at the early days of modernism. Avant-garde art was not yet taken for granted then, having instead to be legitimized, interpreted, and taught. One influential example of such a strategy of legitimization is Wassily Kandinsky's *Concerning the Spiritual in Art* (1911). The book posits an equivalence between art production, art theory, and art teaching, in order to render art rational and scientific, with the aim of establishing it as an academic discipline. Over the course of his artistic career, Kandinsky made various attempts to give an institutional form to his ideas. Der Blaue Reiter (The Blue Rider)—both the group and the almanac of the same name—can be seen as the first such attempt. Following his return to Russia from Munich at the outbreak of World War I, and especially throughout the postrevolution years, Kandinsky engaged in extensive institutional activity, teaching as a professor at Vkhutemas (Higher Art and Technical Studios, from 1918), as well as founding and directing the Moscow Institute of Artistic Culture (InKhuK, 1920–21) and GAKhN (State Academy for the Scientific Study of Art, 1921). During his time at the Bauhaus, from his appointment in 1922 until its closure in 1933, he pursued his analysis of art as a science and academic discipline, as reflected in *Point and Line to Plane*, a theoretical treatise published by the Bauhaus in 1926.

The rigor and determination with which Kandinsky pursued the academicization of art has often been overlooked due to misunderstandings caused by his choice of words. His use of "the spiritual" is a prominent example, since it implies certain religious themes and attitudes that he did not necessarily share. Rather than "the spiritual," it would be better to speak here of "the affective." Kandinsky's book begins with a distinction between art as the representation of eternal reality and art as a means of conveying emotions and moods. Right at the beginning of the book, Kandinsky claims that the representation of external reality leaves us cold as viewers. He describes a typical exhibition of the time: "Animals in sunlight or shadow, drinking, standing in water, lying on the grass; near to, a Crucifixion by a painter who does not believe in Christ; flowers; human figures sitting, standing, walking; often they are naked; many naked women, seen foreshortened from behind; apples and silver dishes. [...] The vulgar herd stroll through the rooms and pronounce the pictures 'nice' or 'splendid.' Those who could speak have said nothing, those who could hear have heard nothing. This condition of art is called 'art for art's sake.'"[1] This description clearly shows that what Kandinsky found irritating about naturalist painting was its formalism. When the motif is dictated from outside, all that matters is *how* it is executed—the formal skill of the artist. Kandinsky opposes this formalist vision of art: only when one has defined *what* art is can one inquire into the *how*.

For Kandinsky then, art is a medium for conveying affects. Rather than portraying external facts, art should visualize and transport inner states of mind. Consequently, he makes inner necessity the criterion for evaluating art: a picture is successful if it adequately expresses specific emotions and moods. And if a picture does this, it is of no consequence whether or not it is a faithful rendering of external reality. A picture may be figurative or abstract—what matters is that it uses only those forms and colors needed for the visualization and efficient transmission of certain emotions. The greatest misconception with regard to the notion of inner necessity is that it is often understood in Expressionist terms, as an inner urge compelling the artist to paint this picture and not that one. The most important aspect of the argument is thus overlooked: for Kandinsky, the emotions and moods reside not in the person but in the picture. The ability of the picture to express and transmit certain moods to the viewer has nothing to do with whether or not the artist "actually" experiences the mood in question. Which is why Kandinsky later spoke of inner necessity in more functional terms: it is purely a question of which means an artist considers necessary to infect viewers with a mood, to create an emotion in them. The artist is a specialist in the production and transmission of emotions, not their subject. Looking back, Kandinsky states that "brainwork" needs to "outweigh the intuitive part of creativity" ending, perhaps, with "the total exclusion of 'inspiration,'" so that future artworks are "created by calculation" alone.[2]

In this light, it is clear why Kandinsky equated art and art theory: he wanted to develop a visual rhetoric that would be similar to discursive rhetoric. One should not forget that rhetoric was one of the principle academic disciplines. Ever since the early Sophist schools in ancient Greece, there has been an interest in how particular beliefs, views, emotions, and moods can be transmitted to others. This question was (and remains) especially important to lawyers. Before deciding to make a name for himself as a painter, Kandinsky worked as a lawyer. So he knew only too well that the truth of a matter and the way this same truth is communicated are two different things. The communication obeys rules of its own, and it was the rules of art, understood as a visual rhetoric, that Kandinsky sought to reveal through his own

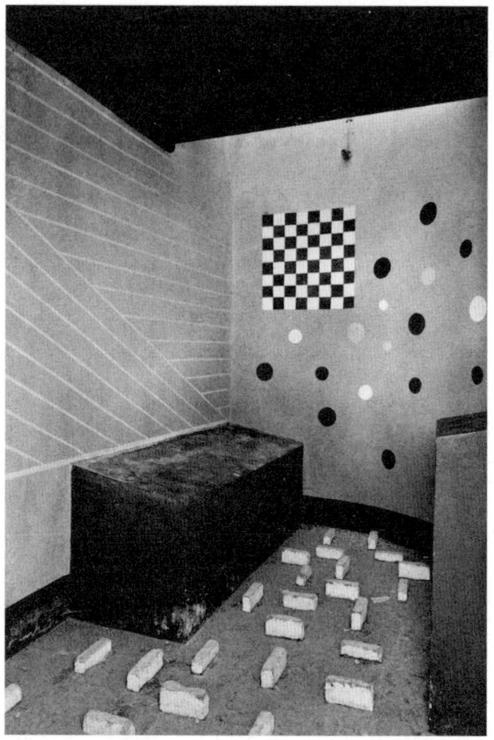

Prison cell designed by Alphonse Laurencic,
Barcelona, 1939

art and writing. This task is indeed both artistic and scientific. If an artistic portrayal of affects can be "calculated," then it can also be taught and learned. All of Kandinsky's paintings can thus be understood as teaching materials, examples of how visual rhetoric works. This is also the significance of the remarks on the psychological effects of colors and forms that make up the greater part of *Concerning the Spiritual in Art*. They can be read as prolegomena to the art science of the future, framed as a study of the rules of visual rhetoric.

Like Sophism before it, rhetoric has always been viewed with suspicion on account of its ability to serve evil ends. Which is why Kandinsky repeatedly underlined the artist's ethical duty to make sure his rhetorical forces serve the good. As history was to show, this warning was not unfounded. During the Spanish Civil War in the 1930s, Alphonse Laurencic, a French artist and architect of Slovenian origin, used the ideas in *Concerning the Spiritual in Art* to decorate cells at a prison in Barcelona where Francoists captured by the Republicans were held. Each cell looked like an avant-garde art installation. With the compositions of color and form in the cells, Laurencic aimed to cause the prisoners to experience disorientation, depression, and deep sadness. To achieve this, he relied on Kandinsky's theories of color and form. And prisoners held in these psychotechnic cells really did report extreme negative moods and suffering due to their visual surroundings. One can say, then, that Laurencic had a better grip on the meaning of Kandinsky's treatise than many Expressionist-minded artists and art theorists, as he used Kandinsky's ideas not expressively, but for a purpose— however dubious this purpose may appear in retrospect.

Traditionally, rhetoric has an implacable enemy: the claim to truth. Ever since Plato, it has been asserted that truth has no need of additional rhetoric, being persuasive on the basis

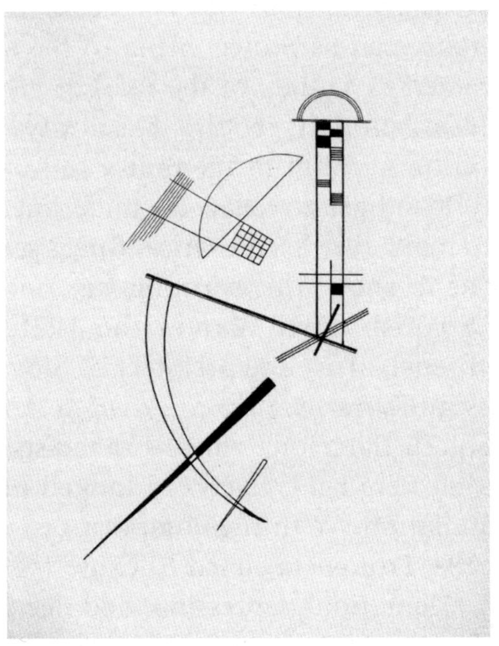

Wassily Kandinsky, *Double sound — cold tension
of the straight lines, warm tension of the curved lines,
the rigid to the loose, the yielding to the compact,
from Point and Line to Plane*, 1926

of it own immanent evidence. In his first major treatise, Kandinsky claims that the effect of a picture on the viewer does not depend on the artist's ability to truthfully portray the external world. A picture makes its impact solely thanks to the emotions it produces in the viewer via its composition—i.e., by specific deployment of purely painterly means. Later, Kandinsky was confronted with another, far more radical claim to truth: both the art of the Russian avant-garde (in particular the Suprematism of Kazimir Malevich) and geometric abstraction in the West (like that of Piet Mondrian) once more laid claim to pictorial truth. But this time it was not the truth of referentiality, but that of self-referentiality: now, the picture was to explicitly manifest both itself and its medium. Kandinsky's response was not unlike the strategy he had already developed in *Concerning the Spiritual in Art*; he wrote *Point and Line to Plane* as a critique of the new avant-garde dogmatism.

Instead of accepting the geometric constructions of the radical avant-garde as entities that are immediately evident, Kandinsky analyzed their geometric lines and figures as vehicles that transport specific affects. The point, in all of its variations (square, circle, etc.), is thus interpreted not as an elementary self-contained form, but as an element removed from its usual context in writing where it marks a moment of interruption: silence in the middle of speech.[3] This meaning remains even when the point is placed on the "basic plane" of the picture. Moreover this independent position of the point, performing an interruption beyond what is usual, is interpreted by Kandinsky as a "useless, revolutionary state of affairs,"[4] not a neutralization but a radicalization of the usual function of the point. Kandinsky de facto interprets Malevich's *Black Square* (1915)—a black square inside a white square—as a symbol of the ultimate silence: death.

The straight line, on the other hand, is interpreted as the manifestation of a specific constant force. Kandinsky writes, "The entire field of straight lines is lyric, a fact which can be explained by the effect of a single force from the outside."[5] Surprising as it may seem at first, this interpretation of strict geometry that negates its claim to self-evidence then permits Kandinsky to speak of jagged and curved lines as "dramatic" because they give the impression of being influenced by a number of different forces. Thanks to this transition from the lyric to the dramatic, the supposedly self-evident geometric construction is subsumed as a special case under the concept of composition. Once again, the principle of inner necessity prevails: rather than contenting himself with geometric forms alone, the artist must use all forms that allow him to express and convey specific constellations of forces and the corresponding affects.

Kandinsky is especially elegant and persuasive in how he undermines the avant-garde's claim to address the specific media of the individual arts, in particular the medium of painting (a claim that, after World War II, was to extend far beyond these avant-garde beginnings, thanks especially to Clement Greenberg's championing of the "flatness" of the "modern picture"). But Kandinsky shows that one can only speak meaningfully about the medium of the canvas if this basic plane is understood as infinite, or at least of indeterminate size. The basic plane of any individual painting however only ever has a single finite configuration, a specific form with its own expressive force, being limited by two vertical and two horizontal borders that are "lyric."[6] Moreover, the picture plane may be shaped like a square or dominated more by horizontal and vertical borders. Each of these configurations of the picture plane has a specific mood-generating effect. This critique of the usual concept of the medium, or the mediality of the medium, is indeed a profound and radical one. The medium only becomes the message if the medium is infinite—which it can never be. As something finite, the medium is subject to its respective particular form.

Kandinsky practiced his critique of art's claim to truth in the name of a visual rhetoric understood as a positive science. This visual rhetoric aimed to study the artistic means that transport specific affects—with the goal of accurately calculating the emotional impact of art. But like discursive rhetoric before it, whose failure led to its demise as an academic discipline, visual rhetoric was not destined to last. Nonetheless, Kandinsky has shown that every artistic form is emotionally charged and thus also manipulative. There is no such thing as pure, autonomous, self-referential, and totally transparent art. For Kandinsky, behind all art there reigns a dark force that manipulates the viewer's emotions. The role of the artist consists in taking control of this force— which can only be achieved partially. But at least the artist is capable of exploring the workings of this force—and thus focusing attention on it as such. Kandinsky's visual theory remains just as relevant as it was in his day—however, not as a positive science, but as a critical analysis of art's claim to truth.

Notes

1.   Wassily Kandinsky, *Concerning the Spiritual in Art*, trans. M. T. H. Sadler (Mineola, NY: Dover Publications, 1977), 3.

2.   Cited in Max Bill, introduction to Wassily Kandinsky, *Über das Geistige in der Kunst* (Bern: Benteli Verlag, 1952), 10–11 (trans. Nicholas Grindell).

3.   Wassily Kandinsky, *Point and Line to Plane*, trans. Howard Dearstyne and Hilla Rebay (Mineola, NY: Dover Publications, 1979), 25.

4.   Ibid., 28.

5.   Ibid., 67.

6.   Ibid., 129.

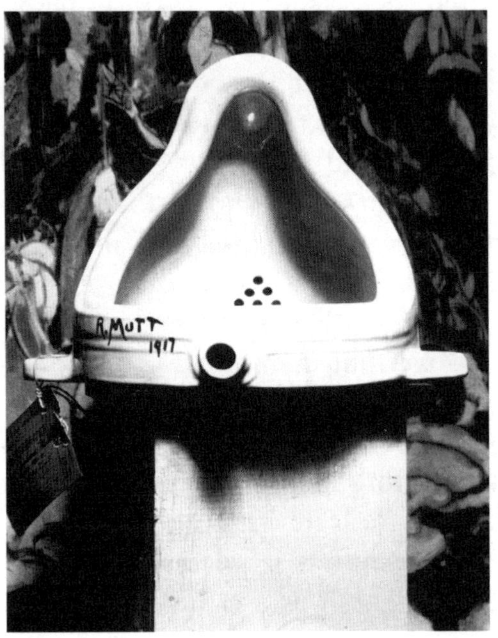

Alfred Stieglitz, *Fountain by Marcel Duchamp*, 1917

2
Marcel Duchamp
Absolute Art

While Marcel Duchamp's artistic practice has served—especially in the last few decades—as one of the main reference points for contemporary art, or at least contemporary Western art, the technique of the readymade is still understood as one particular artistic technique among many. However, the use of readymades was, for Duchamp, merely a way of revealing the mechanism of production of the new as such—not only in art, but also in culture in general. It is especially true for the cases in which Duchamp chose to make no changes to the physical appearance of the profane objects he used. When a culturally valorized object can be physically distinguished from everyday things, the temptation arises—altogether understandable from a psychological standpoint—to interpret this physical difference as the reason for the discrepancy in value between the "art object" and those ordinary things. When, however, one refrains from physically transforming the object, the question of the mechanism that produces a revaluation of values is posed in an appropriately radical form.

Friedrich Nietzsche was the first to posit the revaluation of values as the principle informing cultural innovation in all its forms. According to Nietzsche, culture functions by distributing and redistributing values—and not by merely producing new objects. Hence Nietzsche did not formulate a new "philosophical system" but revaluated "profane" life (the Dionysian, erotic impulse) and the will to power—and devaluated traditional philosophical thinking as such. In like manner, Duchamp did not offer any new way of art production but revaluated objects of profane life—and devaluated the traditional métiers of art. Both Nietzsche's philosophical discourse and Duchamp's art practice exemplify the breakthrough to a new—modern as well as contemporary—understanding of innovation.

The advantage of the readymade technique consists in the fact that both levels of value—of traditional culture and the profane world—are clearly displayed in every individual work. Both are present in the readymade at the same time, but they by no means fuse; they are not canceled out and do not build a unity. Their irreconcilability determines the way the work is produced and received. The readymade is usually interpreted as a sign of the total freedom of the artist, who is supposedly free to put anything in an artistic context and thus valorize it. None of the traditional criteria of quality, beauty, or expressivity apply any more. Whether something is classified as art or nonart seems to be the result, in the final analysis, of a free decision taken by the artist or certain social institutions concerned with art, such as museums, private galleries, art criticism, or academic art history. But is the decision to reevaluate artistic values really free? To answer this question let us consider the opposite case. Let us consider the case of a "normal" artist who follows the established rules of artistic production.

At first glance, nothing seems to be easier than to produce art that can unambiguously be identified as such; indeed, such art is constantly being produced. Most of it, however, is not deemed valuable and worthy to be admitted to the museum, and is not considered original or innovative. Instead, it is treated as kitsch. The decision to use profane things in an artistic context is thus not free but compulsive: our culture incessantly devalorizes art that looks like art, and it valorizes art that does not look like art. The revaluation of values is a principle that regulates our cultural practice—independent of our subjective decisions. Nietzsche and Duchamp did not invent this principle. They simply made it explicit—by following it in the most explicit way.

This cultural logic of revaluation of values is dictated by the modern, secular, post-Christian desire to find a cultural signifier for the totality of the world—after the death of God. For Nietzsche it was the will to power. For Duchamp, a urinal—his "Buddha of the Bathroom" (as Louise Norton described it at the time). In both cases the sign for totality was constructed in such a way that the valorized (philosophically, artistically) level coexisted with the profane level—without being mixed but also without either being clearly distinguishable. The will to power became conceptualized and integrated into the philosophical discourse—but remained somehow wild. The urinal was displaced and put into the artistic context, but it remained identifiable and potentially usable.

Many of Duchamp's contemporaries thought that his readymades heralded the "end of art." They understood the act of assigning a profane thing the same value as valorized works of art above all as a declaration that not only all the art of the past, but also all artistic practice of the present, is useless and without value. Art seemed to be totally absorbed by the profane realm. However, the totality can never be reached by a simple disappearance of one of its parts. As Duchamp's readymades began to assume a place of honor in art history, their interpretations began to put the accent less on the devalorization of art than on the valorization of the profane; increasingly, therefore, a pessimistic tone gave way to a quite optimistic one. The readymade now seemed to offer the possibility of raising the profane realm as a whole to the level of valuable art. However, the aesthetic of the readymade has long since ceased to appear original or innovative.

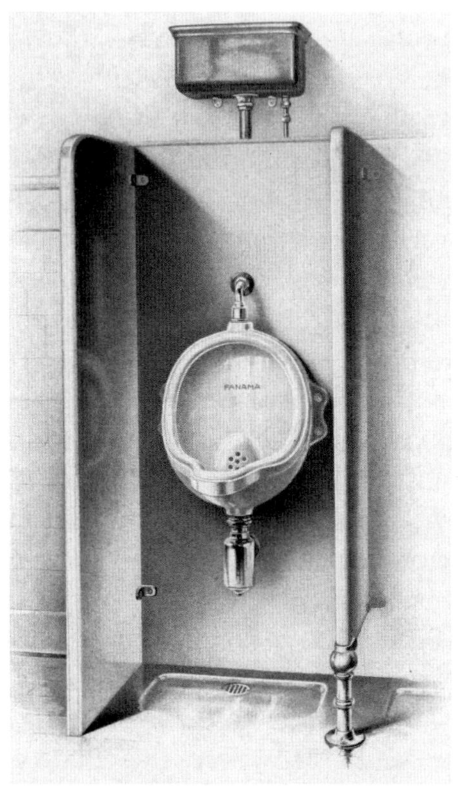

"Panama" urinal, from the J. L. Mott Iron
Works catalogue, 1908

Duchamp not only opened up a new possibility for artistic practice; he simultaneously eliminated this possibility, since the art of the readymade necessarily appeared—after some time—as conventional, trivial, and even uninteresting. To keep the path taken by Duchamp open, artists shifted the discussion from the plane of cultural-economic innovation to that of personal content, interest, and desire.

Accordingly, contemporary criticism tends to seek out, before all else, the hidden, unconscious, libidinal forces that are said to have dictated Duchamp's choice of readymades. It is true that we can easily interpret his choice of a urinal for *Fountain* (1917), and others among his readymades as well, in a broadly understood psychoanalytic context, and also with an eye on his close ties to the Surrealists, in the context of their common interest in the objet trouvé. (The chosen model was a standard one by J. L. Mott Iron Works, whose name seems to have provided inspiration for the R. Mutt pseudonym.) When we do, the transgression of the value boundary between valorized art and the profane realm becomes no more than a secondary effect of the secret labor of desire, not a strategic goal established from the very start. This displacement of interpretation from the plane of conscious strategy to that of the unconscious and desire explains why it has proven possible to continue the production of readymades after Duchamp.

If we assume that every readymade simply represents the profane realm as such, then there can indeed be only one readymade: anything at all, in the context of art, can represent the whole profane realm. A single readymade, such as Duchamp's *Fountain*, would suffice to prove that value hierarchies have been abolished, and would mark the end of art or, as one likes, the end of the profane. It is a different story if readymades manifest artists' hidden desires, their unconscious rituals and fetishistic fixations. In that case the profane realm, ceasing to be homogeneous, becomes the field of articulation of the unconscious.

Duchamp's aesthetic of the readymade—considerably modified, of course—became, for all practical purposes, the dominant aesthetic of our time, since it offered art the possibility of once again becoming powerfully expressive, individual, and rich in content. Duchamp himself wanted to reduce all levels of expressivity and introduce into the valorized cultural context an object that, situated as it was outside the artistic tradition, did not belong to the complex system of cultural associations, meanings, and references. This strategy typified the classic avant-garde approach, which preferred to make use of nontraditional, profane, "insignificant" objects to get rid of the ballast of traditional cultural symbolism. However, since structuralism, psychoanalysis, and Wittgenstein's theory of language—and other theories that in one way or another operate with the concept of the unconscious—have convincingly shown that neutral, purely profane things do not exist, and that everything has a meaning, even though it may not be apparent to a superficial gaze, the original avant-garde's orientation toward a pure, meaningless thing, uncontaminated by culture, would no longer seem to be possible.

Today's art, as a consequence, is once again understood and described in terms of artistic individuality and expressive power, the significance of the ideas it expresses, the richness of the individual world it creates, and the uniqueness and depth of the individual artistic experience that finds expression in it. In this perspective, the technique of the readymade turns out to be a new version of the international art salon, which is reminiscent of the late nineteenth-century Paris salons. The sole difference is that the goals of subjective expression and relevant content are now attained by way of a particular strategy for selecting objects from the profane world, not by their representation on canvas or in stone.

Yet it would surely be unfair to reduce the innovative practices of contemporary art to such psychological trivialities. Today's art diverts the observer's attention from the chosen objects in order to direct it toward the context in which they initially function. New art after Duchamp is concerned with the previously neglected social, political, semiotic, or mass-media contexts of art. In this case, an artist's choice of object is not dictated by personal preference, but becomes subject to cultural-economic logic: this choice is supposed to draw attention to broader contexts in which art appears and functions. Here again the attention is shifted from normative, "autonomous" spaces to the profane contexts of art and the profane ways it is used. Every profane space in which art is situated becomes a sign for the total space of life, social activity, and political struggle.

It can be argued that our culture is still determined by the desire to find a signifier for totality under the conditions of our post-religious, secular age. To find such a signifier for totality does not mean to valorize everything profane—or to devalorize everything traditionally valuable. Rather, it means to find an object, a concept, or a space that would be valuable and profane at the same time—and reveal the tension between these two value levels without bringing them to any kind of unity, to a synthesis. Even if both Nietzsche and Duchamp understood themselves as being programmatically post-Christian, their strategies of revaluation of values were seen as a way to find the signifier for totality, to imitate—to a certain extent—Christian symbolism itself.

Let us consider the discussion of Christianity by Søren Kierkegaard in his 1844 work *Philosophical Fragments*. Kierkegaard states that the figure of Christ initially looked

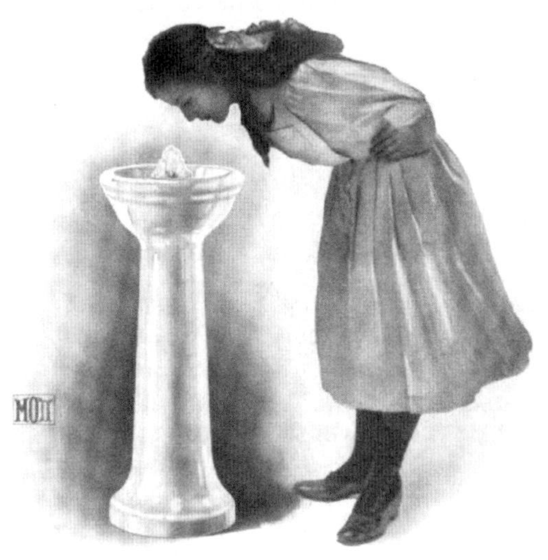

"Puro" drinking fountain, from the J. L. Mott
Iron Works catalogue, 1913

like that of every other ordinary human being in his historical time. In other words, an objective spectator at that time, confronted with the figure of Christ, could not find any visible concrete difference between Christ and an ordinary human being, any visible difference that could suggest that Christ was not simply a man, but that he was also a God. For Kierkegaard, Christianity is based on the impossibility of visually, empirically recognizing Christ as God. Furthermore, this implies that Christ is *really* new, and not merely different. Here, the values are newly distributed without and beyond production of any particular new image: an ordinary human being acquires infinite value. We put the figure of Christ into the context of the divine without recognizing his figure as divine—and that is new. Therefore, for Kierkegaard, the only medium for a possible emergence of the new is the ordinary, the "non-different," the similar.

If we look more closely at the figure of Jesus Christ as described by Kierkegaard, it is striking that it appears to be quite similar to what we now call "readymade." Here too we are dealing with newness beyond identifiable difference—now understood as difference between the artwork and the ordinary, profane thing. Accordingly, we can say that Duchamp's *Fountain* is a kind of Christ among things, and the art practice of the readymade a kind of Christianity in art. Christianity takes the figure of a human being and puts it, unchanged, in the context of religion, the pantheon of the traditional Gods. The museum—an art space or the whole art system—also functions as a place where newness beyond difference can be produced or staged. The figure of Christ is a signifier in which the level of the profanely human coincides, but does not merge, with the level of the divine. The same can be said of Duchamp's readymades. The new artwork looks really new only if it resembles, in a certain sense, every other ordinary, profane thing. And the art space can be seen as new only if it resembles any other profane space.

Kierkegaard called Christianity the "absolute religion" because it was not based on any objectively provable difference between Christ and any other human being. In the same sense, one can see Duchamp as opening a way for the "absolute art" that valorizes the profane and devalorizes the traditionally valuable at the same time—without abolishing either of them.

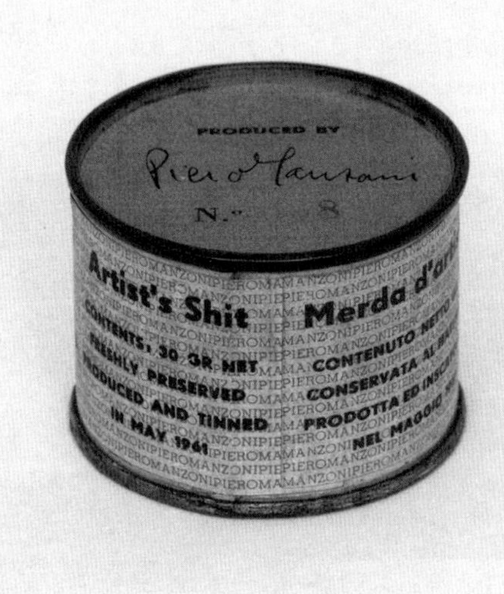


Piero Manzoni, *Artist's Shit no. 68*, 1961

3
Piero Manzoni
The Inner Life of a Can of Preserves

Few works of art in the twentieth century have gained real cult status. After Marcel Duchamp's *Fountain* (1917) and Andy Warhol's *Campbell's Soup Cans* (1962), we can count Piero Manzoni's *Artist's Shit* (1961) as one of them. The fact that some of the best-known modern artworks involve everyday objects is clearly no accident. There's something magical about the ability to represent these objects as out of the ordinary and even make them into a big success. We get the feeling we are faced with a miracle—and only what is perceived as a miracle can become a cult object.

In this respect, Manzoni's work differs from the works by Duchamp and Warhol. *Artist's Shit* does not fit the category of the readymade. It is not a question of selecting just one example of a mass-produced object and calling it an artwork. Instead, Manzoni produced ninety cans of artist's shit, a number that potentially could have been increased. So here we have a new mass product, a new brand, with a market range not necessarily limited to the art world. This is also the difference between the can of preserves produced by Manzoni and the replicas of the Campbell's soup cans or Brillo steel wool turned out by Warhol in his day. Both Duchamp and Warhol play with the boundary between "high" art and mass culture, which appears obvious to both. To Manzoni, though, this boundary is far less evident. He launched his brand of cans of preserves in the same way a designer would launch a new collection, and yet *Artist's Shit* is essentially different from every kind of art design. In this work, the crucial element is not its form but its content. And here lies another important difference separating Manzoni from Duchamp and Warhol. The latter are interested in the form of modern mass culture, but Manzoni is interested in the content. Here, however, the content is not presented as theme, narrative, or ideology, but as matter. In this sense, *Artist's Shit* is above all an ironic comment, at the same time perfectly accurate, on the main strategy of modernism, which explicitly thematizes the materiality of the artwork.

The dominant concern of art is usually its relationship to reality. For a long time this relationship was understood in mimetic terms, as the artist's ability to represent reality faithfully. Ever since modern art rejected mimesis as its main goal, the specific materiality of the work of art itself—the material it is made out of—has been the sole element relating art to reality. And this is the reason why modern art is tenaciously anchored to the thematization of its own materiality: through this, modern art acquires a truth of its own, if by truth we understand its relationship to reality. In this way, abstract art loses its status as pure form and gains content—not a literary or narrative content, but a real and material one. Every modern artwork can thus be interpreted as a can of preserves whose content is concealed in the form of the artwork itself. Through its form, modern art seeks constantly to refer to this hidden material content. This is why Clement Greenberg wanted a painting to look flat, without depth, to reveal the flatness of the canvas covered, and therefore concealed, by paint. Numerous modern sculptors similarly thematize the material their sculptures are made out of rather than concealing it in the outward form of the sculpture.

But the whole laborious work of modern art (which has only approximated the concealed materiality of art without ever expressing it directly) is manifested as superfluous by the gesture performed by Manzoni in *Artist's Shit*. Manzoni explicitly states the content of his work of art: shit. The pure relationship between form and content, so long sought by modern art, has apparently been achieved, and in the simplest way: the surface of the work of art provides exhaustive information about its hidden content. This information appears to be convincing, clear, definitive. But why, precisely? There are some important psychological reasons. When something is concealed, almost automatically we are led to conjecture that it is something disagreeable, disgusting, and potentially dangerous. Our attitude toward what is hidden is by definition an attitude of suspicion—a suspicion that can be suspended only when it is confirmed. Only when the hidden content is revealed to be just as disgusting and dangerous as we had thought it to be all along (or even more so) are we willing to believe it.

The truth of what is hidden therefore becomes credible only when it is an ugly, disagreeable truth. The revelation of the inner content succeeds when it takes the form of an unmasking. In a way, we have always harbored the suspicion that everything sold in cans is properly shit, because we have no idea where the contents come from. On the other hand, the general public has had the idea that modern art, since its inception, is real shit sold at steep prices—in other words, that modern art is a gigantic fraud, that it consists in selling some piece of waste for the price of gold. But this is just what Manzoni proposes to do: sell cans of preserves that he guarantees contain his shit at a price amounting to their weight in gold. The attraction of the work thus lies primarily in the fact that it confirms directly and unequivocally all the antimodernist suspicions of the general public. In this respect, Manzoni belongs to a long tradition of modern art, which has always managed to turn antimodernist prejudice to its

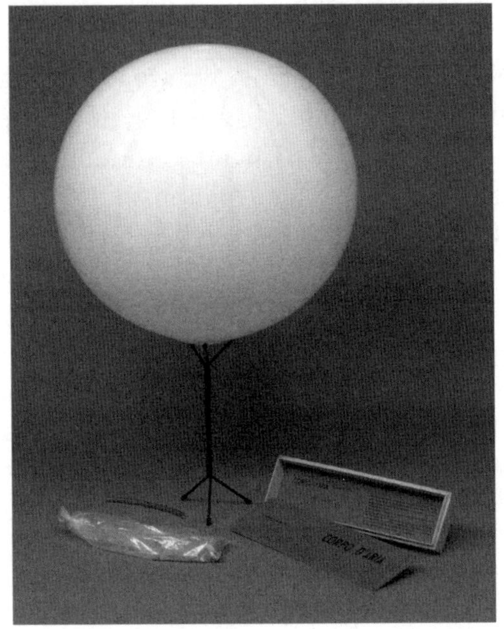

Piero Manzoni, *Body of Air no. 28*, 1959–60

own advantage. Many modern artists, from Marinetti, Dalí, and Picasso, to Duchamp and Warhol, have played ironically with antimodernist propaganda, which always represents the artist as con man, manipulator, and illusionist. And it is hardly an accident that it is these very artists who are now immensely popular.

But we should not be deceived by the seeming relationship between form and content in *Artist's Shit*. Manzoni only apparently supersedes the gap between form and content. In fact, he radicalizes it. The question is not whether the cans of preserves Manzoni sells really contain shit or not, as has recently been conjectured. The crucial point is that Manzoni thematizes and reinforces the taboo that prevents the viewer from knowing what material a work of art is really made of. Generally, the work of art that confronts the viewer in a museum or gallery is there only to be seen, to be observed, not dismantled and destroyed. The body of the work of art, protected by the conventions dominant in the art system, therefore remains inaccessible because the unauthorized viewer is not allowed to look inside it. The true material nature of the artwork is taboo for the art viewer: the viewer's gaze cannot probe beyond the surface of the work because that would amount to destroying it.

This taboo is further reinforced by Manzoni because he fills the inside of the work with his breath (*Body of Air*, 1959–60) or his shit (alleged or real). If the surface of a balloon inflated with the breath of the artist were to be pierced, the air would be lost and the work permanently destroyed. The information that shit is contained inside the work of art, however, directly discourages viewers, and succeeds better than any taboo in preventing them from probing around inside. The result is that the inviolability of the work of art is secured even when it begins to circulate outside the art system, as Manzoni foresaw in the case of his cans of preserves. So we can say that *Artist's Shit* is not a desecration of the work of art but, on the contrary, its sacralization.

*Sacer* in Latin is applied to everything forbidden and prohibited—because set aside for the gods—but also everything impure and defiling. As Roger Caillois points out in his 1939 book *Man and the Sacred*, the sacred is ambivalent: it is pure and impure, holy and polluting. As Manzoni fills the work of art with substances drawn from the human body, the work of art is also humanized—and its inviolability is on par with that of the human being. The taboo that forbids us to kill and dismember human beings to see how they are made is likewise ambivalent. This prohibition clearly has an ethical foundation, which forbids us to kill because killing is evil, but an equally strong, if not stronger justification of this taboo is the fear of seeing inside the human body, which arouses a sense of dismay. The analogy created between the work of art and the human body is therefore Manzoni's most interesting and radical gesture in his art, as he fills the inside of the work of art with breath or shit, substances that we all expect to find inside a person. People can also be interpreted as two-legged cans of preserves—cans of preserves filled with breath and shit.

This equivalence between the human body and the work of art has a long prehistory. The destiny of modern humanism is closely bound up with that of modern art in at least two ways. Firstly, according to the dominant conventions of European modernity, art is only what has been created by a human hand. Secondly, what distinguishes a work of art from other things is primarily the fact that the former can be observed and interpreted, but not used. The fundamental maxim of humanism, that people should always be considered as ends and never as a means, already shows that it sees human beings first of all as works of art. Human rights are, properly speaking, the rights of art applied to human beings. And in the wake of the Enlightenment, the human was no longer conceived mainly as spirit or soul, but as a body among other bodies, and in the last instance as a thing among other things. On the level of things, however, we have no other concept except that of art that would enable us to privilege some compared to all others, meaning to accord them a specific dignity of physical inviolability that is not accorded to others.

For this reason, in the context of European culture, the question "what is art?" involves more than just the art world. The criteria that we use to distinguish artworks from other things are not very different from those we use to distinguish what is human from what is not. In the European tradition, the two processes are indissolubly linked—recognizing certain things as works of art and recognizing specific bodies, together with their behaviors, actions, and attitudes, as human. So it is hardly surprising that the concept of biopolitics, introduced by Michel Foucault and developed by other authors, particularly Giorgio Agamben, should have acquired a critical connotation from the start in the context of European culture. To conceive humanity as a sort of animality, or rather cattle, means almost automatically debasing it, especially when this concept is used to be able to better provide for the physical well-being of the human animal. The true dignity of human beings emerges only when they are conceived as works of art.

This understanding of the human underpins all humanistic utopias, where not just mankind but society as a whole is seen as a work of art. Therefore only by answering the question about the nature of the work of art can we answer the ancient question: What truly is a human—that modern individual recognized as the possessor of rights and the subject of democracy? Human beings and works of art are inseparably united by a dense network of metaphors and metonymies, a network that becomes especially clear to us in the work of Manzoni. The artwork begins to appear to us as the "conserves" of a person, or at least as the "conserves" of a person's insides. In this way, the humanization of art is taken even further, but the same is true of the mirrored process of the further transformation of the human being into a work of art.

Since its beginnings, art has essentially been a process of preservation. Works of art are not only treated differently from other profane things, they even survive them. Ordinary things end up on the garbage heap when they are no longer of any use. But works of art are preserved in museums and archives, repaired and restored. Art is thus presented as an institution that governs the promise of earthly immortality—the only promise of this kind left to us since God, or the gods, have lost all responsibility for our immortality. Philosophy, as founded by Plato, was also firmly anchored to religion, since over the course of its long history it represented nothing more than the attempt to anticipate the survival of the soul after death—in other words, to achieve metanoia, a conversion from the prospect of the here and now to the prospect of the beyond, from the prospect of the mortal body to the prospect of the immortal soul. This type of metanoia is in fact the indispensable premise for becoming metaphysical, for taking up a meta-position toward the world, for being able to contemplate and conceive of the world as a whole.

When metanoia—namely, the anticipation of one's own immortality—becomes impossible, the individual loses the ability to contemplate the whole. In fact, this perspectivism is now seen as almost self-evident, so that whenever someone begins to speak we tend to first ask ourselves where he or she comes from and which point of view he or she is speaking from. Race, class, and gender generally act as coordinates to position whomever is talking. This kind of original positioning also serves as the cultural concept of identity. Even when these parameters are understood not as "natural" determiners but social constructs, their effect remains largely unaltered. Social constructs can be deconstructed but not abolished or replaced arbitrarily by other constructs.

At any rate, when the body ceases to be living and animate, when the soul dies, the body does not disappear but becomes a corpse. If there is no life for the soul after death, the body continues to live as a corpse. In ancient Egypt, of course, bodies were mummified and preserved, and in a certain sense we can say that modern art continues this tradition. This emerges in a very clear way with Manzoni. To the extent that substances from the body of the artist are preserved and placed in museums, he has achieved the dream of individual immortality, without any need for the traditional promise of religion. We can use the well-known concept of heterotopia in this respect, a term introduced by Foucault, to speak of hetero-metanoia. Foucault lumped the museum together with the cemetery, library, hospital, prison, and ship, among "other places," or heterotopias. The body transcends the place where it was found in life when it is placed in a cemetery or museum. This entails a rather drastic shift in perspective, because from the point of view of the cemetery, museum, or library, the world itself is seen in a different perspective—heterotopic, to be precise. Works of art are the living corpses of things. Things are preserved and exhibited in art museums only after their deaths, meaning after they have been defunctionalized, cut off from practical life. The existence of artworks in a museum is life after death, a vampire life that has to be protected from sunlight.

Modern art museums clearly manifest the difficulties facing those who aspire to hetero-metanoia. The stated purpose of the European avant-garde was and remains that of producing a "living" art, as opposed to the "dead" art of museums. Modern art seeks to achieve this aim by displaying the material dimension of art, its pure corporeality, which usually remains hidden behind the surface of the image—properly, the bodily or cadaveric nature of the images and things. By means of art, certain things are detached from the context of their living use and placed in the artificial, cemeterial, heterotopic context of the museum, precisely in order to display their pure materiality, their bodily valence. The life of living art is therefore the eternal life of the corpse, which transcends all the living uses of things.

The heterotopic perspective of the museum can also be interpreted as a sort of meta-perspective. We can experience a hetero-metanoia to the extent that, when we are still alive, we anticipate the coming status of our bodies as preserved corpses, thus attaining a heterotopic perspective. And it is not difficult for us to represent ourselves as corpses, because in our lifetimes we are already subject to an irreversible decline—our participation in an eternal, infinite physical decline, which has neither a beginning nor an end. Uniting ourselves with this endless decadence means performing another metanoia, a hetero-metanoia—a change of perspective that enables us to take up a meta-position toward the world as it is without having to invoke the immortality of the soul. A corpse is immortal by definition: it has left death behind. Instead of the metaphysics of the immortal soul, a new metaphysics opens up before us, the hetero-metaphysics of the body. If you ask someone who has experienced this other metanoia where they come from and what perspective they speak from, they will be able to answer calmly that they speak only from the heterotopic perspective of the cemetery, library, or museum.

Nevertheless, modern art can also evoke rather than just demonstrate the advent of radical materialism, of hetero-metanoia, the metaphysics of the body. Precisely for this reason, modern art is constantly in search of a new image that can serve as the icon of pure materiality, of pure profanity. Creating such icons of radical profaneness can, however, only succeed for a short time—when the violence with which a thing is torn from life is still perceptible. In every individual historic period it thus becomes inevitable to seek some other new icon of corporeality that has not yet been exploited, the perception of which, as the Russian Formalists said, has not yet been automatized. And yet, even after the passing of a specific historical time, in particular when we see a ready-made work of art in a museum, we still perceive its nature as a corpse very clearly. We know that this urinal will never again find its usual place in a lavatory, that Warhol's soup cans will never arrive on the supermarket shelves, will never be bought and eaten.

From this stems the atmosphere of melancholy that sur-rounds all readymade works of art, quite apart from the playful character they often have. Manzoni's *Artist's Shit* also belongs in this category. This work can be considered a successful joke alluding to the mechanisms of the art mar-ket (a perfectly legitimate interpretation). At the same time, however, it is a deeply melancholic work, one that reveals the universal destiny of organic matter exactly to the extent that it promises a new form of preservation, of immortalization, of our living substance. In fact, it shows what remains and what can be preserved of a human being in our neo-Egyptian civilization: not much, but more than nothing.

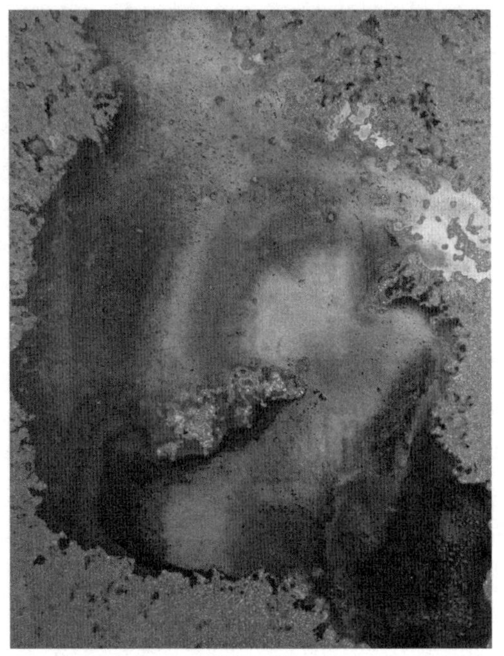

Andy Warhol, *Oxidation Painting*, 1978

4
# Andy Warhol
## In Search of Suspended Time

Andy Warhol has emerged as one of the very few historically known artists who have profoundly changed our understanding of the ways in which artistic subjectivity defines itself and its relationship to the world, artistic tradition, and society. Warhol, of course, was initially part of the Pop art movement and shared many of its attitudes, but his late work reveals a radical difference in artistic strategy that separated him from mainstream Popism.

Pop art was a reaction against the Romantic image of the artist that remained fundamentally intact until the late '50s. In the context of modernity, the fine artist was understood as a lonely creative individual, defined by his or her rejection of socially established norms and conventions as well as subjugation to the powerful socioeconomics of modern industrial and cultural production. Such an act of rejection needed to manifest itself openly and explicitly to be recognized as a sign of genuine artistic subjectivity. In this sense, the appropriation of mass cultural images by the Pop generation could moreover be interpreted as a continuation of the modernist tradition because it was also a rejection of the norms and conventions defining the "high" art of the previous, modernist epoch.

From the beginnings of his artistic career Warhol practiced his art beyond the mere oppositions of negation and affirmation or rejection and appropriation. Instead of defining artistic subjectivity as being manifested through an individual, irreducible act of creation of the new or appropriation of the old, Warhol developed the strategy of variation, which operates as a middle course between negation and affirmation. His art almost always starts with a certain image borrowed from American commercial culture or the art-historical canon; he then proceeds to modify it so that every such step of the process remains clear and understandable for a potential spectator. Warhol's serial technique acts as a formalized algorithm, producing reiterations and modifications, repetitions and shifts, identities and differences. Artistic subjectivity is no longer defined here by a unique, mysterious act of creation, but by a series of choices that can be easily identified and repeated. Warhol writes, "Even when the subject is different, people always paint the same painting."[1] This statement is, obviously, an invitation to the viewer to see his oeuvre as a series of modifications of topic, style, color, or size applied to a painting that never takes final shape. In Warhol's case the images themselves are not of central importance—even if they are in most cases truly powerful and imprint themselves deeply in the memory of the spectator. Rather, the importance lies in the space and time between these images in which artistic subjectivity operates.

In Warhol's late work his modus operandi is even more explicit than in his earlier artistic production. Like the other members of the Pop generation in the '50s and '60s, Warhol made the new and vast territory of American consumerism and commercial mass culture a field of operation for his art. This discovery gave new energy and optimism to the art of the era. But the enthusiasm of the '60s began to cool during the next decade. In Warhol's case, the end of the '60s sensibility arrived in 1968, at its peak, when he was shot and almost died. In the ensuing decades the theme of death became more and more persistent in his work. He began to move away from mass-culture imagery toward traditional symbols of melancholy (skulls) or symbols of violence (guns and knives). He also turned his attention to images that belong to the art-historical canon, such as Leonardo da Vinci's *The Last Supper*, or religious and ideological symbols—Mao Tse-tung, the hammer and sickle, crosses. At the same time he expanded his painterly technique in a way that reflected his concern with painting as a medium, as in the *Oxidation Paintings* (1977–78) or *Camouflage* (1986) works. In this change of topics and techniques, one can clearly see the symptoms of Warhol's desire to establish himself as an artist within the grand tradition of the international arts and beyond purely American cultural references. Even more important, this expansion of his visual vocabulary demonstrated Warhol's artistic method in a more explicit way than his early work did.

The serial technique was, of course, recognized early on as a hallmark of Warhol's art, but it was interpreted primarily as a reaction to the proliferation of images, to the triumph of the mass-produced copy over the original—and therefore as just another means of addressing the mechanisms of mass culture within the context of high art. However, Warhol's series rarely if at all imitate the mechanical reproducibility that defines the operations of commercial mass culture. They are rather a lineup of the potentially infinite variations to which individual images of that culture, like a portrait of Marilyn Monroe or a Campbell's soup can, may be subjected. Nor do these variations reproduce the modifications that certain images have, or might have, undergone through their mass dissemination. Warhol's variations certainly do not testify to the commercial exploitation of the "small difference" that undoubtedly prevails today in the cultural markets.[2] The artist's late works, in particular, clearly demonstrate that his visual variations are the specific product of his own individual strategy. Variations on symbols, like the hammer and sickle or the cross, take a turn that one would not likely encounter in the commercial mass reproduction of these symbols in the real world—for example, the hammer and sickle becoming three-dimensional in Warhol's paintings. Their variation must therefore have a reason and significance beyond merely pointing to the mechanisms underlying the mass dissemination of images. In fact, Warhol's deploying of variation *reverses* the conventional practice of image production that is at work in commercial art.

The core procedure of commercial art is image selection, which precedes its mass reproduction. The commercial artist ordinarily offers a client several variations or options, be it in the form of paintings, drawings, or photographs. One of those options is then selected for use in, say, newspaper advertising. It seems that Warhol, who started out as a commercial artist and must certainly have suffered from this selection procedure, capitalized on his position as a fine artist to suspend the act of selection and show all of the variations of an image at once. Warhol's serial technique does not demonstrate the process of multiplying a source image but rather a return to the time prior to its selection.

"I always like to work on leftovers, doing the leftover things," Warhol said. "Things that were discarded, that everybody knew were no good, I always thought had a great potential to be funny."[3] When it comes to image selection, Warhol is an anti-Darwinist. He does not trust the real business of selection; he prefers the unselected, extinct variants, the ones that couldn't compete, that didn't make it. He wants to give them a second chance by displaying a virtual series of such variants. In fact, he explicitly refers to the practice of revising the selection procedure of commercial art when he talks about "Business Art." As he put it, "You're recycling work and you're recycling people, and you are running your business as a byproduct of other businesses. Of other *directly competitive* businesses, as a matter of fact. So that's a very economical operating procedure."[4] Warhol's Business Art dispenses with the selection that is operative in conventional business practice and returns to the options that have been deselected by the art trade. Business Art essentially functions as a reversal of normal competitive business, as a kind of antibusiness, and it is motivated not only by pragmatic considerations but by ethical concerns as well. It is especially interesting in this respect that Warhol returns to the leftovers of his own artistic practice to create variants of his early works in the *Reversal* and *Retrospective* series.

Such leftovers should not, of course, be necessarily understood as real, material ones. Rather, they build a virtual, subjective archive of modifications, shifts, and differences that cannot be fully realized but only imagined by the artist. Artistic subjectivity can be defined—and is de facto defined by Warhol—as owner and administrator of such a virtual archive of all possible image modifications. Warhol understands individual artistic imagination to be vaster and richer than commercial mass culture. The adequate answer to mass culture's overproduction of images is not rejection, reduction, or negation, but the demonstration of the power of artistic subjectivity to imagine more possibilities than mass culture can ever realize.

Warhol is not alone in defining this virtual archive of image variations as a true site of artistic subjectivity. Linguist Roman Jakobson, one of the most important scholars of the twentieth century, has described every act of communication as an act of selection from a virtual archive and the reversal of the selection process not only as a specific artistic device among many but as the very source and origin of art. In

"Linguistics and Poetics," first delivered at a 1958 conference, Jakobson introduces the concept of the poetic function to elaborate the precise distinction between the usual communicative text and the poetic artistic text.[5] Jakobson observes that in ordinary written and spoken language we engage in two fundamental operations: selection and combination. Through the act of communication we select the word we want to use from a set of synonyms, all of which basically have the same referent. Jakobson illustrates as follows: When we want to talk about a child, we choose from a set of more or less similar nouns—child, kid, youngster, tot, and so on. Having made our selection, we combine it syntactically with a verb—sleep, doze, nod, nap—to produce a message. Jakobson writes, "The selection is produced on the base of equivalence, similarity and dissimilarity, synonymity and antonymity, while the combination, the build up of the sequence, is based on contiguity."

Jakobson further defines the poetic function as a conscious suspension of the act of selection: "The poetic function projects the principle of equivalence from the axis of selection onto the axis of combination."[6] In other words, the message itself becomes an enumeration of all the word options at the speaker's disposal prior to having selected and incorporated any particular option into a communicative statement. Such an enumeration, says Jakobson, is exactly what we call a poem and, more generally, a work of art. It follows that the function of the poem does not consist in conveying specific content but rather in suspending the linguistic selection in which speakers ordinarily engage to expose the process of selection that would otherwise remain concealed. That process, in fact, reveals the number of options that speakers select from and that form every speaker's virtual, inner archive. Jakobson claims that art, especially poetry, is generated by projecting the axis of selection onto the axis of combination. This theory suits Warhol's art perfectly.

Warhol's serial technique can best be described as a display of the virtual axis of selection that is activated in the mind of any commercial artist or art director who is trying to determine the most effective means of transferring an image to the surface of a poster or the page of a newspaper: Black and white or color? If color, then which color? Fine-grained or coarse-grained? Lighter or darker? And so on. The final image does not readily reveal the process of selection from which it originated. When Warhol begins reconstructing, or rather imagining this process of selection by placing all possible visual variations of an image side by side—all its virtual leftovers—he is actually dissolving the solid form of the image. Through variations of this image he achieves a state that is more original than any original image because he precedes the act of selection from which the original image emerged. This is the state prior to the origin of the image. A de-incarnation of the image is at work here; the "real" image has been transformed into a state of pure potentiality. The image loses its solidity, its materiality; it becomes an unstable and extremely questionable equivalent to a potentially infinite series of image options, which are mutually intertwined in a complicated network of "similarity and dissimilarity, synonymity and antonymity," as Jakobson said. And not only does the image itself become variable, but so does everything that is related to it: context, medium, referent. Subject *Mona Lisa* or Marilyn Monroe to enough variations and they will mutate into combinations of pure form and color, obliterating the subject matter in much the same way as the meaning of a word is obliterated if we repeat it often enough—converted into a pure combination of sounds. The interpretation of the image has thereby also been projected from the axis of

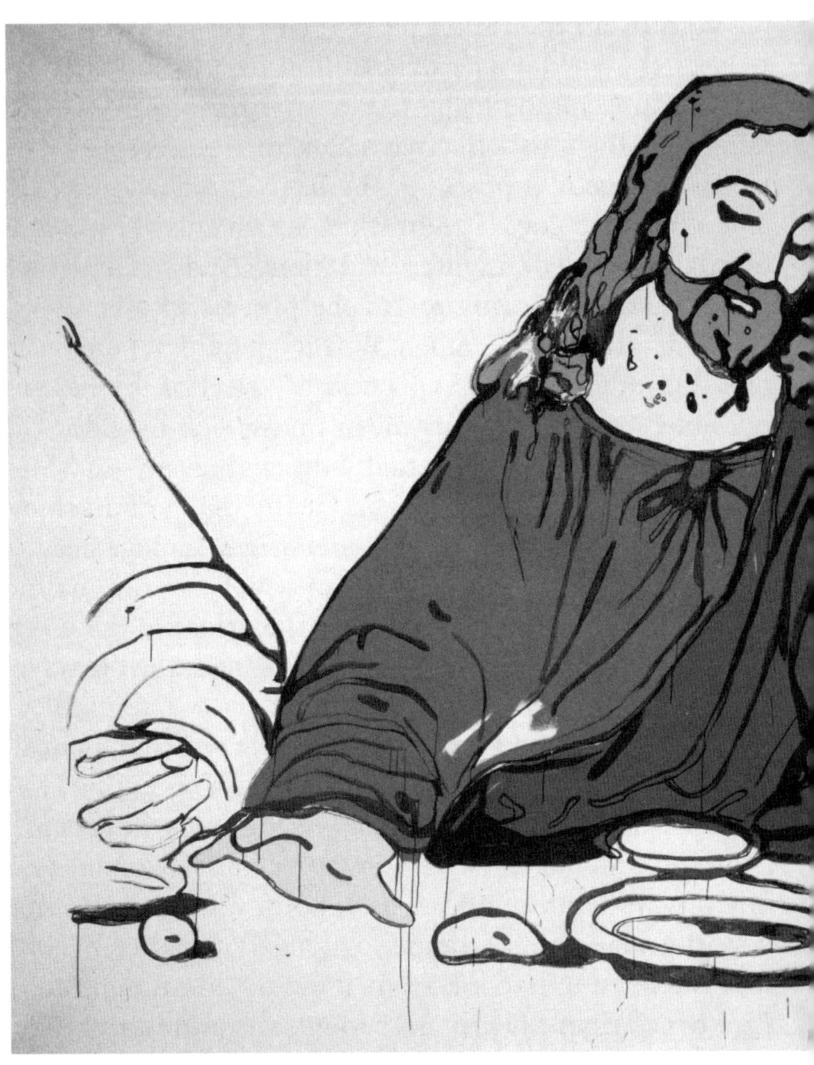

Andy Warhol, *Detail of The Last Supper*, 1986

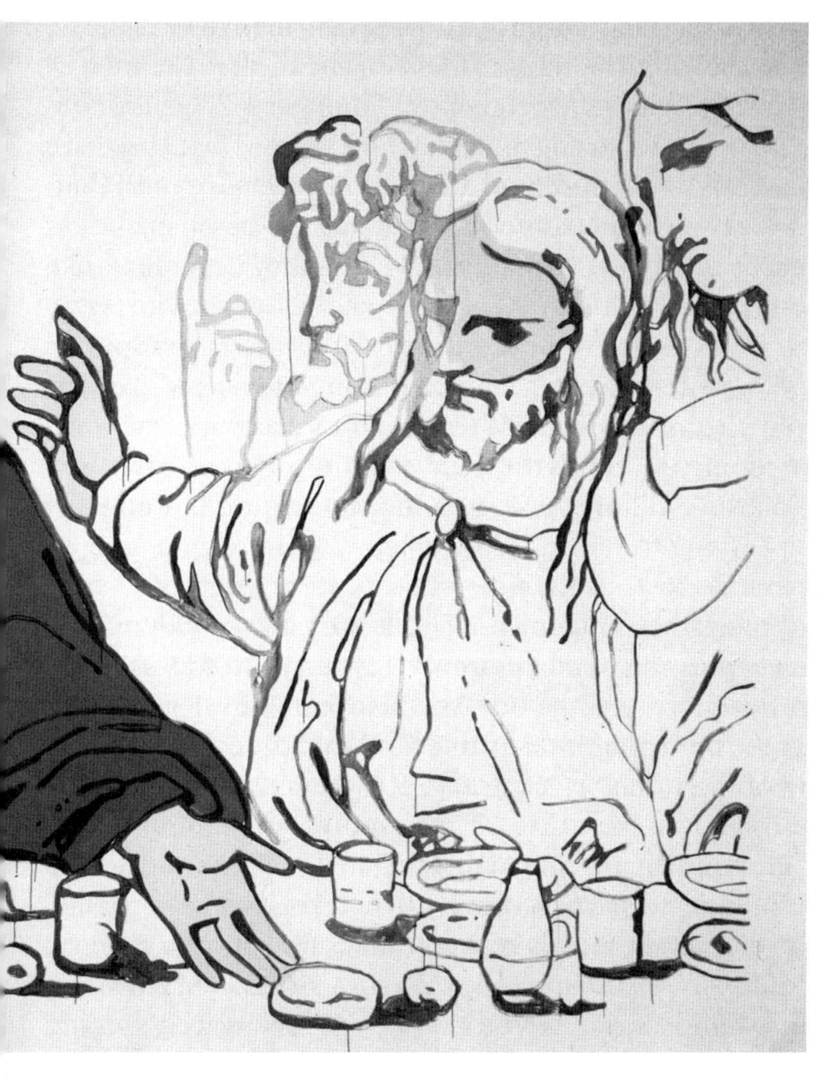

selection onto the axis of combination. Warhol's images can legitimately be read as figurative or abstract, as representing high art or popular culture, as being affirmative or critical.

Destabilizing the image does not mean that the images produced by Warhol are somehow "immaterial." On the contrary, they have a strong immediate presence. Their sheer size does not allow the spectator to overlook them; beyond that, they are powerful in painterly terms, and are based on a clear and easily graspable visual formula. Yet they never look like just one possible ultimate choice. Warhol refuses to choose, to select. He does not want to pin himself down to one specific option; he wants to be open to all options at once. Moreover, he wants to return to a state prior to selection even when others confront him with their selection. People often say that Warhol willingly accepted the status quo, but actually he kept trying to return to the imaginary status quo ante, to the paradise lost, to the time of suspended judgment—be it moral or aesthetic judgment. This suspension of judgment is not an expression of an immoral or cynical attitude, as it was often misinterpreted to be. Art historian John Richardson compares this (pre)moral attitude of Warhol very aptly to the figure of the *yurodivyi*, central to Russian medieval spirituality and modern literature.[7] The yurodivyi is an anonymous, profane saint living on earth as if he were in paradise. He never judges, he reacts positively to everyone and everything, but at the same time his reaction takes a form of a strange, we could say, dadaistic joke. Warhol states, "My instinct about painting says, 'If you don't think about it, it's right.' As soon as you have to decide and choose, it's wrong. And the more you decide about it, the more wrong it gets."[8]

This artistic strategy of Warhol can also be compared to another well-known religious figure in recent history. In *Concluding Unscientific Postscript to "Philosophical*

*Fragments"* (1846), Søren Kierkegaard writes that a true Christian can only be one who is capable of imagining the situation prior to the appearance of Christ—that is, the situation of choosing between Christ and the many other more or less similar itinerant preachers. That entails being able to imagine a situation in which the faithful are faced with a selection that has not yet been historically decided. More importantly, this selection cannot be based on any visually recognizable opposition between the human and the divine. The figure of Christ has nothing specifically divine compared to an ordinary human figure. Here again it has to do with only small differences and variations that make our choice purely subjective and unfounded. The selection of the figure of Christ as described by Kierkegaard can be compared to the production of art by selection, and to the readymade technique as Duchamp initiated it. In both cases the act of selection is understood as being purely arbitrary. After Kierkegaard and Duchamp, everything—religion and high art included—appears to be a matter of choice.

Warhol is heir to this modern tradition of making choices. He characteristically insists that even his *Oxidation* paintings are a matter of technique and choice—namely, the proper pissing technique, which requires conscious control. He specifies, "If I asked somebody to do an *Oxidation* painting, they just wouldn't think about it and it just would be a mess. Then I did it myself."[9] Warhol undoubtedly thought that any art produced "without thinking about it"—in other words, authentic, spontaneous, ingenious art—was also a mess. And above all he thought of himself as the kind of person who meticulously considers and controls all of his decisions and actions. But in a seemingly paradoxical way this predominance of conscious choice is seen by Warhol as a chance to reverse the selection process, to return to the initial, innocent, free state of mind.

Indeed, if everything is a matter of technique, and if technique is essentially a process of selection, then Warhol's artistic method as the reversal of selection becomes universally applicable and as such highly critical or at least deconstructive, because it shows that the same thing can always look different. This deconstructive thrust comes to the fore especially when he applies his technique to images that viewers have learned to accept unquestioningly, "without thinking about it." At the same time he almost always chooses the images that were initially produced in a very conscious, controlled way. Leonardo da Vinci is especially known for his scientific method of art production based on studies of geometry, mechanics, and anatomy. But Warhol's variations of *The Last Supper* turn the original work into one option among many by subjecting the original image to a series of variations relating to all visual aspects of this image. Warhol's 1986 serialization of *The Last Supper* creates an archive of the variations where Leonardo's original becomes one of many items. The demonstration of the axis of selection is here invested with a certain irony, because it relativizes and undermines the familiar, immutable, and—as the Russian Formalists would have put it—"automatized" image of Leonardo's work.

There are, of course, more instances of the same strategy. Warhol reminds us, for example, in a 1976–77 series, that the hammer and sickle, which have become a visual formula, an immutable ideological sign, are not merely a political symbol but tools with a practical purpose. By creating combinations that deviate from the conventional rendition of the hammer and sickle in its function as the emblem of the Communist movement, Warhol makes his automatized version look purely accidental. Moreover, as components of the Communist symbol, the hammer and sickle appear flat and two-dimensional; in Warhol's pictures they become three-dimensional, and the sickle is labeled "Champion No. 15 by True Temper," which definitively deprives it of any symbolic function. So what we see are two tools, a hammer and a sickle, in different compositions, without really knowing whether we are looking at a still life or at something that is politically symbolic. And if they are meant to be political, then is their treatment critical or affirmative? And so on.

The hammer-and-sickle combination ordinarily appears as a two-dimensional image, but the cross in the Catholic churches of the West conventionally presents itself to the faithful as a three-dimensional object. Warhol reverses that convention by showing a two-dimensional cross in a 1981–82 series of works that also bring to mind Malevich's flat Suprematist crosses. Once again ambivalence prevails, this time between a religiously coded object and a purely geometrical, abstract shape. As in the case of the hammer and sickle, the viewer is free to choose between religious/ideological and secular interpretations. Both options vie equally for our attention. Hence, Warhol's variations on the portrait of Mao, which echo his early portraits of Marilyn Monroe, encourage viewers to see the chairman not only as a hero of the revolution whose countenance has mutated into an ideological icon, but also as a celebrity, just another figure of commercial mass culture.

Warhol's double images unmistakably demonstrate the ethical and political dimensions of his take on variation. Because we traditionally associate white with goodness and black with evil, the aesthetic choice between the white and black variations on the picture is informed with ethical and political implications. The political aspect of Warhol's use of variation is even more explicit in *Vote McGovern* (1972), in which the appeal to vote for Democratic candidate George

McGovern is combined with a portrait of Republican candidate Nixon. This picture perfectly illustrates Jakobson's theory. The choice between Nixon and McGovern is transported directly from the axis of selection to the axis of combination. The aesthetic function has transformed the conventional campaign poster into a poem. One can of course claim that such a device aestheticizes the political election and therefore deprives it of political content, an assessment that reinforces the widespread opinion of Warhol as a preacher of indifference. But let us not forget that by treating visual production as an act of selection—that is, as a series of choices—Warhol conversely engages in a radical "politicization of aesthetics," as Walter Benjamin so famously put it. In Warhol's words, "Politics can mean doing a poster that has Nixon's face on it, and says 'Vote McGovern.'"[10]

Just how radical Warhol was in politicizing art can be best illustrated with what would appear to be an apolitical example. In a conversation with Robert Nickas about his *Rorschach* paintings, Warhol insisted that he did not use any of the standardized cards of the Rorschach test (and he supposedly didn't even know that there were standardized cards). He simply wanted to make pictures that look like the inkblot test but that are not actually part of the official set.[11] Warhol's *Rorschach* (1984) paintings are of special relevance because he pushes his method to extremes by adding another layer of uncertainty to images that have already been designed to produce the effect of indetermination—or of the inability to come to a decision—by suggesting a whole series of interpretations, none of which the viewer can choose to the exclusion of all others. In the final analysis, viewers are not merely uncertain as to how they should view and interpret the *Rorschach* paintings but wonder whether they even see them as Rorschach images at all. A kind of double axis of selection has been created here. Warhol treats not only artistic images or political/ideological symbols but even scientifically established pictures as the result of decision-making processes and undoubtedly debatable choices, thereby effectively destabilizing them.

In a comparable way, Warhol uses military camouflage patterns in his *Camouflage* paintings to make them look like modernist abstract paintings. Here again the visual richness and the immediate aesthetic appeal of the image are ironically subverted by the suspicion that this image is not a product of spontaneous artistic inspiration but an effect of planning strategies and decision-making process effected by a military bureaucracy. On the other hand, there is no guarantee that Warhol's *Camouflage* paintings use actual camouflage patterns instead of merely simulating them. His method invariably postulates the total dominance of a rational, strategic, and politic subjectivity, which perceives nothing, including itself, as nature, as ineluctable fact, but rather considers and treats everything as variable—in short, the dominance of a thoroughly modern subjectivity.

But then how is this kind of subjectivity constituted? That question, raised time and again in the course of modernism, has been answered in a variety of ways, and one of those answers shows an astonishing relevance to Warhol's practice and life. In his 1929–30 lectures on the fundamental concepts of metaphysics, Martin Heidegger proposes that a modern calculating subjectivity is born of the experience of "profound boredom," which is at its most radical at a dinner invitation or, in contemporary terms for Warhol's context, at a party.[12] In contrast to other forms of boredom, as defined by Heidegger, such as the boredom experienced while waiting for a train, profound boredom is all-inclusive. The reason for this lies in the fact that by accepting the dinner invitation, one has chosen to take time, to cut a piece of time out of the general flow that is ordinarily dominated by daily chores, and to devote it exclusively to pure entertainment, the passing of time. This makes us more acutely aware of time because when we are involved in daily chores we overlook its passage. The time spent having dinner is "suspended" time, time as a quotation that separates us from the natural world around us, driven by constant worries.

According to Heidegger, profound boredom, as a state in which everything is equally boring, creates a distance between the subject and the world; boredom makes the world appear as something alien, as an object. Heidegger even considers boredom a mood that actually generates man as such; animals cannot suffer boredom because they are so preoccupied by the world that they are unable to experience the world as world. Therefore, in Warhol's case, boredom is not to be confused with a dandyish or blasé attitude. Heidegger's analysis in fact shows that profound boredom, the experience of suspended time, constitutes a subjectivity that takes the entire world as its operative domain.

Warhol, one might say, not only experienced suspended time at parties but, above all, he created it in his art. The projection of the axis of selection onto the axis of combination, as in Warhol's art, can also be interpreted as a ritual of return to suspended time—the time prior to selection, the time of indecision, of doubt, of repeatedly listing all the available options. As a rule, this is time that appears to be lost, wasted, boring, because it prevents settling on a single specific option and therefore taking practical steps and embarking on the passage to action. In truth, however, this is about the time in which a modern, technical, and strategic subjectivity is actually constituted; this is the time when that subjectivity catches sight of the extensive and steadily growing archive of lost possibilities, missed chances, and unrealized utopias, which testify to the fact that everything that is could also be different.

Notes


1.  Andy Warhol, *THE Philosophy of Andy Warhol (From A to B and Back Again)* (New York: Harcourt, 1975), 149.
2.  See Rosalind Krauss, "Carnal Knowledge," in *Andy Warhol: Rorschach Paintings* (New York: Gagosian Gallery, 1996), 11–12.
3.  Warhol, *Philosophy of Andy Warhol*, 93.
4.  Ibid.
5.  Roman Jakobson, "Linguistics and Poetics," in *Style in Language*, ed. Thomas A. Sebeok (Cambridge, MA: MIT Press, 1960), 350–77.
6.  Ibid., 358 (both quotes).
7.  John Richardson, "Eulogy of Andy Warhol," in *Andy Warhol: Heaven and Hell Are Just One Breath Away! Late Paintings and Related Works, 1984–1986*, ed. Charles F. Stuckey (New York: Gagosian Gallery, 1992), 140.
8.  Warhol, *Philosophy of Andy Warhol*, 149.
9.  Cited in Benjamin H. D. Buchloh, "An Interview with Andy Warhol, May 28, 1985," in *Andy Warhol: B&W Paintings; Ads and Illustrations, 1985–1986* (New York: Gagosian Gallery, 2002), 39–41.
10. Warhol, *Philosophy of Andy Warhol*, 15.
11. Robert Nickas, "Andy Warhol's Rorschach Test," *Arts Magazine*, October 1986, 28–32.
12. Martin Heidegger, *The Fundamental Concepts of Metaphysics: World-Finitude-Solitude*, trans. William McNeill and Nicholas Walker (Bloomington: Indiana University Press, 1996), 106.

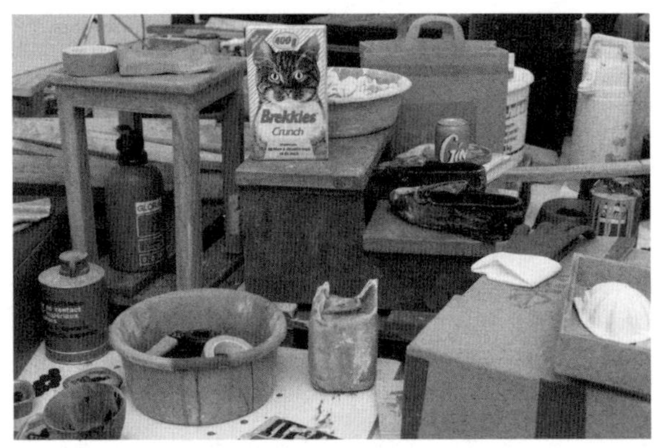

Peter Fischli and David Weiss, *The Table*, 1992–93

5
Peter Fischli and David Weiss I
Simulated Readymades

The insight that reproduction, more than production, suits human subjectivity is one of the oldest in the history of human thought. Nature produces and a person who lives in and with nature produces as well—the wise, however, reproduce. Plato wanted to reproduce the eternal ideas in his soul; the true believer wants to reproduce the Passion of Christ; Freud believed in the reproduction of sexual traumas in dreams; Peter Fischli and David Weiss reproduce milk cartons, drills, and saws in polyurethane. Subjectivity is something invisible, which is why it must not and cannot become visible, identifiable, objectified. Actually, the reproduction of things without any observable difference indirectly reveals subjectivity through the very absence of productive intervention.

When we first look at Fischli/Weiss's exact polyurethane copies of ordinary objects—they might best be called "replicants," after the 1982 film *Blade Runner*—we find that they are indistinguishable from the originals. Only upon close inspection will the viewer perhaps realize that they are not the "real thing," but artificially made replicants. In fact, the viewer has to know this to begin with—from the artists themselves, from their friends, or at worst from a catalogue. Fischli/Weiss's replicants refuse to give us any insight into their inner nature and structure, which we, as products of a scientific age, automatically want to investigate. Instead, we are radically confronted with a surface that cannot be penetrated because it conceals nothing but a void. The polyurethane used by the artists is merely a physical metaphor for this void; it is, of course, no accident that the items weigh practically nothing. Fischli/Weiss thus create a situation that obviates study and insight, a situation in which art alone has power over us. They reproduce a pre-scientific, pre-philosophical world that was interested only in two things: what we see with our eyes and, additionally, how what we see with our eyes has been created out of nothingness. It was once possible to find this information in the Bible—nowadays people look for it in exhibition catalogues.

But the greatest, most immediate effect of Fischli/Weiss's objects and installations lies in undermining certain expectations entertained by contemporary viewers. We are all familiar with the practice of the readymade, and when we see the simple things of daily life on view in a museum we tend to believe that they are indeed "real things." In fact, our faith in their thingness is even greater on seeing them in a museum than in reality. We know how hard it was for the practice of the readymade to garner acceptance; we know how long it took the artist to earn the right to put real things, and not only their representations, on display in museums. Then why should someone come up with the idea of simulating the readymade itself? And one can argue that Fischli/Weiss simulate readymades rather than the real objects allegedly used as readymades, because in real life these object-replicants would immediately be exposed for what they are—namely, useless in actual practice. In a museum context, however, the readymade is not required to pass a test of authenticity or practicability thanks to a firmly established convention that only its surface may be viewed, for we are not allowed to touch, take along, or use the objects on display. It is this convention that has made it possible to simulate the readymade.

In general, our perception of readymades in a museum is determined by the assumption that they are real, genuine things that could potentially be returned to reality. Fischli/ Weiss's replicants disclaim this assumption by demonstrating that we have been deceived by a convention that cannot give us a guarantee of reality, for readymades travel a one-way street from reality to art. Once the classic readymade crosses the invisible threshold in our culture that separates art from reality, the possibility of retracing its steps becomes purely theoretical. The threshold has been inscribed in the inner structure of the readymade replicants; the act of becoming art precludes their return to reality. But how does this practice enhance our understanding of art? What is the point of copying a copy or of reproducing a reproduction?

Actually the practice of the readymade is itself an act of copying, of duplication: everyday objects are duplicated by the mere fact of being placed in a museum. Marcel Duchamp's discovery consisted of demonstrating that it was no longer necessary for art to resort to painting or sculpture in order to depict reality: the context in which an object is presented suffices for us to perceive it as an artistic copy of itself. The ordinary object that escapes our attention precisely due to its everyday use, captures our attention in the context of the museum and acquires new meaning. Its utilitarian value gives way to a new symbolic value: the object becomes mysterious, fraught with meaning, mythical. It begins to inspire obscure religious associations, to imply a ritual function—in short, it begins to carry the entire weight of our culture. It becomes erotic. It becomes pure presence. It becomes spiritual. It puts Joseph Beuys into play.

Here the threshold between art and reality is given a spiritual and mythical interpretation: it is defined by the individual's inner, purely mental decision to see things differently. Crossing it begins to resemble a religious conversion, an inner enlightenment that allows us to see the familiar from a new

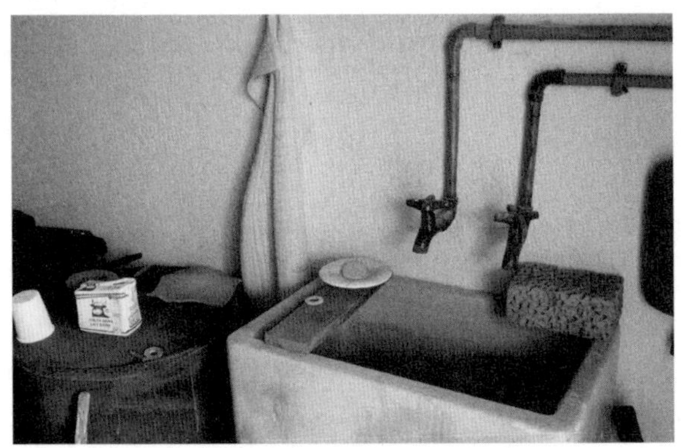

Peter Fischli and David Weiss, *Untitled Room*, 1990–92

angle and to contemplate what is hidden below the surface of the things. Thus, the classical practice of the readymade has the aspect of a mythical experience, which Fischli/Weiss obviously have misgivings about. Their strategy seeks to desecrate the distinction between art and reality. A thing made by Fischli/Weiss becomes art by virtue of the fact that it has been carved out of polyurethane. This definition replaces the old one, according to which a thing becomes art upon being seen in the light of transfiguration. The astonishing thing about this substitution of polyurethane for a higher spirituality is that the effect remains the same: divested of any practical, ordinary functionality, the thing can be used only as an object to be viewed.

By simulating readymades—that is, by reproducing a reproduction—artistic subjectivity becomes suppressed even more, and therefore becomes even more subjective. In installations like *The Table* (1992–93) at the Museum für Gegenwartskunst in Basel or *Untitled Room* (1990–92) on Hardturmstrasse in Zurich, Fischli/Weiss exhibited copies of the tools of their trade that were carved out of polyurethane. Thus previously, in their studio, they carved replicas of their tools and utensils using these same tools and utensils. The objects manufacture themselves, carve their own self-portraits, convert themselves into art. The will of the artist no longer plays a critical role, as it did in the classic practice of the readymade, where artists presided over the fate of objects by determining which ones were to be elevated to the rank of art. Instead, things reproduce themselves as art by producing themselves. One is reminded of Fischli/Weiss's film *The Way Things Go* (1987), in which things are given the appearance of having been left to their own devices to play out their own dynamics of inertia and motion. In more recent works, things not only move autonomously, they also seem to generate themselves in a purely physical process that eliminates anything that might be construed as spiritual, metaphysical, profound, or mythical—except perhaps the greatest pre-Platonic mythos of a self-producing and self-reproducing *physis*. But we must not forget that the greatest and supreme power consists of giving one's creations independence and freedom. In this sense, Fischli/Weiss present themselves as divine creators, albeit with a grain of irony.

At the same time, their works are not without idyllic undertones. Their staged universe of tools seems to be self-contained and self-sufficient. Human beings living in its midst live in familiar, homely surroundings. An invisible human presence is tangible in all of Fischli/Weiss's installations: the things they make all show traces of use and domesticity as part of everyday life. But humans do not figure as masters of these things; their activities have no external purpose to which the tools and other utensils must submit. *Untitled Room*, for example, shows the unassuming atmosphere of what might be a little workshop. The room has not been installed in the museum but rather in an old industrial building, behind a door facing the street. Pedestrians chancing to glance through the window in the door will not realize that what they see is a work of art, especially since it is not labeled as such. They will assume that the owner has locked the door and just stepped out for a moment. At most, they might wonder what the workshop is for, what sorts of things are made or repaired there, for the owner's trade and the purpose of the establishment are not immediately apparent.

Only our acquaintance with other Fischli/Weiss works, in particular *The Table*, will supply the answer. Here the same or at least comparable objects, spread out on the table, are unmistakably marked as products of Fischli/Weiss's artistic craftsmanship, and not as the tools themselves. The work of the anonymous craftsman, embodied by Fischli/Weiss, is the medium of the self-reproduction of the instruments of the work. The only purpose of their craftsmanship is to perpetuate itself, ceaselessly reproducing the circumstances and instruments attendant upon their way of life. One is reminded of Wittgenstein's *Lebensform* (form of life) or Heidegger's *Seinsweise* (manner of being). Every activity is described as self-sufficient self-reproduction, eternally repeated by people living in the midst of this activity and acting it out, thereby producing a superfluity that ultimately guarantees a kind of immortality. Since people are completely integrated into a process that does not require their decisions, personal will, or even existence, the radical menace of death loses its thrust. But this menace becomes acute again as soon as the unalloyed repetition of a way of life leads to efforts to improve, modernize, accelerate, and enhance the efficacy of life. This is why both Wittgenstein and Heidegger were so firmly opposed to the modern technological world.

Fischli/Weiss do not like modern technology either—its products do not figure in their installations. Above all, they reject the technological improvement that has been so successfully employed in the enhancement of artistic efficacy— namely, the practice of the readymade—so that the speed of the fine arts today easily rivals the speed of all modern technology. And indeed, is there anything faster than changing one's inner gaze? It is only because such change has become the essential technology of art in our century that modern art learned to compete in the economic arenas of our society. Fischli/Weiss want to decelerate modern art. Their readymade polyurethane replicants not only wax ironic over the mystical pretensions underlying the practice of the readymade, or merely desecrate the distinction between art and nonart; these objects are also products of a slow process

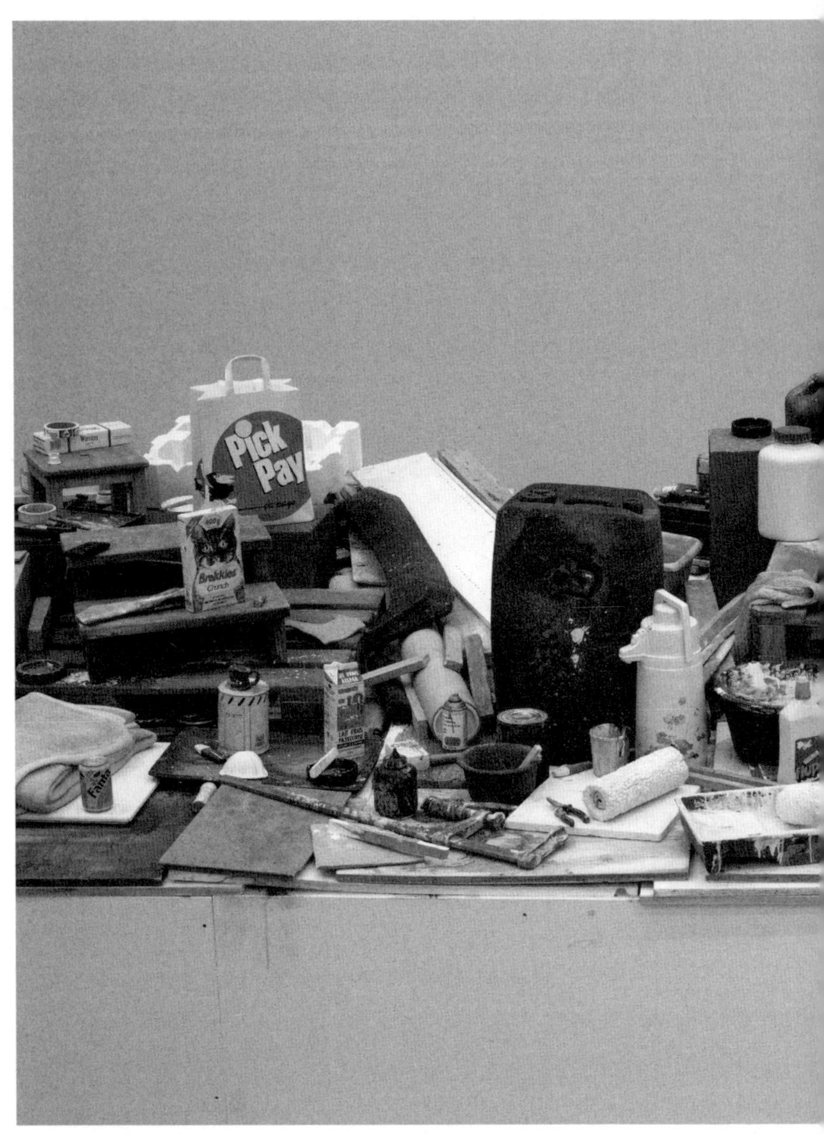

Peter Fischli and David Weiss, *The Table*, 1992–93

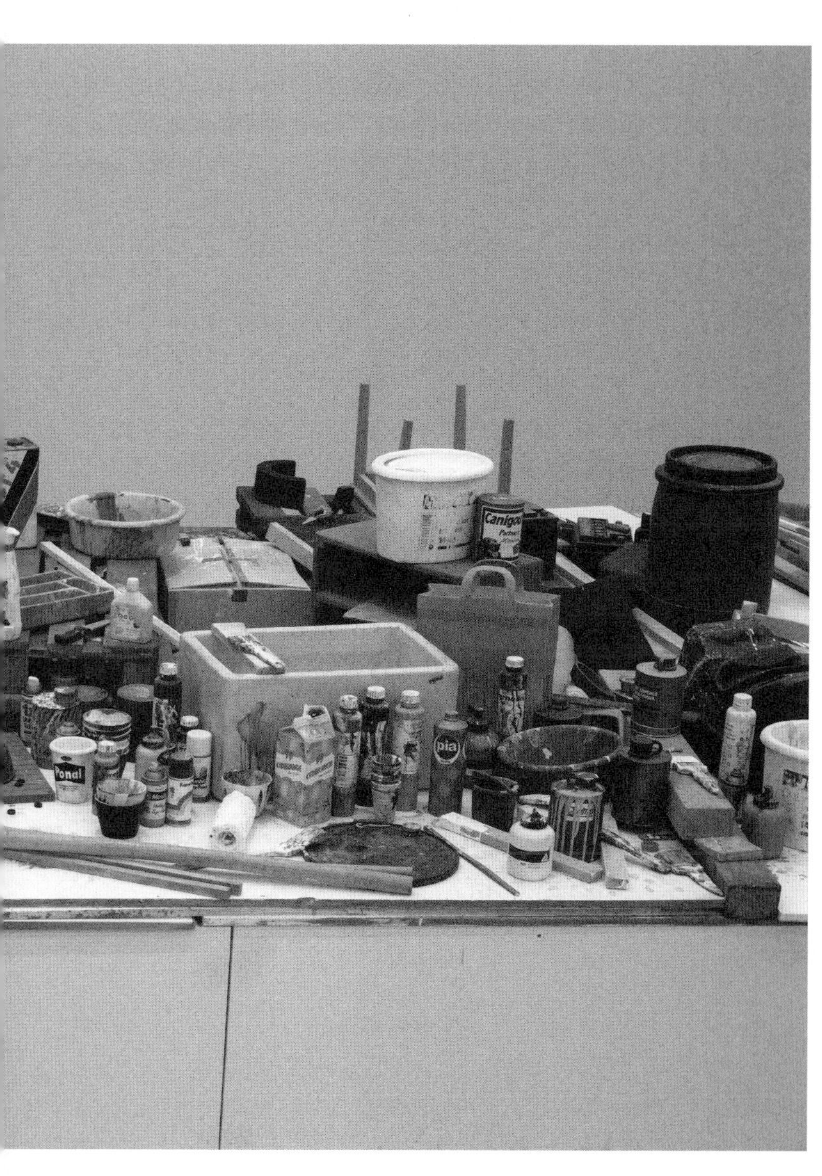

that revives the ethos of the artist as a working craftsperson who once again duplicates the things of reality.

Except Fischli/Weiss's replicants are obviously not the original things of this world but, as we know, mere simulated readymades. The traditional artistic ethos can only be reproduced today under the cover of irony: Fischli/Weiss render their things not in marble but in polyurethane. It is difficult to say whether Fischli/Weiss use the reproduction of the traditional role of the artist as an ironic device or whether irony is deployed to make this role acceptable again.

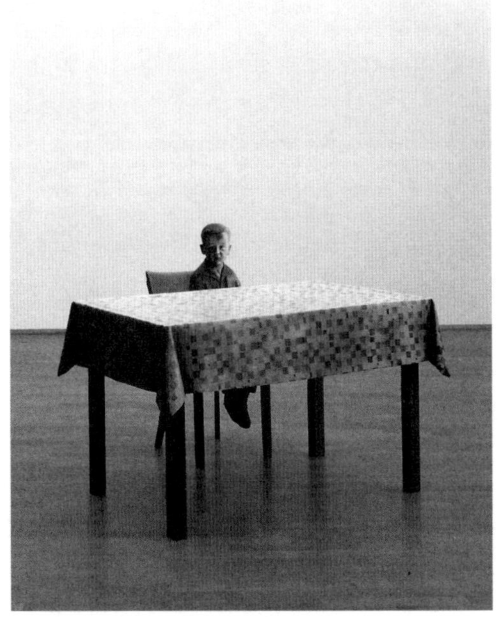

Martin Honert, *Photo*, 1993

6
Martin Honert
A Self-Collector

Most of Martin Honert's works have their source in memories that bring the artist back to his childhood. Of course, he is not unique in this respect, neither in the history of art nor on the contemporary art scene. But the way he treats images from his past is thoroughly original. It follows from a radical artistic questioning of the way in which the continuity of our memory can be achieved and secured. To put it another way, how and to what extent is it possible for us to return to images from our childhood?

Many artists nowadays fashion their work as an obsessive occupation with genuine or putative childhood traumas, which apparently not only guarantee the possibility of returning to past images but exert an all-but-inevitable compulsion to make that return. Insofar as the concept of trauma—and especially childhood trauma—is universally recognized, and makes every other rhetorical effort superfluous, it provides an easy answer to the question of why these artists operate in their art with this subject and not another, and with this particular formal vocabulary and not another. In today's era after postmodernism—that is, in an age after the end of all artistic ideologies and programs—the suggestion that traumatic experience is inescapable, imponderable, and hence beyond criticism is apparently the only possibility left to justify a particular artistic practice to society. Finally, and most of all, the reference to trauma offers a plausible explanation for why these artists remain perpetually captive to their themes and forms. In positing a traumatic compulsion to repeat themselves, it refutes the suspicion that in holding to a particular form of production they are driven by a commercially dictated adherence to a certain well-established brand.

One can, if one wishes, interpret Honert's art as a deconstruction of this currently prevalent discourse on trauma, exceedingly subtle yet all the more effective for just that reason. The images that Honert uses in his art, as we have noted, usually refer to memories from his childhood. But they are memories beyond trauma, beyond obsessiveness, beyond the usual range of psychoanalysis. In fact, the images cannot be traced back to a horrible or even unpleasant experience. Rather, the atmosphere they suggest is idyllic; it is neither excessively burdened with emotion nor an account of the ecstatic experiences that might have been summoned by a return to one's own past. Instead, the images and objects that Honert produces with the help of these memories appear to be emotionally neutral, objective, and artistically well controlled. In addition, they refer to everyday things and events (*House*, 1988, *Starling*, 1992, or *Fire*, 1992), to a photo album belong to the artist's parents (*Photo*, 1993), or to the artist's own drawings from childhood (*Nikolaus/ Santa Claus*, or *Gang*, both 2002). In none of these cases is it really possible to ascertain the psychological reason why Honert found precisely this or that mnemonic image worthy of being reproduced as an artwork, in what is often a strenuous and tedious process. The selection seems almost arbitrary—and as a result it resists any attempt to give the images a psychoanalytical interpretation by treating them as symptoms of a traumatic experience. The selection of mnemonic images is too heterogeneous, too disparate, and too aleatoric to permit such an interpretation. It is immediately evident that any attempt at a homogenizing hermeneutics of these images is condemned to failure from the start. Rather, the images signal that they contain no mystery, that they are not symptoms of traumatic experiences, and that they offer no revelation of anything interior or hidden. Their only mystery is that they programmatically lack any mystery; their only manifest trauma is their lack of any trauma. If they are at all open to being interpreted as obsessive, it is only an obsessive resistance, if you will, to any possible discursive interpretation—a claim to stand exclusively for themselves, alone and isolated.

This aura of deliberate seclusion distinguishes all of Honert's works. The idyll that they suggest is a secluded one. All of Honert's images, objects, and installations assert and illustrate their radical spatial and temporal isolation; they quite obviously have no wish to share their space or time with others. Hence these works can be understood as images of childhood, but of a childhood, as Honert interprets it, that is a time of radical seclusion. And the images of seclusion that the artist preserves as childhood memories are employed as metaphors for the seclusion that ultimately distinguishes any artistic creation. Paradoxically, however, this metaphorical use presumes that the images cannot come entirely from inside, cannot derive solely from the artist's own memory, but must be taken at least in part from external reality. This is the crucial aspect of the way Honert grapples with the problem of memory: he fundamentally distrusts "inner images," including traumatic ones. For him, memory always refers to something that can—and should—be found in external reality. When the artist recalls a house, a bird, or a fire, he asks what this house really looks like, objectively; he photographs the house and uses the photograph as a model for the work in question. Or he consults an encyclopedia to find out what a starling looks like, objectively. Or he builds a model to find out how fire really works, and so on. And even when the memory is entirely personal, Honert consults his archive, or that of his parents. Thus the memory as such is not yet an image for Honert. Implicitly, the insistence that the invisible inner world of subjectivity be made visible—something proposed by many theories of modern art—is meaningless, because there are no images in the interior of memory. The space of memory is empty; it contains only references to images that must be sought elsewhere, in external reality. Individual memories are precisely references to images found in the external space of reality, and must be integrated into the space of memory by means of art.

Hence Honert's relationship to the archive of his memory is emphatically distanced and objective. Just as many other artists, particularly in the United States, use the world of the mass media strategically, citing images from it as readymades and thereby creating something like an archive of the collective consciousness or collective memory, so Honert uses his own memory, secluded and idiosyncratic though it may be, as the reference system for a personal memory archive that he can deliberately compile. In his work with his childhood memories, Honert is not an Expressionist artist subject to an unconscious compulsion to express himself; rather, he is a Pop artist who draws readymades into his memory and collects them there.

To a certain extent, this strategy of the distanced, readymade-like approach to one's own memory demonstrates Honert's affiliation with a certain artistic milieu based primarily in Düsseldorf. Emergent in the 1980s, the group comprises such artists as Katharina Fritsch, Thomas Schütte, and Thomas Ruff, who practice a neutral, objective, distanced treatment of the European painting tradition, or of individual mythology, or of everyday objects and impressions from their immediate surroundings. For all their individual differences, these artists are united by their distance from the "hot" Neo-Expressionist painting of the Neue Wilden, like Albert Oehlen or Martin Kippenberger, the neo-Fauves who also came to prominence in the 1980s and were able to quickly conquer the German art market. The Düsseldorf artists, by contrast, were fascinated by Pop art and its attempt to come to terms with the myths of mass culture and everyday American life. They wanted, however—even, to a certain extent, like in the previous generation, with artists like Gerhard Richter and Sigmar Polke—to develop a European and even specifically German way of confronting their own cultural surroundings, one more influenced by history, be it political or artistic, than the American version. To that end these artists could call on the Neue Sachlichkeit tradition of the 1920s and '30s, which also practiced a neutral, objectifying approach to the surrounding world and to art, and thereby differentiated itself from the Expressionism that dominated at the time. The Düsseldorf artists, however, lack the sarcastic, critical, and accusatory attitude of Neue Sachlichkeit. Instead their art is marked by a certain cool, neutral distance more characteristic, as we have noted, of Pop art in the United States.

Although Honert's art is part of the Düsseldorf art scene in many respects, it is also rigorously independent. Honert is not explicitly concerned with the tradition of German painting, everyday life in contemporary Germany, or the political and social attitudes of his generation. One might say that Honert is a "self-collector." It is, of course, only possible to be a self-collector if one is inwardly divided, if one takes the position of an observer of one's own remembered life. This inner tension has nothing to do with individual traumatic experience, however. It cannot be said—and Honert emphasizes this in his interviews and commentaries—that the artist is pursuing a narcissistic drive and practicing or celebrating uncritical self-examination. Rather, Honert insists on the exemplary and universal character of his art. He sees his confrontation with his childhood as a practice permitting him to obtain general insights into the relationship between the experience of childhood and the creation of art. For that reason too, he avoids all allusions to an individual trauma, allusions that could lessen the universal claim of his art. The inner division of artistic consciousness that Honert has diagnosed in his oeuvre is a division characteristic of contemporary art generally—but Honert's art thematizes it in an especially interesting and persuasive way.

At least since the dawning of the Romantic age, in the late eighteenth century, artistic creation has been stuck in a dilemma that is easy to describe but difficult to escape. According to the modern view, the artwork should faithfully capture the moment of artistic inspiration. Hence, if it is to be considered an authentic artistic achievement, it must be created spontaneously and without visible effort. Anything that smells of sweat, that betrays the investment of strenuous work—in short, anything that resembles a craft—is met with contempt. Modern art ultimately strives for the miracle of a work beyond work, but this effort repeatedly proves futile, for every artwork inevitably presents itself as the product of an investment of labor—and this simultaneously undermines its claim to spontaneity and authenticity. Unfortunately, art cannot work without craft—and hence modern art is stuck in this dilemma: it wants to be art, now as ever, but at the same time a kind of art that does not look like the result of a craft.

Many attempts to escape this dilemma have led to the creation of spontaneous Expressionist painting. In Germany in the 1970s and '80s a declaration of the truth of immediate expression was made by the generation of "princes among painters" such as Georg Baselitz, Anselm Kiefer, and Markus Lüpertz, who claimed to be creators whose art was due only to themselves and to their own genius, not to any model or craft. Even in this case, however, the craft of painting could not be entirely overcome—something that is confirmed indirectly by the fact that these artists always insist on the "quality" of their work. The ostensibly opposed strategy of using readymades or photography in art, a strategy that at first glance appears to contradict the Expressionist claim to authenticity, actually follows the same logic of Romantic spontaneity: here too the artwork should be created in the moment through a pure act of free artistic decision—namely, the decision to place an object or image in the artistic context and to preserve it there. But this method is insufficient on its own to overcome the original dilemma: the work is simply delegated to others, to those who produced the objects and images that artists use as readymades, and to those who built the spaces that artists can occupy with their readymades in a momentary, spontaneous decision.

This is precisely the dilemma that Honert tries to escape in his art—namely, by explicitly separating momentary inspiration from craft. Accordingly, he rigorously presents his works as the sum of two artistic operations that are clearly distinguishable from each other. On the one hand, Honert uses images that draw his attention momentarily and by chance, such as a house, a bird, or even the images that he simply finds in his own archive—the drawings he made as a child, without any conscious artistic or professional intention. On the other hand, he invests a considerable amount of craftsmanship in these images, which makes them into artworks that he can then present as his own. This enables him to strictly distinguish the spontaneous and "personal" from the artisanal and "alien" in his work.

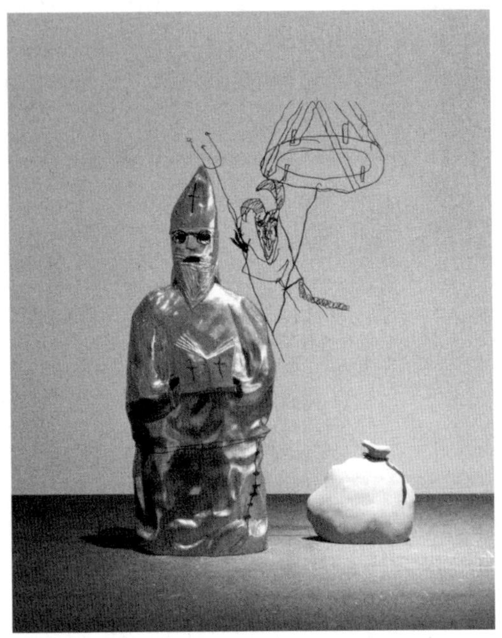

Martin Honert, *Nikolaus/Santa Claus*, 2002

Honert alludes first of all to the Romantic ideal of the artist as eternal child—creating images spontaneously, playfully, and without any explicit brief, whether from the market or public, but as an immediate expression of his or her joie de vivre. To engage in a creative activity in a paradisal state of innocence, of not knowing what one is really doing, is to be indebted only to oneself for one's images and to no one else. Because these images are supposedly created without the intention of being used in the art system, as if they emerged on their own, they cannot be criticized by art criticism's usual rhetorical means. To be sure, children will inevitably use models from films, magazines, or other children's drawings for their drawings. Particularly in our day, when the entertainment industry has specialized in producing artificial worlds for children that are brought into their rooms by means of television or mobile technology, we can hardly speak of the pictorial world that a child uses for his or her art as autonomous. What is important here, however, is that one cannot criticize children for using this or that image, technique, or procedure in their drawings, nor for how they use them. Children's drawings are innocent in the sense that they are art outside of all professional artistic intention, and also outside of the art market. Such a children's (non)art, one that remains on this side of the threshold to standard professional art, is precisely what Honert uses as readymade material for his "adult" art. Even if these images are not invented but rather found among his own childhood works, the ways that he reworks and places them are of course dictated by professional and strategic considerations that owe their validity to a knowledge of the art world today.

Hence Honert's art can also be interpreted as not only cultivating and illustrating the artist's own memory but also arguing polemically against practices that define our approach to childhood today. For example, the art that Honert pursues does not look infantile, wild, or naive. On the contrary, he rigorously avoids any stylization of the childlike or any artistic convention that might have served in modernism to suggest the naive gaze of the child; his works look thoroughly mature, professional, and thought-out. He is even proud of his artisanship: in a few works he cites the drawings from his childhood faithfully and literally, precluding any kind of belated artistic stylization of the childlike. In citing these drawings Honert is also following a strategy aimed at using the drawings to create spatial installations. These installations are too well planned, artistically and technically, to be mistaken for "children's art"—even though their construction follows the model of Honert's corresponding childhood drawings in every detail. The adult artist thus takes the skill that he has gained in the course of his artistic life and places it in the service of a drawing that he himself sketched as a child. As a practiced artisan, employing his professional experience and skill, he repeats an image that he made at a time when he did not possess that experience and skill. This gesture of literal repetition manifests an unswerving fidelity to himself—and specifically to himself in a state of childlike innocence. Even so, it is only possible—and only necessary—because Honert does not believe that he, as he exists here and now, has any "inner" connection to the child that he once was. One prerequisite of this kind of fidelity is the conviction that adulthood means an absolute and irrevocable break with childhood—or to put it more generally: the conviction that every memory is ultimately false, that we cannot have inner access to our own past, that the continuity of our subjectivity is an illusion. In his day, Siegfried Kracauer criticized photography for preserving only a superficial memory of others and ourselves—and hence for negating and killing off our inner living memory.[1] Honert, however, no longer possesses this faith in the possibility of an inner living memory—not even in the form of an unconscious trauma that could be pulled out of the depths of one's psyche.

Consequently, Honert feels obliged only to the external, artificial, and artistic documents of memory. Through his actions as an artist he confesses his faith, as it were, in his own memories. That recalls the faith in the image of Christ, an image that Kierkegaard once remarked was necessary to guarantee the continuity of faith—precisely because it is an image one cannot recall.[2] Fidelity to the external sign of one's own existence, one's own life history, becomes equally necessary if one no longer believes in the continuity of one's own subjectivity. One might say that it is this lack of faith in the continuity of his own self that drives Honert's artistic production. An insight into the death of the subject, into the impossibility of obtaining a guarantee of one's own identity, has seduced many artists into making this identity loss an explicit theme of their work—by means of stylistic leaps, or by using heterogeneous forms, materials, and artistic methods. Honert, as we have seen, proceeds from the same insight into the discontinuity of his own subjectivity, the impossibility of finding an identity. But this does not lead him to postmodern patchwork. Instead, he attempts to compensate for the lack of inner continuity by remaining faithful to an external continuity in his own life. Using the artistic means of repetition, he creates an external continuity where an internal one is lacking. He artificially constructs an identity precisely because he does not believe in this identity's reality. Honert has told me:

> I don't think that I'm involved in the problems of my childhood—I am indirectly of course, but I'm not directly stuck in that emotional world. That is an important point. Childhood is a theme for me not because I think my childhood was especially eventful, or bad, or good; my childhood was exactly as dull and boring as every other childhood.

> Childhood is a theme for me because I think it's important to discover what's long past but still in the memory as an image. The memories that remain from farthest back become the most important for me. This has nothing to do with psychoanalysis; there are certainly ugly and beautiful things in my childhood, things I want to overcome and things I want to or have to live with, but those things don't interest me as an artist. People have asked me whether my work has a therapeutic side, but I consciously distance myself from that side of art.[3]

The use of new artistic material for the repetition of the same artistic form is thus as much an act of self-commitment as it is an act of self-distancing.

It is also possible to detect a certain artistic evolution in Honert's attempt to come to terms with his own history. The most important change—at least from an external perspective—took place in 1995, when the artist, who had been mainly occupied with isolated images or objects up until that point, moved to the art form of the installation when he exhibited *A Model Scenario of the Flying Classroom* in the German Pavilion of the 46th Venice Biennale. The work takes its title from Erich Kästner's *The Flying Classroom*, a children's novel written in 1933. Honert remains faithful to Kästner's text, both in the installation's details and in its basic mood. A section of Kästner's novel tells of a play, also called *The Flying Classroom*, staged by the novel's hero, Martin; Honert's installation reconstructs the play's set as Kästner describes it. What Honert depicts, then, is not reality, not the everyday life of the child as that life is described in Kästner's novel. Rather, Honert is interested in the way the hero of the novel dramatizes himself in art. In Kästner's novel, too, this dramatization is the central event: real life revolves around art. The mnemonic image that Honert seeks is therefore, from the start, an artistic image, an artistic vision—ultimately a theatricalization of the self. For this self-dramatization shows more clearly than so-called reality (which in the end, after all, can only be grasped and described from outside) how the child views, organizes, and experiences the world.

Hence, memory leads not to life but to art, although they are the same thing in a child's eyes. Children are not innocent because they see reality as undisguised or unstaged, but on the contrary because they do not distinguish strategically between life and theater. Our culture still functions largely under the Romantic assumption that the child sees the world, reality, and life with "new eyes"—seeing through the cultural mise-en-scène. That is why it is only the child who sees that the emperor has no clothes in Hans Christian Andersen's famous tale. But, de facto, it is precisely the staged world of our civilization that the child experiences as the only reality—and thus the child becomes this civilization's vanishing point, where reality and fiction merge. The return to the past, and the repetition of a memory by means of art, are possible only because our memories are, from the start, memories of our own theatrical invention of the self. The chain of memory is a chain of self-theatricalizations whose continuity is guaranteed only through fidelity to prior mise-en-scènes.

In the installation *A Model Scenario of the Flying Classroom* Honert identifies with a doppelgänger, a literary figure; in later installations, however, he uses his own drawings from childhood, which are unmistakably theatricalizations of the self. This is particularly clear in the installation *Gang* (2002). This childhood drawing (made when the artist was somewhere between eight and ten) presents the young Martin as the nameless and secret ruler of his gang of friends. They all have names, and they appear in a row. He, however, exists in a different space—more a protective god than an earthly leader. Obviously the young Martin already had an access to the world that differed from that of his rather

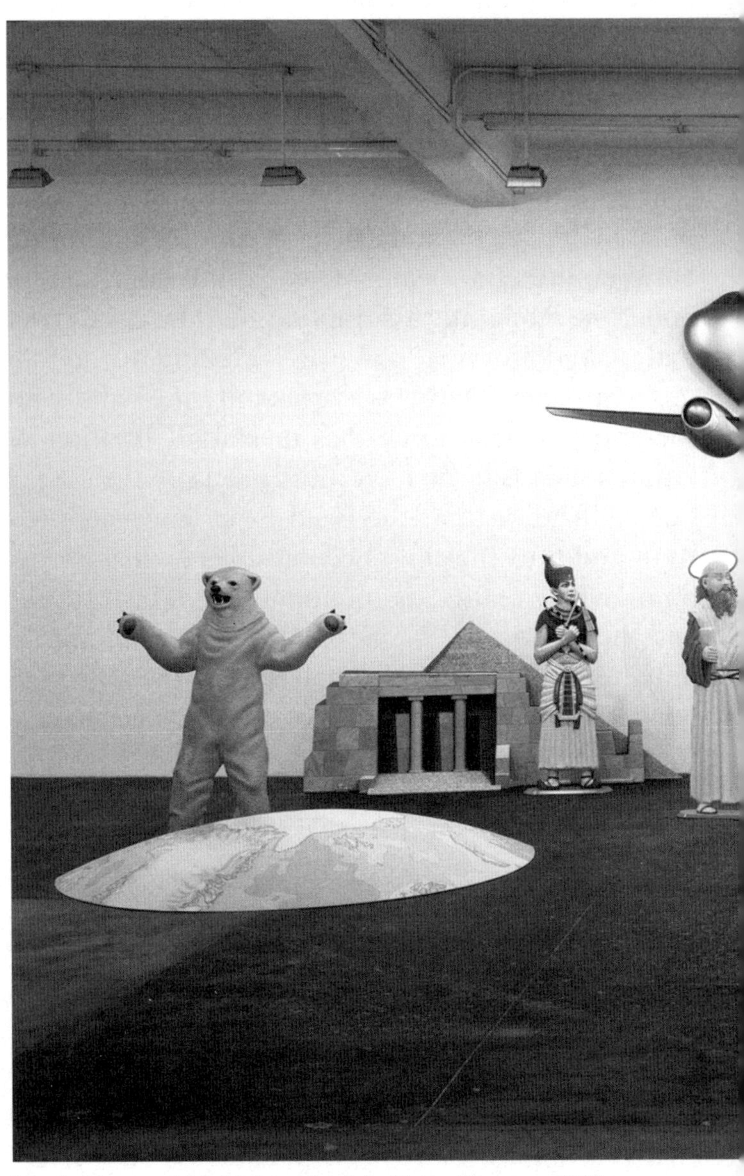

Martin Honert, *A Model Scenario of the Flying Classroom*, 1995

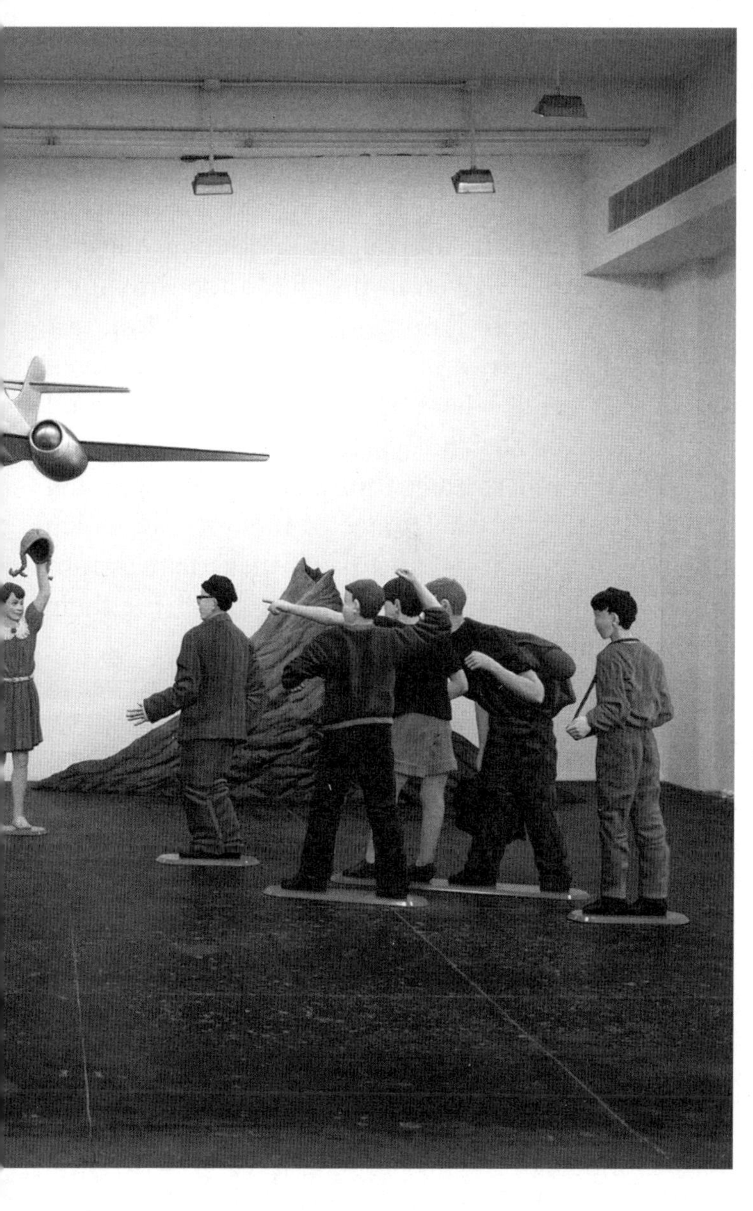

ordinary-looking friends. This "other world" is presented in drawings like *Nikolaus/Santa Claus* and *Ghosts* (both 2002), which also serve as models for Honert's eponymous installations. Both drawings place the viewer in a ghostly realm, their iconography pointing to the pictorial world of the German Catholic tradition. For Honert, however, this reference is clearly less important than the thoroughly subjective interpretation that this tradition is given in his childhood drawings. Santa and his helper Knecht Ruprecht float in the void, just as ghosts do.[4] Like the heroes of *A Model Scenario*, or even the members of the "gang," these figures seem weightless and without context. This is clearly the feature of his childhood drawings that Honert most values today: from the beginning they seem to create the abstract space of memory, in which individual things, impressions, and (self-)theatricalizations can float freely—until the artist uses his craft to bring them down to earth and archive them.

The viewer of these installations cannot help but recall that the year in which Kästner's novel was written, 1933, marked the beginning of a traumatic epoch in German history. And neither can we help but remark that the childhood drawings that form the basis of the later installations date from the phase of rebuilding that followed German defeat in the war. Consequently, the play of decontextualizing and recontextualizing, of staging and restaging the self, that revolves around this traumatic time can be interpreted as an attempt to deal with a collective history in which Honert did not take part but that was nevertheless of defining importance for his generation. We could equally understand the implicit reference to the innocence of childhood as a response to what is usually called "the question of German guilt." There can be no doubt that the artist intends such an interpretation, at least in part. Yet it would be misguided to seek hidden political content in Honert's art. Rather, we can assume that the constant discussions of personal and collective guilt that were held in Germany during the postwar period led Honert—and other contemporaries as well—to pursue the question of individual guilt with particular attention. For example, to whom is one indebted for one's own art? To oneself, the individual genius—or to one's cultural context, tradition, education, milieu?

Walter Benjamin, in his well-known fragment "Capitalism as Religion" (1921), which describes capitalism as a religious cult whose rites are continuously observed by modern society, remarks, "Capitalism is probably the first instance of a cult that creates guilt, not atonement. [...] A vast sense of guilt that is unable to find relief seizes on the cult, not to atone for this guilt but to make it universal, to hammer it into the conscious mind, so as once and for all to include God in the system of guilt and thereby awaken in Him an interest in the process of atonement."[5] Obviously Benjamin is not speaking solely of the financial indebtedness that is a structural feature of capitalism, which famously lives from credit. Rather, his concern is that economics has entered all aspects of modern culture, whose central task is now to establish as precisely as possible the exact amount of debt carried by every individual, by society, and by all other active subjects, including God. Psychoanalysis also belongs to this economy, in Benjamin's view: "Freud's theory, too, belongs to the hegemony of the priests of this cult. Its conception is capitalist through and through. By virtue of a profound analogy, which still has to be illuminated, what has been repressed, the idea of sin, is capital itself, which pays interest on the hell of the unconscious."[6]

Proceeding from Benjamin's position, one can say that Honert's art analyzes the internal economy of artistic creativity by distinguishing strictly between what his work owes to the unconsidered sketch whose origin can be found in his childhood and what it owes to his later artisanal execution. At the same time, the origin of this artistic sketch is not to be sought entirely in the child. In order to stage themselves, children necessarily use the means provided by their immediate cultural surroundings. The imagination of the child thus proves to be too staged, too "artistic" from the start, to be reduced in all seriousness to the "real" guilty imagination and to be banned to the hell of the unconscious. At the same time, this imagination, in its status between reality and art, is also too indeterminate to be examined for its indebtedness to the political and economic conditions of the current art industry. Thus the artist causes the ghosts of his imagination to hover in the empty space of memory that lies between hell and paradise— neither originally guilty nor definitively atoned.

Notes

1.  Siegfried Kracauer, "Photography," in *The Mass Ornament: Weimar Essays*, ed. and trans. Thomas Y. Levin (Cambridge, MA: Harvard University Press, 1995), 47–63, esp. 50–51, 58–59.
2.  Søren Kierkegaard, "Truth Is Subjectivity," in *Concluding Unscientific Postscript*, trans. David F. Swenson and Walter Lowrie (Princeton, NJ: Princeton University Press, 1968), 169–224.
3.  Martin Honert, quoted in Boris Groys, "Mind's Eye Views: Boris Groys Talks with Martin Honert," *Artforum*, February 1995, 104.
4.  [Translator's note: In some German traditions Knecht Ruprecht is a companion figure to Nikolaus (Santa Claus). He is usually depicted as the one who punishes the bad children.]
5.  Walter Benjamin, "Capitalism as Religion," trans. Rodney Livingstone, in *Selected Writings*, vol. 1, *1913–1926*, ed. Marcus Bullock and Michael W. Jennings (Cambridge, MA: Belknap Press of Harvard University Press, 1996), 288–89. [Translator's note: Rodney Livingstone comments in a note that the German word *Schuld*, which he translates here as "guilt," also means "debt." The present essay plays on this ambiguity as well, but I have used forms of "guilt" and "debt" respectively.]
6.  Ibid., 289.

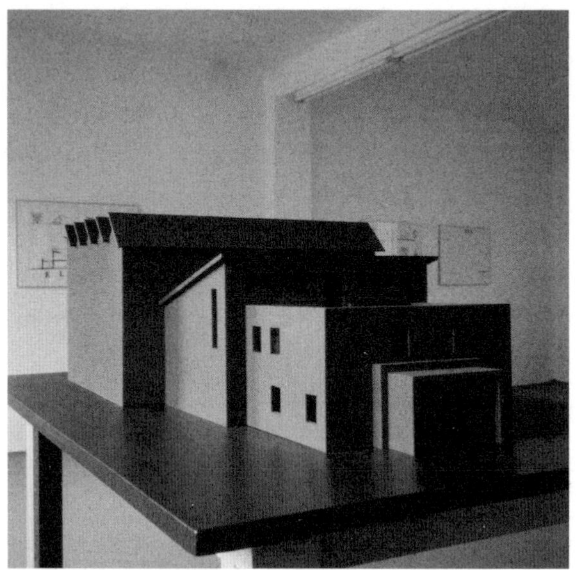

Thomas Schütte, *E.L.S.A.*, 1989

7
Thomas Schütte
Escaping the Prison of a Style

It is not an easy task to address the oeuvre of Thomas Schütte, since it cannot be analyzed using the usual terms to describe an individual style, a clearly defined artistic program, or a recognizable attitude. Imagine an exhibition of Schütte's complete body of works: such a virtual exhibition looks like a collection of heterogeneous objects reflecting extremely different artistic styles, programs, and attitudes—like an exhibition not of an individual artist but of several artists. In this exhibition, separate groups of artworks can be identified. And the works have common styles and attitudes within each group, but there is no clear or understandable connection between the various groups.

Many artists do change their attitudes and methods during the course of their careers, and such changes can be significant, which is why art-historical writing predominantly deals with the development, the history, of an individual artistic project. Such a development is usually described in Hegelian terms as a movement of self-reflection. Artists reflect on their previous works and move on further, considering their own achievements and failures, formulating new goals, or reinterpreting old works. This self-reflection can be—up to a certain degree, but nevertheless in a more or less plausible way—understood and described by a spectator, art critic, or art historian.

However, in this virtual exhibition of Schütte's collected works, the change from one group to another betrays no clear progression; it does not seem to represent a process of self-reflection on the artist's side. Instead the spectator confronts abrupt, seemingly unmotivated changes, shifts, and gaps that cannot be described as a continuous development or an individual artistic project. Rather, as spectators, we encounter a Foucauldian notion of the historical archive of different paradigms. The shifts from one paradigm to another seem to just happen. It is difficult to imagine a conscious and subjective self-reflection—self-reflecting subjectivity—unifying all these heterogeneous artistic strategies. The collection of Schütte's works look like the result of transferring the Foucauldian notion of a universal historical archive to an individual artistic archive. Here the archive of the individual creation presents itself as a combination of continuities and ruptures that does not allow understanding and explanation in the traditional terms of an art-historical analysis. Every such homogenizing and unifying interpretation must function as an act of violence, ignoring the fundamental heterogeneity of Schütte's work.

The strategy of creating a personal collection consisting of ostensibly incongruous objects by following obscure, hermetic, or even random rules of choice is well known and established in the context of contemporary art. But, as a rule, contemporary artists who create their own collections and personal museums do so by using readymades, photographs, or videos, which provide the possibility for these artists to collect the world rather than produce it. The contemporary artist thus acts not as a creator but as a consumer, as an appropriator of things produced by modern technology that circulate anonymously in our mass culture. This artistic practice is often characterized in terms of the "death of the author," but it may be more apt to describe it as the emergence of a different type of authorship, which manifests itself not through an act of production but through an act of consumption, of appropriation—a deferred, assumed authorship post-factum. The mechanism of such a deferred assumption of authorship has been suggested long before Marcel Duchamp. This alternative notion of authorship was proposed much earlier by Søren Kierkegaard, who described authorship as taking ethical and social responsibility for something that one has not done or has done "unknowingly"—that is, not as a conscious subject or as producer of one's own actions.[1]

The case of Schütte is much more complicated. He produces all the objects of which he claims to be author. When he speaks about his own work, he stresses the point that his methods of art production are traditional and do not relate to or rely on contemporary technology. Schütte does not appropriate. He is an author-creator. Still, the obvious discontinuities and gaps in his artistic production suggest the loss of the traditional notions of artistic identity or creative subjectivity. Schütte is able to demonstrate the fate of artistic subjectivity in modernity precisely because he does not reject the traditional role of the artist as creator, as many other artists do. Schütte consciously takes on this traditional role and, at the same time, he presents the collection of his own works as a kind of *Wunderkammer* consisting of disparate and disconnected sets of objects and images.

A complicated interplay between two different notions of authorship—artist-creator and artist-appropriator—determines the inner dynamic of Schütte's work. His strategy is not one of self-reflection but of self-appropriation, as if two different authors are living and acting in one and the same authorial inner space—the post-Foucauldian author-collector appropriating the pre-Foucauldian author-creator. It is as if the artist picks up images from different parts of the individual world of his creative personal imagination and memory, but he does it in such a way that the general topography of this world as a whole remains concealed, and the history of the creative development of his imagination also remains hidden. As spectators, we are confronted, in the first place, with gaps and shifts that deny any possibility for the usual reconstruction of the inner landscape of the artistic imagination. Therefore, we become the spectators not of the death of the traditional author but of his calculated and carefully staged suicide. The whole world of the creative, personal, and Romantic imagination is shown by Schütte as debris of the past, which we cannot understand or reconstruct but can only collect.

It is important to recognize the similarities between the artistic strategy of Schütte and the Foucauldian description of historical memory as an arrangement of gaps and ruptures. The fact that all the objects produced by Schütte are also produced by him, and are not simply chosen as readymades, makes the experience of a loss of self-reflective subjectivity and of the possibility of a continuous historical narrative much more acute, much more immediate. The absence of continuity, of a unifying project, of the subject of universal history as stated by Foucault, seems to leave us more or less cold. The news that history has no subject and that historical memory cannot be organized according to a dominant narrative seems, at first glance at least, to be even liberating, optimistic, and prospective in its promise of a new individual freedom in the handling of history. But, as the art of Schütte shows, if we accept this Foucauldian model, we immediately confront the same problems in relation to our own personal history. Our personal development suddenly loses its logic and its memory, and it turns into a heap of heterogeneous objects open to a more or less unmotivated and random choice of collected items.

This parallel between universal and individual histories is underlined by Schütte's complicated citations of art history.

The images he uses in his production are derived from a world whose phenomenology is primarily familiar to us not from our own inner psychological experience, but from art history, dream analysis, and popular culture. The objects crafted by Schütte suggest, in a certain way, private traumas and obsessions, but at the same time they are placed in cold neutral spaces that make them look like collector's items. The art-historical references are never direct and explicit but are always present, always suggested, and thus Schütte's works never pretend to be immediate or eruptive manifestations of the artist's compelling personality. Schütte does not follow Duchamp, but neither does he present himself as a postmodern "genius" like, say, Georg Baselitz or Markus Lüpertz.

Schütte is not especially fascinated by modern technological civilization or commercialized artistic production. Like many European artists of his generation he associates the latter with the United States, specifically with the art of the last few decades and the American art market. In this sense, his art also attempts to formulate an alternative, distinctly European way of aesthetic reflection and art making—in effect, as a polemic against American art. The following questions are raised by his art: What has actually happened to traditional European art and artistic attitudes in our time? How can an artist, raised within and by the European cultural tradition, work under the contemporary (that is, American-dominated) conditions of art production and distribution? How can the artist deal with the seemingly irrelevant disparate remnants and traces of the old European tradition? Schütte does not rely on easy answers, as do some of his French and German colleagues—who seem to believe that in order to restitute the concept of the "true artist" in the European tradition all they need to do is look deep into their own souls. However, although Schütte acknowledges the death of the old European artistic subjectivity, he still tries to collect its remnants and traces from his personal memory and imagination.

The entire history of European art, German art especially, in the twentieth century is characterized by the conflict between, on the one side, a direct expressive gesture, an individual revolt, a violent eruption of inner passion directed against its suppression by the coldness of the modern age, and, on the other, a neutral and objective, yet ironic, description of the conditions of modern life. Consider, for example, the opposition between Expressionism and Neue Sachlichkeit in the 1920s. Schütte takes no sides in this old conflict, which resurfaced in the 1980s in Germany with the rise of Neo-Expressionism. Instead he avoids this rigid opposition by delivering his personal emotional statement in the form of an understatement and by distancing himself from the ready-made aesthetics that dominate internationally, as well as from the pathos of Expressionist painting. At the center of Schütte's work is not an artistic genius but a certain void, an absence—an inner space presented in a way similar to the neutral space of a modern museum—not an eruptive space, as found in the work of many of his colleagues. He ironically demonstrates his subjectivity by demonstrating a loss of subjectivity. His work gathers up the lasting residue of the purely subjective, free, dreamlike European imagination, and what's more he performs a eulogy, or a bereavement, for this lost subjectivity. One can say that new contemporary subjectivity and authorship are founded on this sacrifice of the traditional notion of the artist as genius.

In his well-known theory of "symbolic exchange," Marcel Mauss describes the role of sacrifice in so-called traditional cultures as a freely induced loss of one's wealth by means of a sacrifice or a gift, which brings with it symbolic compensation in the form of honor and glory.[2] Within the framework of his "general economy," Georges Bataille applies this model of voluntary loss to art, suggesting that the artist acquires utmost glory when he loses himself most radically in his work. Bataille describes the particularly spectacular forms of such loss of self through the excess and delirium that characterizes the poète maudit in the French tradition.[3] But there are more subtle, and even more radical forms of sacrifice; for example, producing art through one's own physical work in this time of rampant technological and readymade production. By using traditional methods, Schütte's handwork does not simply return to the traditional personae of the artist—that is, his methodology is not a reactionary movement back to the notion of art making as it existed before the technological era. Rather, his manual work manifests itself in our time as an unnecessary, excessive, superfluous act—as pure sacrifice of time and vital energy. Precisely this subtle effect of excess and sacrifice is central for his artistic strategy.

In this respect, it is notable that early in his career Schütte established an immediate relationship between collection, museum, and sacrifice. From 1981 to '82, he drafted and constructed *Model for a Museum*. The model is conventionally impressive, but closer inspection reveals it to be a huge crematorium with ovens installed to burn the collected works. The museum functions not as an institution for collecting and preserving art but as a machine for consuming and destroying art. With *Model for a Museum* Schütte advances a long-standing metaphor: the museum as cemetery, a comparison that poses the scenario that what is already presented in the museum is automatically regarded by our culture as belonging to the past—as already dead. If we encounter, outside the museum, something that reminds us of the forms, positions, and approaches represented inside, we will not see this thing

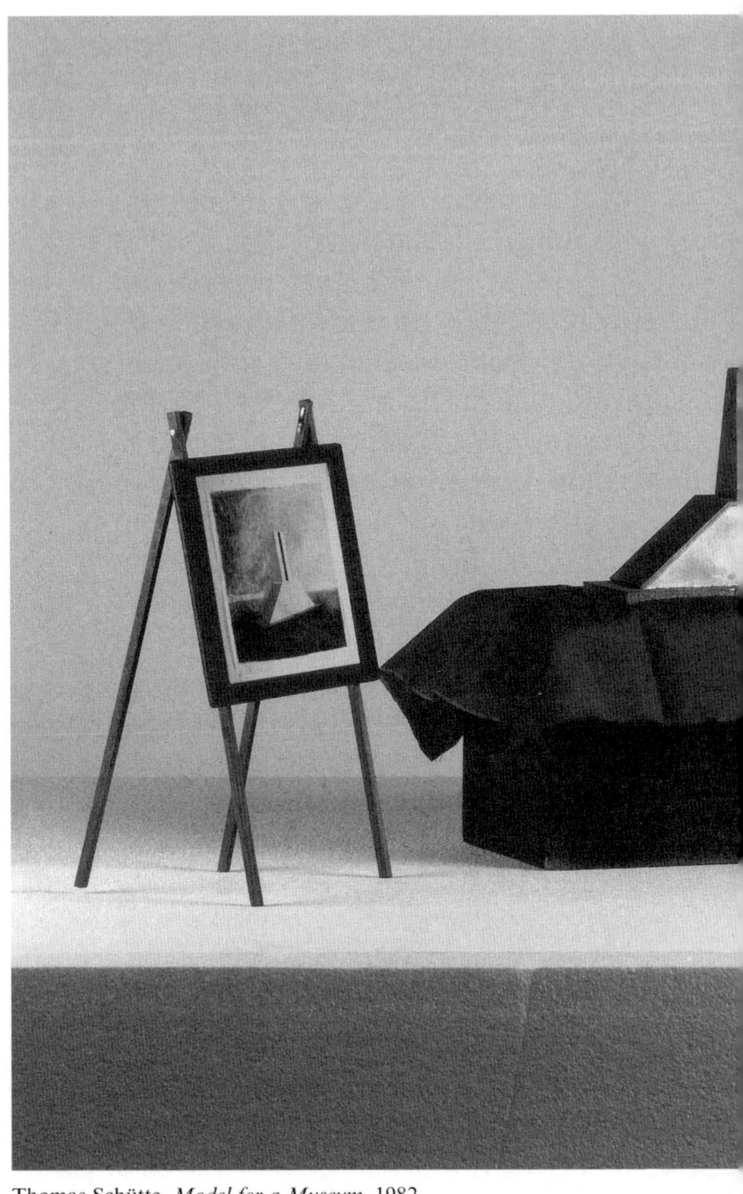

Thomas Schütte, *Model for a Museum*, 1982

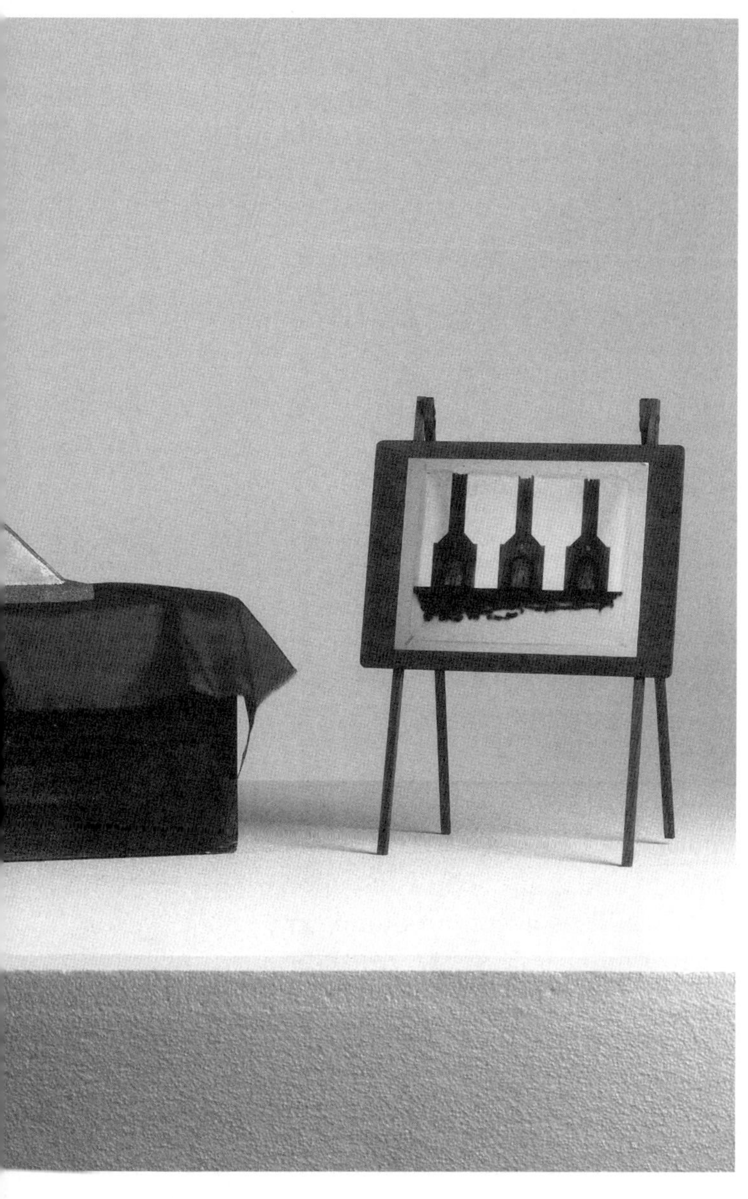

as real or living, we'll see it as a dead copy of the dead past, incapable of being truly present or relevant, like a walking corpse. In 1981 Schütte employed the analogy—the museum as cemetery, and curators, art critics, and art historians as gravediggers—in a design for his own tomb, upon which he assigned a date for his own death: March 25, 1996. But, with *Model for a Museum*, Schütte takes on a different, much more radical metaphor: the museum as crematorium.

In so doing, he brings to mind a short but important text of the early avant-garde, Kazimir Malevich's "On the Museum" (1919). At the time the text was written, the newly established Soviet government feared that the old Russian museums and art collections could be destroyed through the civil war and the general collapse of state institutions and the economy, so the Communist Party tried to secure and save these collections. Malevich protests against the regime's pro-museum policy and calls on the state not to intervene on behalf of the old art collections because their destruction would open the path to a new truly living art. Malevich writes: "Life knows what it is doing, and if it is striving to destroy one must not interfere, since by hindering we are blocking the path to a new conception of the life that is born within us. […] In burning a corpse we obtain one gram of powder: accordingly thousands of graveyards could be accommodated on a single chemist's shelf."[4] Schütte materialized the conflation of the museum and the crematorium, but its conception had in fact already emerged with the birth of the avant-garde.

This truly modern way to deal with corpses of history fascinated many artists and intellectuals in the nineteenth and twentieth centuries, and many of them actually professed a desire to be cremated in order to obliterate any traces that could connect them to history and the past. They believed this sacrifice would open the way for a new conception of life, as Malevich describes it. Nevertheless the cremains are still collected, and that is the subject of a later project, which Schütte titled *The Collector's Complex* (1990), a work that implies the housing and presentation of the ashes of burned old works. It is a kind of museum-pharmacy that enumerates, arranges, names, and titles. Malevich also concedes to the establishment of an archive of ashes that could provoke memories and "ideas" in the imagination of the spectator.

Indeed, collection, cataloguing, categorization, and description have deep and clear connections to burial, destruction, and cremation. To be identified and classified, singled out and categorized, corresponds to being endangered, thrown away, destroyed, or even eliminated. Categorizations, classifications, and identifications, which seem to facilitate the smooth functioning of historical memory, allow for judgments on both the individual work and the individual artist— potentially dangerous and destructive judgments, or even convictions. These arbitraments are made, of course, not only in art, but also in political and social life. On the contrary, the ability to evade or escape identification can save the work and the person. Losing identity is here not just a negative loss, it is instead a calculated sacrifice that promises survival. Nonclassification makes it possible for one to sneak through borders—and remain alive.

The tendency and even struggle to avoid classification and categorization is characteristic of many German artists working after World War II—including Gerhard Richter, who was Schütte's teacher at the Kunstakademie Düsseldorf in the '70s. The calculated, consciously performed loss of identity is seen by many artists not as tragedy but as opportunity. Their relationship to the archives of history and memory is ambiguous and complicated: on the one hand, the museum gives the system of historical memory a chance to be preserved, especially in our secular times, when we no longer can rely on the eternal memory of God; on the other, the same archive, the same system of categorization, can be used and in fact is used to destroy, isolate, and kill. Historical experience in Schütte's work is in many ways tenuous in its relationship to collection.

Schütte's particular will to escape identification sometimes takes on an obsessive form, leading to artworks that are invisible, unrecognizable, and unidentifiable. One group of works, including *E.L.S.A.* (1989), *Studio* (1983–86), and *W.A.S.* (1989), resemble Bauhaus projects. They could be taken and interpreted as utopian urban spaces of the future. Half functional and half nonfunctional, they are situated between an artwork and an architectural project. On further consideration, though, these models are anything but utopian. In fact, in an interview with writer and curator James Lingwood, Schütte admitted that while he was strongly influenced by Russian Productivism, by Constructivism in general, and by the Bauhaus, he also blames the Bauhaus for being responsible for the monotony of contemporary cities, claiming postmodern architecture as a liberation from modernist dogma.[5]

These are complicated negotiations. Though Schütte shares the interest of the Bauhaus to bring art into life, these models are nevertheless postmodern precisely in their quotation of modern architectural styles. At the same time, they do not share in the postmodern celebration of exclusivity and the classical tradition. Schütte's art is rather "cheap," a kind of Arte Povera architecture. This approach characterizes "second modernity"—the catchword that became popular in Germany in the 1990s (in art as well as architecture) to identify what comes after postmodernity, which was a modernity that stylistically reflected the art of the twentieth century, a modernity that had gone through a period of (postmodern) self-reflection and had evolved into a second modernity.

I also tend to interpret this second modernity as a second-hand modernity, a boring, uninspired, shabby modernity that follows everyday life, while still determining it. This modernity is our destiny, our fate. It does not expose any hope or project for the future, but it typifies the inescapable condition of everyday existence. I would say that Schütte constructs precisely this second modernity—the secondhand modernity—in his models. The main opposition, at least in immediate art-historical terms, that Schütte tries to escape with these models is precisely the opposition between modernity and post-modernity. It is an intense, sharply formulated opposition, which dominated the consciousness of the German art scene in the '80s. Schütte withdraws from this *neo* or *post* attitude and instead embraces humdrum reality.

The series of works titled *Great Spirits* (1995–2004) reminds us of the cyborgs of the 1991 film *Terminator 2: Judgment Day*, as well as of Umberto Boccioni, the sculptor of Italian Futurism, who demanded that artists free themselves from the past and embrace modern technological civilization. Using both art-historical and pop-culture icons, recognizable and unrecognizable, the artist employs an obvious irony, combining his fascination for the fluid condition of Futurist culture and the "evil" Terminator's corporeal fluidity, for filmic and virtual fluidity. Schütte asks us to imagine a body with no clear structures, a virtual body, a transient body, an *Übergang*, a stage, a momentary still from a series of transformations. This work relates art to the infinite perspective of metamorphosis, which is ancient as well as modern.

The centrality of the protean dimension of Schütte's artistic project is also clearly formulated in the series of works

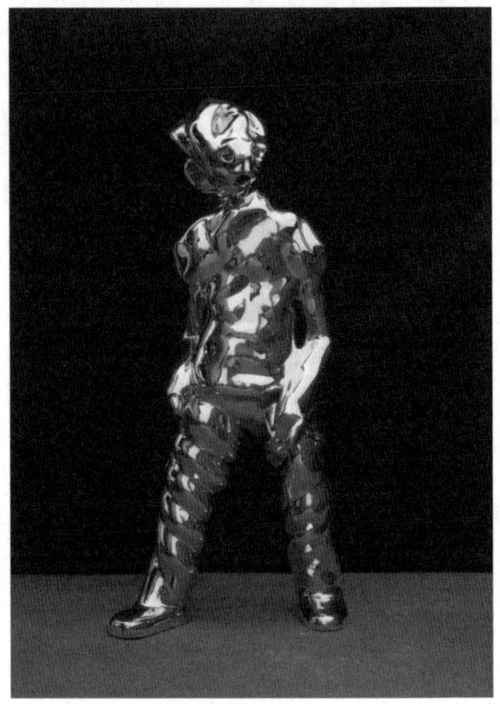

Thomas Schütte, *Great Spirit No. 1*, 2003

*United Enemies* (1992–2010), which readily quotes from art-historical tradition. Though it appears to be his most "postmodern" work, the artist is cautious to distance himself from this impression: he claims to have been inspired to make the work by events that occurred in Italy in 1991, where he was living at the time. He describes these events as a peaceful revolution—when prominent corrupt politicians were exposed and sent to jail. In his conversation with Lingwood, Schütte described his *United Enemies* figures as "sticks with a head on top and another stick that builds the shoulders." He continued, "I used my own clothes to wrap them in and form the body. For me they were puppets and not related to classical art."[6] When Lingwood suggests that they look classical, Schütte reacts negatively and distances himself from the characterization. The role of tradition seems less important to him than the actual message of the work. The figures of *United Enemies* have an expression of aggression and contempt; they have old faces immobilized by animosity, and it is this hate that unites them. It is struggle, not love, that provides their common ground.

This work reminds me of Ernst Jünger's description of the war between Germany and France as an expression of an ecstatic unity more intense than all peace declarations.[7] Such a vision of history makes the idea of a unified history utterly superfluous, a peaceful unity achieved through the Hegelian *Aufhebung* (sublation) of old historical conflicts. History happens, it changes—but not in a peaceful, predictable way. Shifts, gaps, and ruptures are internally connected to this vision of history as battle, as a struggle that intimately connects adversaries—the destiny of a battle is unpredictable and essentially happenstance. The battlefield moves from one place to another, from one configuration to another, without clear logic, without making a difference.

Looking at a series of these works, one gets an acute sense of their inner rhythm. The position of the figures shifts, their faces and their poses change, but the facial expression and the body language remain the same. They embody transformation without movement. The enemies are encapsulated in the same topology all the time—they are transforming themselves, but they remain in the same place. The history presents itself as a protean movement incapable of changing place, incapable of producing a real difference.

In the first chapter of *Creative Evolution* (1907), Henri Bergson writes that there are two kinds of movement. One is a movement of a body in space and the other might be described as the dissolution of sugar in a glass of water.[8] Something has happened to the water; it became sweet. But this change is invisible. Gilles Deleuze gives two similar examples in *Cinema 1: The Movement-Image* (1983): movement in space as opposed to a freer and transformative flow.[9] For Schütte, the movement of history is more like the dissolution of sugar in water than it is the progression of, say, a car down the street.

Schütte's overall artistic strategy presents itself as subtle protean movement undermining the classificatory art-historical and art-critical discourse, by the wish to escape external categorization and historical judgment and make it difficult to define his work. For me, this wish to escape classification and art-historical judgment is the most interesting aspect of Schütte's work. It does not result in a particularly hermetic imagery that has to be revealed by an interpreter. Rather, every attempt to theoretically interpret the work inevitably confronts the artist's conscious intention to avoid this very possibility, because he creates a permanent situation in which every definition and conceptualization seems to be irrelevant and pointless. In fact, the only adequate way to address Schütte's work, to recognize and to take seriously the will of the artist, seems to be to stay silent. The art critic is then confronted with a hopeless situation: every attempt to identify and categorize Schütte's work demonstrates a misunderstanding of the artist's main idea. But how can a critic say anything at all without using categorizations and identifications? I, of course, haven't remained silent. It's my job as a critic to find a way to speak even if an artist tries time and again to prevent me from doing so.

One obvious critical strategy could be to say that Schütte has not fully achieved his goal, and that his art retains a certain identifiable style, but such a solution is not especially interesting and, in fact, employs a line of false presuppositions. The wish to avoid critical appreciation is a strategy that by no means characterizes only Schütte's art, or even, more generally, German art after World War II. At first glance, this wish contradicts the classic modernist strategy to rely on theoretical manifestos, rigid programs, strong commitments, clearly defined and explicitly formulated aesthetic principles, and clearly demarcated lines.

But in fact, from its beginnings, the artistic avant-garde was driven by two contradictory desires: to be absolutely modern and simultaneously to elude confinement in its own time to avoid being superseded by the next step in a historical progression. Modernist artists and theoreticians strove to be free from the burden of history, from the necessity to take the next step, from the obligation to conform to historical laws and the requirements of the new. In struggling against the dominance of the spectator, the avant-garde artist used the device of aesthetic provocation, the "shock of the new," which was calculated to disconcert and disarm the viewer. The avant-garde wanted to be new to avoid judgment by the spectator on the basis of established criteria of taste, mastery,

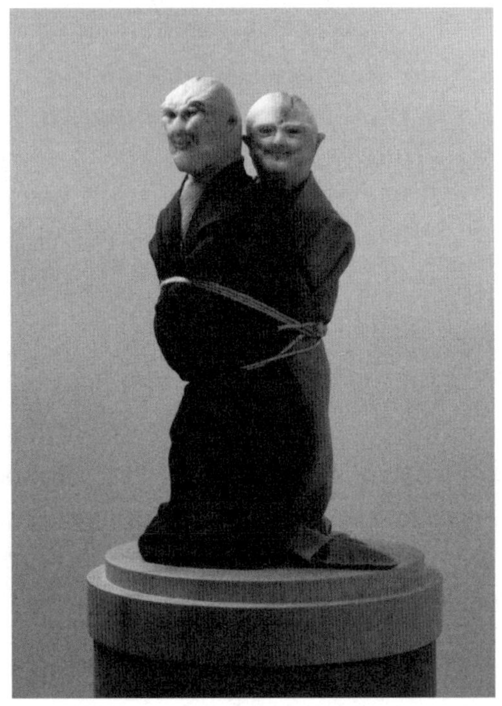

Thomas Schütte, *United Enemies*, 1995

and traditional classifications of art production. But it was precisely this desire that paradoxically subjected the avant-garde artist to the art-historical narrative, which is, of course, inherently based on differentiating between the old and the new, on the premise that new art can emerge only through a comparison to old, already known, already collected art. The writings of avant-garde artists consistently protest against this predicament, and argue that any neutrality controlling art-historical progression is spurious.

Wassily Kandinsky asserts in *Concerning the Spiritual in Art* (1911)—one of the earliest and most radical manifestos outlining avant-garde strategy and practice in Germany—that specific forms and colors exert a magical, unconscious influence on the viewer, as long as the soul of the viewer is finely tuned, reactive, and receptive enough for such an influence.[10] Only a few souls—the true artists who are gifted with special sensibilities and powers of self-analysis—are able to consciously capture, generate, and manipulate these unconscious effects according to a principle, which Kandinsky defines as the "principle of inner necessity." Modern art, in Kandinsky's view, requires the artist to understand this inner necessity, explore it, and master it technically. The artist who can master the unconscious influence of images has the ability to command the viewer's psyche, and to manipulate and educate him or her to become a better human being. This ability to control marks the artist as an elite member of society. On this deeper level of inner necessity, as Kandinsky states, there is no difference between old and new, between abstract and figurative, between original and trivial, and thus all art-historical descriptions and classifications become useless. The spectator therefore loses the capability to judge a work of art. Quite on the contrary, the work of art begins to judge the spectator. According to Kandinsky, the spectator's soul participates in a cosmic drama—in a battle between opposing spiritual principles—and specific artworks, by stimulating reactions, assign the role of the spectator's soul in this inner drama. Kandinsky's reference to the soul or the unconscious serves here to bridge the aesthetic distance that intervenes between the spectator and the work of art. The illusion of that distance serves only to conceal the unconscious effect of the image—and thus reinforces it. The viewer no longer has control of the image, and the artist, like a magician, manipulator, and educator, wields power over the viewer's unconscious.

Many other twentieth-century artists tried, in differing ways, to seize control from the spectator and critic. Using references to contemporary technology and mass culture in their work, artists from Duchamp to Warhol and beyond refer to the art of the mass unconscious embodied by this technology. Joseph Beuys appealed to cosmic processes and energies to escape critical and art-historical control. Schütte's art is not so aggressive, and he does not present his work as a revelation of the unconscious. The images that Schütte uses are too well defined, too clear, to be misunderstood as eruptive and expressive.

But Schütte's work demonstrates a similar will to break loose from historicity by appealing to a temporal dimension of "uchronia," the state of disruption. He tries to do that by referring to the infinite flow of images and signs that cannot be controlled, described, and categorized by a finite vocabulary of standard art-historical discourse. This seemingly limitless, virtual flow of images should give the artist the opportunity to find at any time an image that can deconstruct known oppositions. Such an image would be neither old nor new, neither traditional nor immediately expressive. Such an image should also be able to navigate through all historical categorizations into an atemporal, uchronic sea, where it could somehow survive historical dangers and changes.

The work of Schütte evokes such an image flow. The individual work groups look like sequences, like fragments of the infinity of virtual transformations, modifications, and variations that flow beyond the museum, beyond personal or collective memory, beyond any art-historical control. Schütte stages his work as a ceremony in which individual authorship is sacrificed; the reward for this sacrifice is access to the uchronic eternal stream of virtual images. There are, however, no purely virtual signs. Schütte himself demonstrates that artworks need a material support—they must be made, produced. And hence they are always finite. By producing his work in a traditional mode of craftsmanship, Schütte makes clear, at the same time, the gap that separates his Romantic aspirations from the reality of a private or museum collection as a final destination of a contemporary artwork. In the end, Schütte cannot escape history: rather, he ultimately joins a history of attempts on the part of modern artists to evade art history. Under the conditions of modernity, the art critic is a spectator of a historical competition to escape art criticism; and the role of the art critic is to record the best results in this competition. In this respect, to follow Schütte's artistic strategy is promising and rewarding.

Notes


1.  Søren Kierkegaard, "The Seducer's Diary," in *Either/Or: A Fragment of Life*, ed. and trans. Howard V. Hong and Edna H. Hong (Princeton, NJ: Princeton University Press, 1987), 301–446.
2.  See Marcel Mauss, *The Gift: The Form and Reason of Exchange in Archaic Societies*, trans. W. D. Halls (New York: Routledge, 1990).
3.  See Georges Bataille, *The Accursed Share: An Essay on General Economy*, trans. Robert Hurley (New York: Zone Books, 1999).

4.    Kazimir Malevich, "On the Museum," in *Essays on Art, 1915–1933*, vol. 1, ed. Troels Andersen, trans. Xenia Glowacki-Prus and Arnold McMillin (London: Rapp & Whiting, 1971), 70.

5.    "Somehow the idea came from the Russian productivist movement after Constructivism, when artists worked with real life objects for mass production, like in the Bauhaus. [...] The Bauhaus got all the credit and made all the mistakes. I mean their disciplines made a lot of cities ugly; nobody wants to live in them." Thomas Schütte, in an interview with James Lingwood, in *Thomas Schütte* (London: Phaidon Press, 1998), 20, 37.

6.    Ibid., 29.

7.    See Ernst Jünger, *The Storm of Steel: From the Diary of a German Storm-Troop Officer on the Western Front*, trans. Basil Creighton (New York: Howard Fertig, 1975).

8.    See Henri Bergson, "The Evolution of Life – Mechanism and Teleology," chap. 1 in *Creative Evolution*, trans. Arthur Mitchell (New York: Henry Holt and Co., 1911), 1–97.

9.    See Gilles Deleuze, *Cinema 1: The Movement-Image*, trans. Hugh Tomlinson and Barbara Habberjam (Minneapolis: University of Minnesota Press, 1986).

10.   See Wassily Kandinsky, *Concerning the Spiritual in Art*, trans. M. T. H. Sadler (Mineola, NY: Dover Publications, 1977).

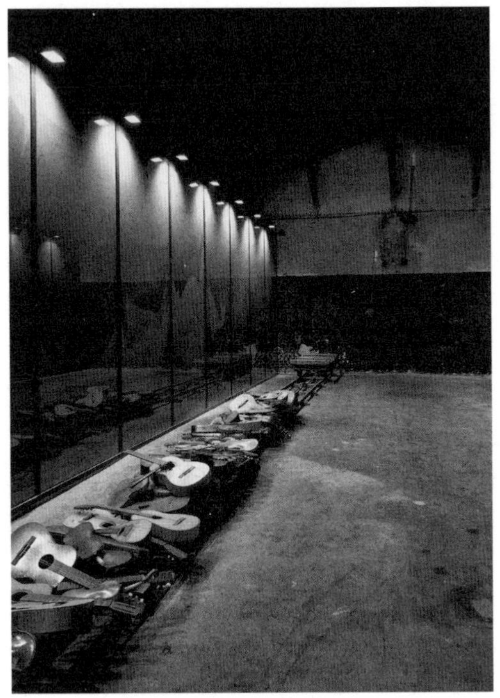

Rebecca Horn, *Concert for Buchenwald*, 1999

8
Rebecca Horn
The Archive of Ashes

The generally acknowledged purpose of every archive is to store evidence of the past and preserve it from destruction. The archive that most successfully fulfills this purpose is one that offers the greatest immunity against the destructive forces of time. The archive of ashes clearly comes closest to this ideal of indestructibility. Ashes cannot be further destroyed, burned, or eradicated; they can only be dispersed. But even in a dispersed state, the archive of ashes still retains its virtual unity—as an opportunity for a new collection. Rebecca Horn's installation *Concert for Buchenwald* (1999) primarily represents such an archive of collected ashes. The ashes are stored in large cabinets that encase the room and are particularly reminiscent of the bookcases found in old libraries, where the books kept behind glass serve as the architectural consummation of the room as well as its embellishment. Just as one's first response on entering such old libraries is the visual attraction to the color pattern of the books on display, once inside Horn's installation, at a former tram depot in Weimar, one is immediately aware that the ash stored inside the cabinets consists of various colors—thereby creating an altogether engaging aesthetic effect. And similar again to old libraries, the strict geometry of the cabinets and the cold uninviting surface of the glass walls are particularly awe-inspiring. At the same time, one's first impression of the ash is not one of an unstructured, fluid, transitory mass, but of something that is compact and fossilized—a massive block or a stone monument. What this represents is an archival collation of ashes that have been drawn from their scattered state—their diaspora—and transported to a place where they can once again constitute a self-contained, cohesive form.

However, this new monumental form that the ashes obtain from having been collected and archived bears no discernable or mimetic relation to the things that were once burned to produce them. Ash preserves no visual memory of the burned objects or organic bodies—as opposed to the "natural" process of decay and decomposition, which throughout all stages of transformation, deformation, reduction, and dissolution always retains some mimetic affinity to the original form. The cremation of a thing or a body also incurs a radical shift into a nonmimetic, abstract, and nonobjective condition. In the custom of keeping the ashes of a cremated human body in an urn, the marked artificial and conventional character of the urn's traditional classicist form further accentuates the radical break with the original form of the human body. In her installation, Rebecca Horn draws attention to this radical loss of the original organic form by showing the ashes en bloc and replacing the classicist urn with rigorously geometric minimalist forms, pointing to the radical break with mimesis performed by the twentieth-century avant-garde by means of geometric abstraction.

Not only all mimetic similarities, but also all material vestiges of the individually incinerated objects have vanished from this archive of ashes. The collected ashes constitute an undifferentiated mass in which the "individual" ashes left over from the burning of specific objects can no longer be identified. The ashes intermingle. The boundaries separating individual bodies and objects disappear. With this diffusion of bodies, all individual, qualifying, and discrete features are dissolved—and are dispersed. The distinction between the individual object and its surroundings ceases to determine this object's fate. The diffusion of all things in their ashen state instantly points to the most ancient—and most modern—of all utopian visions to have governed the political and artistic imagination of mankind over thousands of years. It is the vision of the individual's release from his ontologically determined isolation, the entry into unified and integrated communion with universal totality. The ashes' cold collectivism clearly represents a far more successful fulfillment of this utopia than the much-vaunted ecstatic fraternities aspired to by living beings.

There have certainly been previous occasions where this form of collectivism—Postromantic, but also postmortal—was treated both thematically and aesthetically. Ernst Jünger, for instance, was fascinated by the sight of the mass of human corpses collectively decaying on the battlefields of World War I—as opposed to the familiar process of individual decomposition that occurs inside the grave: "All secrets of the grave were exposed with a gruesomeness in the face of which even the wildest dreams paled."[1] The communal process of decomposition on the battlefield united all those who in life had inevitably been separated. This collectivism of death brought on by war was described almost two decades later by Roger Caillois—with reference to Jünger—as a celebration that destroyed the old world of divisions, restrictions, and isolation and, through the experience of such a radical release from the constraints of the self, made way for a new and vigorous era.[2] Hence the collective decomposition of corpses celebrated by Jünger and Caillois continues to be included in the general process of life. This is analogous to an old saying keenly reiterated in all arable societies, which likens a decaying body to a seed that must be brought under the soil in order for new life to sprout from it. By contrast, however, the collected ashes manifest primarily their radical inorganicity.

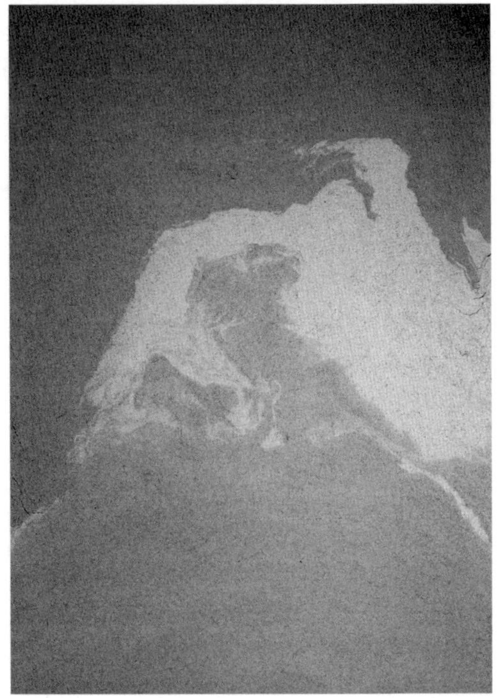

Rebecca Horn, *Concert for Buchenwald,*
1999 (detail)

The ashes call to mind the death wish described in 1920 by Freud in *Beyond the Pleasure Principle*—as a yearning to return to the mineral, inorganic, and dispersed state preceding all forms of life, but primarily one that irrevocably extinguishes any form of individual life and denies the possibility of all memory. Ash can be anything but agriculturally productive—and hence is everything but optimistic. It signals the resignation of any hope for reincarnation. Consequently, no phoenix can possibly rise from the collected, archived ashes, not even a collective phoenix, since these ashes derive from a fire that, far from being cosmic, is nothing more than technically generated.[3]

The inexorable radicality of this work by Horn is undeniably dictated by the installation's immediate proximity to Buchenwald—both through the explicit reference in the title and through the technologically organized cremation of human bodies that was a modus operandi of the Holocaust. Approaching the issues of the Holocaust in artistic terms clearly has a long tradition. However, while this artistic exploration has taken on a wide variety of forms and led to the creation of works of very different aesthetic and conceptual character, it can nonetheless be claimed that the great majority reveal a common wish on the part of their artists to oppose the work of elimination and extinction brought on by the Holocaust with a work of remembrance and restoration. All reflection on the Holocaust is marked by numerous and varied endeavors to compensate and "make good" the suffered loss, to excavate and stabilize the memory of the destroyed and buried past, and to retrospectively repair both the disrupted Jewish tradition and the lost heritage of a "better" Germanness—and to resume this tradition with vigor. This explains why most artistic works that deal with the Holocaust include photographs, inscriptions, or stones similar to gravestones, thereby raising hopes for some kind of eventual resurrection—all emblems of institutional remembrance. What we find are documents, pictures, texts, videos, and film footage being amassed, we come across virtual synagogues being constructed on the Internet and witness museums and documentary centers being opened that simulate symbolic firsthand experience and offer palpable understanding of the destroyed past. In brief, an intensive search has been mounted for vestiges of the past.

Yet whatever view one might take of these numerous scientific and artistic efforts to restore the burned past, it is evident that Horn has adopted an entirely different approach. Her installation is without doubt also an archive, yet with the difference, as we have already seen, that it is an archive not of memory, but of oblivion—a collection of dispersed ashes, not specific ashes somehow located in the course of a purposeful search for traces, but simply some accidently found, random, and radically scattered ashes. The aim of this archive is not to help us repair a historical rupture and bridge the gulf that separates us from those who have perished; quite the opposite, its purpose is to manifest the impossibility of establishing such a link between us and the burned past. Compacted to stone, the ash that has been collected and exhibited here is an impediment to any labor of remembrance. Which is why it is no longer relevant whose ash is on display and where it came from, for all the ash accumulated here acts as a wall irrevocably dividing us from the past. Any attempt to reinstate a link to the past is doomed to failure. The labor of memory must be abandoned at this point—it cannot proceed, because all forms and traces that might direct us toward the past have been scattered.

The immutable destruction of the historical past by means of fire has, incidentally, not entirely been a cause for regret in our culture, it has also been the object of celebration, on par with the burning of bridges that, still intact, might otherwise offer a means of retreat and discourage us from advancing into the future. The fascination exerted by immutable, irreparable destruction certainly represents a significant thread of radical European progressivist thinking. Even Rousseau marveled at the burning of the library in Alexandria in ancient times, a loss that was claimed to have opened up the way for a new school of writing. In particular, an affinity toward the irrevocable rupture with heritage is part of the psychological makeup of the radical artistic avant-garde, a tradition of thinking that has also informed the work of Horn. This image of the irreversible loss of the past is well illustrated by a short text written by Kazimir Malevich in 1919, "On the Museum," in which the author considers the question of whether we should safeguard or destroy the vestiges of our past.[4]

After posing several rhetorical questions—"Do we need Rubens or the pyramids of Cheops? Does the pilot flying in the heights of our new awareness need the damaged Venus? Do we need plaster copies of ancient cities borne by Greek columns?"—Malevich comes to a decisive conclusion: "Immediate life requires nothing more than what is part of it; and only that which grows on its shoulders is part of it." What, incidentally, Malevich is alluding to here is by no means just a purely symbolic and aesthetic renunciation of the past in art. As he points out:

> Life knows what it is doing, and if it decides to destroy something by force we should not try to intervene, since by preventing it we would be blocking the path to the new concept of life that is born within us. By burning a corpse we are left with one gram of ash, enabling thousands of graveyards to be fitted onto a chemist's shelf. We could make a concession to conservative forces by offering to cremate all

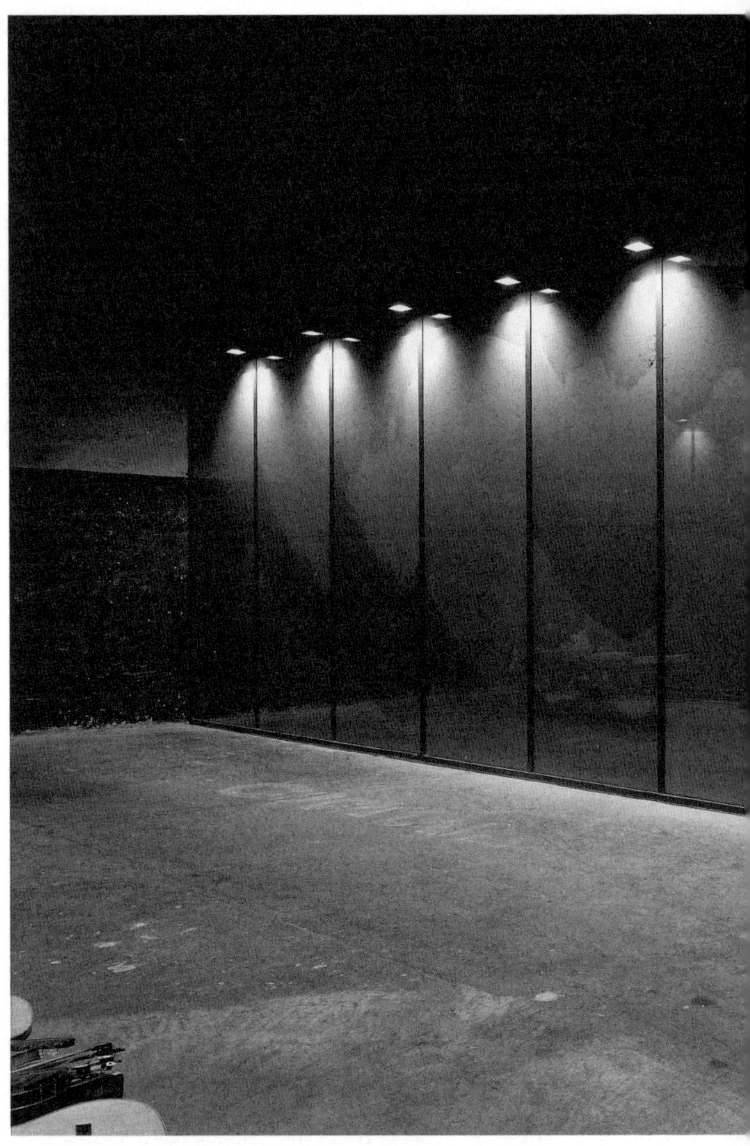

Rebecca Horn, *Concert for Buchenwald*, 1999

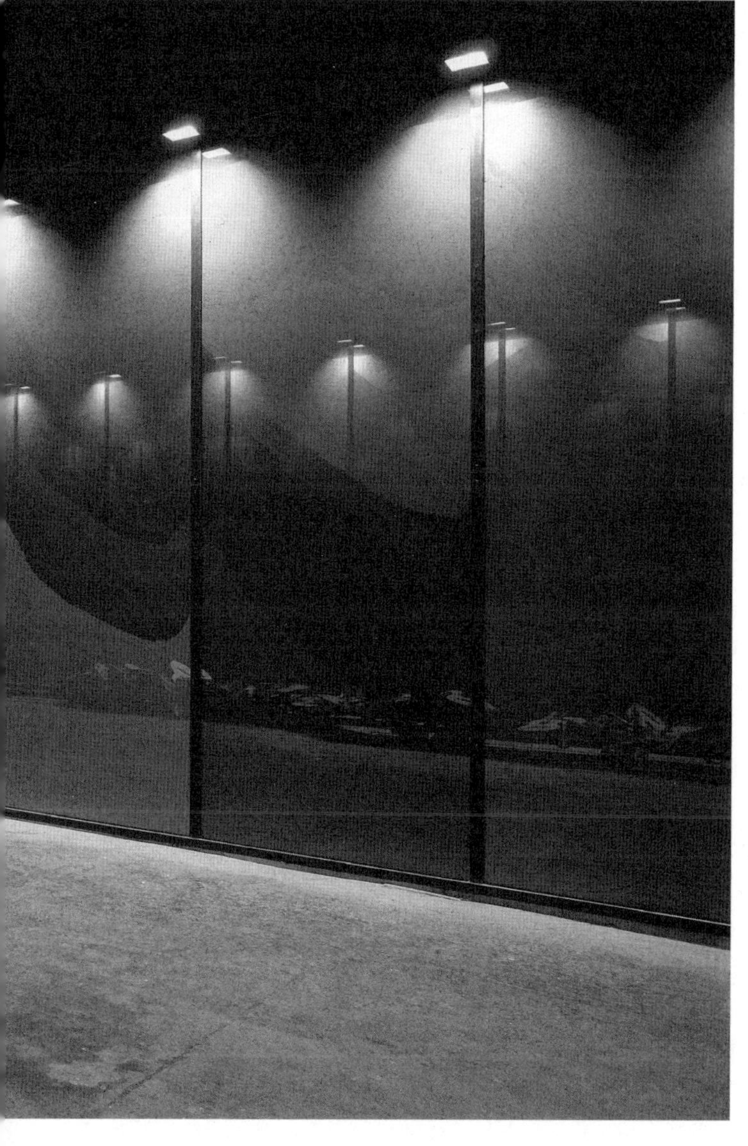

past epochs, since anyway they are already dead, and then open up a pharmacy. [...] This would have the same effect, even if people examined the ashes of Rubens and his entire works—masses of ideas would germinate in them that would contain more life than his actual pictures (and take up less space).

For Malevich, the ideas inspired in someone viewing the ashes of Rubens's pictures are certainly not recollections of the burned past, but instead look forward, prompted by the realization that a return to the past has become impossible. The sight of the ashes obstructing the way back to our origins is meant to point us—indeed, even compel us—toward the future. Malevich happened to write this short text at a time when a widespread surge of enthusiasm for crematoriums took hold of left-wing progressive circles. Cremation was viewed as a symbolic rejection of the church's promise of life after death, depicted in Christian mythology as resurrection from the grave. Anyone prepared to make room for the future necessarily had to consent to the cremation of his body and the scattering of his ashes. Many left-wing intellectuals, particularly Marxists, drew up their wills with this in mind. Above all, the choice between embalmment and cremation proved to be of political relevance. Stalin and Mao both instructed that they should be embalmed, while Trotsky and Deng favored cremation. As it happens, belief in the promise of resurrection, provided the body is preserved (whether in an embalmed or a decomposing state), has ultimately turned out to be more than mere superstition. Advances in modern genetics now offer the possibility of reconstructing the genetic code of even the most thoroughly decomposed corpse. Such research has recently been carried out, for instance, on the exhumed remains of the last Russian Czar's family, and also those of Thomas Jefferson. In the future it is quite conceivable that cloning techniques will enable us to use the deciphered genetic codes of illustrious corpses to reconstruct living replicas of their bodies. On the other hand, as far as we can judge at present, cremation fully erases the genetic code, making it indeed utterly impossible to reproduce the past.

Hence, opting for cremation is synonymous with a repudiation of resuscitation, regardless of whether the choice is made for religious or scientific reasons. Such a radical decision is given further weight by the refusal to preserve old works of art or the historical memories of heroic deeds. Past works would be reduced to ashes, as would the bodies of their authors. In the eyes of radical modernism, with its (left-wing) Hegelian notions of historical progress as the labor of negation, cremating the past (which also comprises self-immolation) is the only service an individual can render unto history. This hygienic and highly industrial manner of dealing with the corpse also fascinated the public imagination in the 1910s and '20s on a singularly aesthetic level. In the progressive fervor that gripped Moscow during these years, artists and writers in particular were invited to take part in specially organized tours to experience the newly built crematoriums in operation—which also demonstrated in what order and manner the various parts of the body were cremated. These guided tours enjoyed great popularity, especially among avant-garde artists who were eager to take their friends and lovers with them to such displays. Highly typical were projects furthering the secondary use of heat emitted during the cremation of corpses, especially for heating public buildings. However, the grave inefficiency of Russian crematoriums at that time was cited as the reason why these projects were ultimately discarded—interestingly, it was generally believed that the best crematoriums and incineration specialists were to be found exclusively in Germany, and when it came to the business of cremation, the Russians, and indeed the rest of Europe, were deemed to be lagging far behind the Germans.[5]

Such manifestations of ethical and aesthetic fervor for the workings of the crematorium are certainly difficult to envisage in the aftermath of the Holocaust. It has been remarked elsewhere that the avant-garde nurtured a specific form of anti-Semitism that viewed the Jews as the race that embodied the Old Testament, and consequently as an incarnation par excellence of the past.[6] There is even reason to claim that the margin between the Old and New Testaments also served as a paradigm for all demarcations between old and new drawn up thereafter in the course of European history, which has been so markedly conditioned by Christianity. As is well known, the Enlightenment also viewed itself as a departure into a new era, a kind of New Testament of reason that annulled all that had characterized the Old Testament—in the sense of a religiously transmitted legacy. It is no accident that various authors of the Enlightenment developed a singularly virulent strain of anti-Semitism—an anti-Semitic belief in innovation and renewal that was felt to be a radical rupture with tradition. Later on, this "innovationist" anti-Semitism was to be found among many proponents of the progressive Left, including Marx. To a similar degree, this same anti-Semitism was also rife among numerous authors of the avant-garde, even in those who, unlike Céline and Ezra Pound, did not openly identify with it.

In many respects, the anti-Semitism of the Nazis also reflected this anti-Semitic quest for a new beginning—a new beginning that in its utter dismissal of the past also demands that the corpse of the past must be burned. Familiar and influential both within avant-garde and Nazi circles, the theosophical doctrine that advocated the succession of cosmic epochs, attributed earlier origins to the Jews than, for instance, to the Aryan peoples. According to this theory, the great fire that was to signal the beginning of the new era of the Aryan race would axiomatically destroy all older races, and foremost the Jews. It is no coincidence that the elimination of the Jews is commonly termed "Holocaust," a word that originally meant nothing other than an immense sacred sacrifice to mark the inception of a new epoch. The fact that this expression has been able to achieve such broad and unchallenged acceptance within Christian culture shows that, even in the present, the occult theosophical meaning of the event described by this word still colors our understanding of what actually took place.

The question remains whether the sacrifice was accepted and a momentous change from one era to the next actually occurred. Many people feel this claim to be exaggerated and, regardless of all prior acts of destruction, believe that the past can be revived—hence their search for similarities and hidden traces, genetic codes, as it were, which promise to restore the continuity of history. By contrast, the archive of ashes displayed by Horn in *Concert for Buchenwald* suggests that the past was definitively and irrevocably destroyed, fully barring the way to any form of restitution. There was indeed a transition from one epoch to the next. This shift precludes the possibility of restoring the link with history, with cultural heritage. It has dissolved and dispersed. For this reason, any notion of the new has been rendered equally impossible, since the definition of the new is contingent on a comparison with antecedent tradition. New developments could only arise if our cultural archive, the Old Testament, were still intact, offering a framework for determining the novelty of what is deemed to be new. Instead, the cessation of tradition creates a world of perpetual new beginnings. In such a world where everything that happened before has now been forgotten, all that remains is the possibility of a project oriented toward the future. This, however, can never be fully realized and brought to a conclusion, since we lack the criteria needed to judge its success—such criteria also presupposing some form of comparison with the old.

The only tenable prospect is the perpetual return to a new beginning that, at some point and for no apparent reason, will be abandoned, only to be continually re-embarked upon. When Adorno states that poems cannot be written after Auschwitz, this is evidently not a moral edict, just a simple statement of fact. For in the aftermath of this temporal shift, there is no longer any tradition, audience, or adequate public response that would enable a writer to complete her or his poem. Nonetheless, this fact certainly does not prevent one from starting the poem over and over again. Writing about Sisyphus, just after World War II, Camus succinctly described this new condition of the perpetual new beginning. In certain respects his analysis has remained valid right up to the present day. Though not necessarily the primary cause of this condition, the Holocaust nevertheless remains its unmistakable symptom. For, as I have argued, the Holocaust is not an event that occurred outside art, or an event that can somehow be symbolically surmounted through artistic means. This event is in itself intrinsically bound up with the very destiny of art. The only appropriate way of remembering the Holocaust is to preserve the memory of the oblivion that irrevocably separates us from it—a memory of the ashes that bar the path of our memory, since this path too has turned to ashes and been scattered. The path leading back has been burned. Horn's installation shows us the archive of ashes as evidence of the dispersal of this path.

Notes

1.  Ernst Jünger, "Der Kampf als inneres Erlebnis" [Battle as inner experience], in *Sämtliche Werke*, vol. 7 (Stuttgart: Klett-Cotta Verlag, 1980), 22 (trans. Matthew Partridge).
2.  Roger Caillois, "War and the Sacred," in *Man and the Sacred*, trans. Meyer Barash (Urbana: University of Illinois Press, 2001), 163–80.
3.  Derrida refers to the "rebellion against the Phoenix" in his book *Cinders*, ed. and trans. Ned Luckacher (Lincoln: University of Nebraska Press, 1991), 59.
4.  Kazimir Malevich, "On the Museum," in *Essays on Art, 1915–1933*, vol. 1, ed. Troels Andersen, trans. Xenia Glowacki-Prus and Arnold McMillin (New York: George Wittenborn, 1971), 68–72.
5.  For a brief cultural history of crematoriums in Russia, see Semjon Michajlovskij, "Krematorij zdravomyslija" [Crematorium of the common sense], *Chudozestevnnyj zurnal*, nos. 19–20 (1998): 12ff.
6.  On the subject of the relationship between the avant-garde and anti-Semitism, see Philippe Muray, *Céline* (Paris: Éditions du Seuil, 1981).

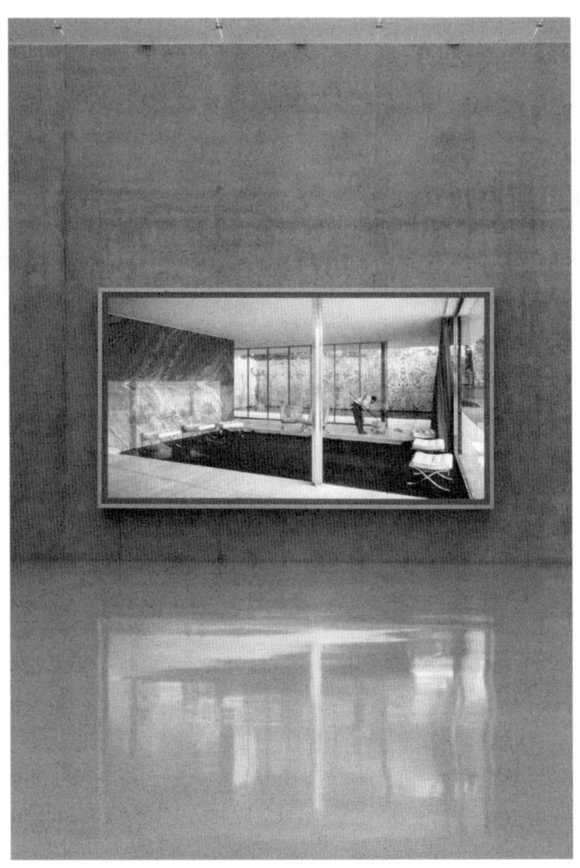

Jeff Wall, *Morning Cleaning, Mies van der Rohe Foundation, Barcelona,* 1999

9
Jeff Wall
Life without Shadows

It's impossible to overlook Jeff Wall's works in an exhibition: they glow. For contemporary viewers this will certainly
be taken as a reference to the glowing advertisements of the
modern city street, but this is by no means the only associa-
tion that comes to mind. Throughout history, the ability to
glow, to shine, has been a sign of holiness, of being chosen,
of being invested with magical powers. Even glowing advertisements lend a magical dimension to any landscape, a fact
exploited by countless filmmakers.

Glowing produces an aura. After Walter Benjamin, everyone knows that modern art, insofar as it can now be reproduced, has lost its aura. Accordingly, photography above
all has no aura because of its potential for infinite reproduction. Works by Wall, however, lose their glowing aura
when reproduced in a catalogue or a book, although they
are photographs. Reproduced, these works cease to glow.
All that remains is their theme, their art-historical or social
relevance. That's a great deal, but it isn't everything. And in
my view it isn't the essential element.

In Wall's originals the glow is technically produced: it comes
from a light box hidden behind the picture. The aura is not
to be understood in a metaphorical sense, as in Benjamin, but
literally—and this continues a long tradition. In old icons the
halos of the saints actually do shine. And the background—in
Byzantine icons, for example—shines too, being made of gold
or silver. One of the most interesting interpreters of icon painting, the early twentieth-century theologian Pavel Florensky,

describes the icon as a semitransparent wall that screens the light on the other side from the viewer, protecting the viewer's eyes from the light's intensity—a description astonishingly apposite to Wall's works. As Florensky continues, the figures on this icon wall mark only different intensities of light, and for that reason cast no shadows. The true iconic technique resides in this absence of shadows: the figures in the icon articulate the light, but they do not resist it. There is nothing dark, opaque, or purely material about them. This, for Florensky, is what distinguishes the icon from post-Renaissance European painting, which stages a play of light and shadow within the painting. Where painting in the modern era is concerned, the world has a dark, opaque core that can only be lit from without; light cannot pass through it.[1]

But the light that illuminates Wall's transparencies from within is definitely a very modern light. It is distributed very evenly—"democratically," you might say—behind the picture's surface. It does not divide the essential from the inessential, the high from the low, the center from the periphery—and in this sense it also casts no shadow. This light knows no hierarchies, it ignores no details. It is the light of modern enlightenment that leaves nothing in the shadows and shines through everything, making everything visible. It is not by chance that this light flows to us through a photograph, the embodiment of the objective gaze of modern science.

In the twentieth century, for this very reason, photography has traditionally been subject to criticism. The neutral scientific gaze is accused of failing to capture the opaque core of the world that constitutes its reality, and of striving only for external control and power. For example, Siegfried Kracauer wrote that photography preserves only an outward sign of the past and reality, its empty shell. Photography is a "general inventory" of these external signs, a sum of everything that must be stripped from people and nature if their true, hidden reality is to be recognized. Humankind, space, and time collapse in the photograph, and are abandoned to death.[2] This critique of photography was later pursued in greater depth by Roland Barthes. For Barthes, photography represents only the semiotics of a purely external social context that denies actual reality—which is everything that eludes that context.[3]

According to this view, photography—in contrast to painting—is not a picture of living reality, but merely an arrangement of dead signs: writing that presents itself as a picture. True reality can only be achieved in painting, which emerges out of a hidden and outwardly uncontrollable piece of memory work. Photography, on the other hand, lacks the time it takes a painting to become a picture of the living world. Life is only possible in time, in duration—but photography is momentary. An experience that can only be gathered over time is inaccessible to photography: photography has no memory. Painting necessarily contains something opaque, insoluble, inexplicable. And it is this element of the irrational, which holds within itself an accumulated time, that gives painting its reality, a reality that photography must inevitably lack.

Of course, such objections to photography historically have not gone uncontradicted. But it is interesting to note that photography's defenders are constantly searching for the medium's element of the opaque and irreducible real. This is to be found not in the opacity of lived experience, however, but in the element of chance to which photography is necessarily prone. For Aleksandr Rodchenko, and later for Susan Sontag, the reality of the chance and fragmentariness of the world—the lack of a total vision, the presence of dark spots in space and time that cannot be overcome by any amount of memory work—can only be proved by photography.[4]

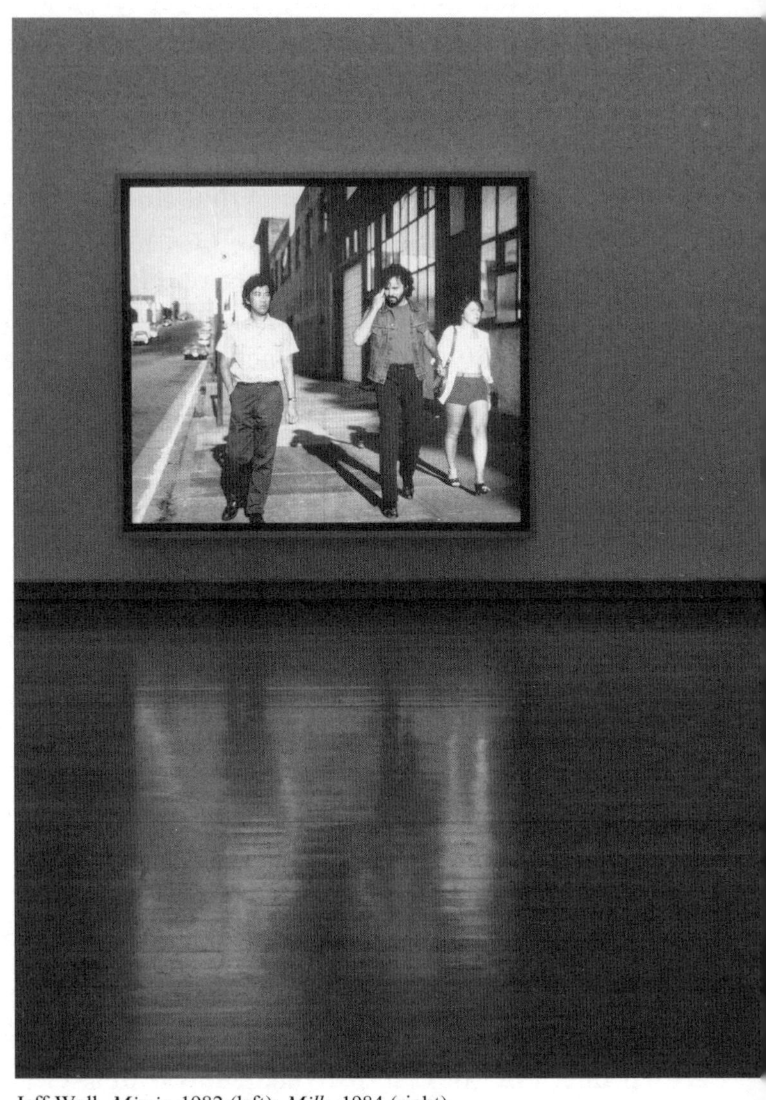

Jeff Wall, *Mimic*, 1982 (left); *Milk*, 1984 (right)
Exhibition view, "Jeff Wall: The Crooked Path," Centro Galego
de Arte Contemporánea, 2011–12

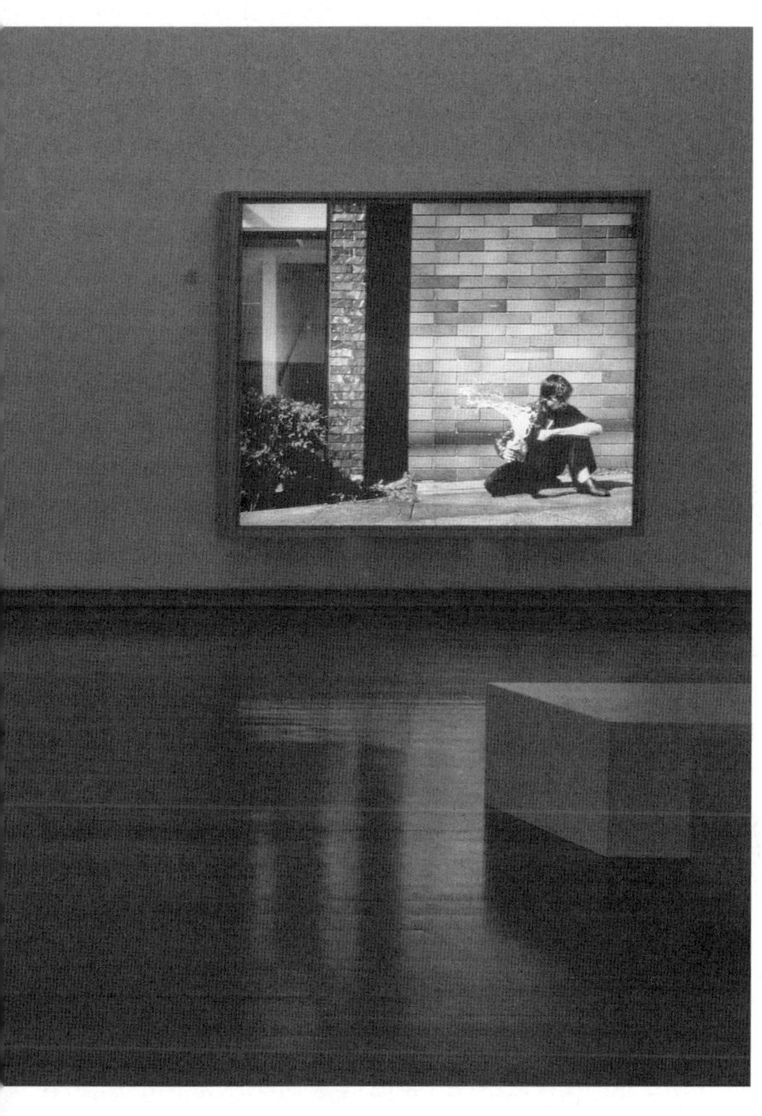

Against the background of this basic discussion about the relationship between painting and photography—in which each side thinks it can best defend its preferred medium by discovering an irreducible, opaque, "deconstructing" remnant of reality—it is particularly interesting to note that Wall uses references to the two media with a view to eradicating all remnants of the opaque and reaching total illumination. All elements of chance and fragmentariness are systematically and consistently avoided in taking the photographs; to achieve this, Wall chiefly relies upon references to nineteenth-century naturalistic painting. His photographs are precisely planned and organized to avoid any chance disturbance. It is particularly interesting that whenever Wall speaks about chance, it consists precisely in its elimination. For instance, when considering a landscape, he suddenly finds himself being reminded of a painting by Poussin— and for that reason chooses that same landscape.[5] Here, the Poussin painting is working as a materialized Platonic idea: a landscape is recognized as a landscape, because this landscape recalls an art-historical model. Wall is using the tradition of painting to free photography from everything that is not preplanned and calculated, to leave nothing to uncontrollable chance.

Every detail is thought through and explained by comparison with the existing store of paintings. Accordingly, history is not thought of as an opaque process in the depths of subjectivity, but as an objectively identifiable difference in representation. Wall also observes that the formal proximity of his own photographs to the paintings of the art-historical tradition gives him the opportunity for a precise measurement of a temporal shift in perception.[6] It is interesting that Kracauer sees this kind of comparison, which photography has made possible, as a crucial threat to historical consciousness.[7]

In using references to the history of naturalistic painting to reduce the element of chance and fragmentariness in photography along with the photographic process, Wall is also eliminating the opacity of painting, its purely subjective, lyrical, dark dimension, seen as the free development of technically uncontrollable signs, which refer to the accumulation of time, and refuse momentary correspondence with that external, controllable reality. Photography ("writing in light," to translate from the Greek) possesses the transparency and controllability of the technical process that eliminates all darkness.

Thus, according to Kracauer, photography becomes an arrangement of pure signs grouped around the great void. And the photographic image as a whole becomes a purely emblematic, allegorical sign of mourning for a reality that has vanished without a trace. Illumination or enlightenment apparently fails here, being obstructed by the surface of things. The inner, hidden, unconscious, dark reality of the world, which Wall himself often describes in his texts and statements as a universal economic law, is not revealed here. The control to which the figures are subjected is twofold: by the artistic tradition and by the technical, photographic process. There is no room left for any additional determination that could itself be observed and critically opposed to visible reality.

Nevertheless, Wall's works have a public, liberating effect. The light of enlightenment, passing through what exists, does not encounter a dark core of reality, but rather another light with which it can mingle. Behind the world, as it is represented in works by Wall, nothing is concealed apart from its visibility as such, an inner light source that flows through its surface. The light of enlightenment proves to be related to the mystical light of apocalyptic illumination.[8] The emblematic nature of photography suddenly refers to the emblematic nature of icons. Both are a form of writing with light, a system of signs that cast no shadow.

The tradition of painting is used here against itself. It is cleansed of everything dark, subjective, and opaque, and is transformed into a system of signs. This turns light into a universal principle of visibility of things that cannot be manipulated. For what is dark and invisible—understood as hidden reality—can always also be invisibly manipulated. While in Wall's work, light becomes a support for reality, that reality becomes irrefutable. We can only see what is shown to us. And if we begin to analyze what we see in the light of enlightenment, we will soon understand that we are merely repeating the original visibility—without penetrating behind that visibility, for behind there is nothing except the very light that produces it.

And what is hidden behind the light? Its source. Maybe a god, maybe a lamp. But this light source obviously is publicly inaccessible and opaque—so there is certainly no point in wasting any further thought on the matter.

Notes

1.  Pavel Florenskij, *Die Ikonostase: Urbild und Grenzerlebnis im revolutionären Rußland*, trans. Ulrich Werner (Stuttgart: Urachhaus, 1988), 160ff.; in English, *Iconostasis*, trans. Donald Sheehan and Olga Andrejev (Redondo Beach, CA: Oakwood Publications, 1996).

2.  Siegfried Kracauer, *Der verbotene Blick: Beobachtungen, Analysen, Kritiken* (Leipzig: Reclam, 1992), 185–202.

3.  See Roland Barthes, *Camera Lucida: Reflections on Photography*, trans. Richard Howard (New York: Hill and Wang, 1981).

4.  See Peter Noever, ed., *Rodtschenko, Stepanowa* (Munich: Prestel, 1991), 234–37; and Susan Sontag, *On Photography* (Harmondsworth: Penguin, 1977).

5.  See the interview with Els Barents, in *Jeff Wall: Transparencies* (Munich: Schirmer/Mosel, 1986), 98.

6.  Ibid., 96–97.

7.  Kracauer, *Der verbotene Blick*, 201.

8.  On the relationship between enlightenment and illumination, see Jacques Derrida, *D'un ton apocalyptique adopté naguère en philosophie* (Paris: Galilée, 1983), 64ff.; translated as "Of an Apocalyptic Tone Recently Adopted in Philosophy," *Oxford Literary Review* 6, no. 2 (December 1984).

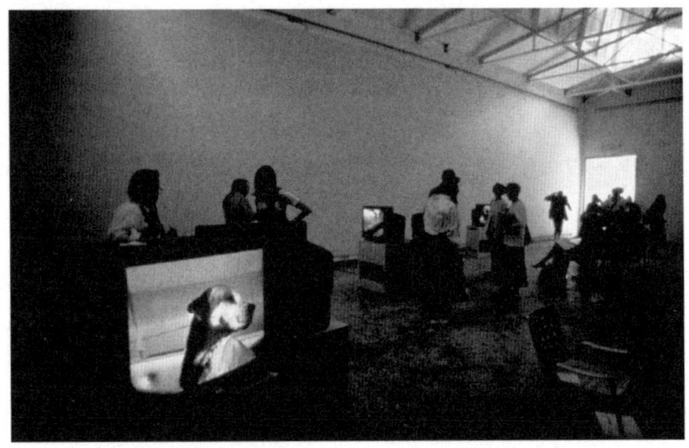

Peter Fischli and David Weiss, *Untitled (Venice Work)*,
Swiss Pavilion, 46th Venice Biennale, 1995

10
Peter Fischli and David Weiss II
The Speed of Art

Art has achieved an unparalleled speed in the last century. I am not talking about the representation of speed in art—an issue that was explored, for example, by the Futurists—but about the speed with which art is produced. It was primarily Marcel Duchamp's readymade technique that dramatically increased this speed. Today it is enough for an artist to look at and name any chosen fragment of reality in order to transform it into a work of art. In this case, art production has virtually achieved the speed of light. The readymade technique is probably the greatest technical achievement of the twentieth century next to the splitting of the atom, if you take speed as the decisive criterion. This acceleration guarantees today's visual arts a certain cultural rank and authority, which become apparent on comparing the speed of producing artworks with, for example, the speed of manually producing texts.

But the increased speed of art production is also considered a menace and kept in check—just as one would not want to deploy the atom bomb. The history of art after its acceleration at the beginning of the twentieth century is the history of its deceleration. The most effective damper on the speed of art is the criterion of newness. Not everything that can be declared art is actually acknowledged as such. We expect the artistic gaze to show us something new; that is, something that has not yet found entrance into existing art archives. Since these archives keep getting bigger, and since the public does not always have the grace to accept deviations from things seen before as signaling something really new, art production is of necessity curbed by the need for the artworks to be new. The economy of innovation checks the rampant growth of art. Thus, the demand for novelty slows art down instead of speeding it up. When compared with existing archives, most of what is produced as art—or rather, presented as art—is found to be tautological, redundant, superfluous, and therefore rejected. But art is not always to blame. Sometimes art moving at the speed of light is simply too fast for its innovations to be registered as such. As they go racing by, the outside world often sees nothing new in these innovative deviations—they seem to be too small, too inconspicuous, too vague—and dismisses them. Artists would therefore be well advised to keep themselves in check and synchronize the speed of their art with the tempo of real life. That way, others will be better able to perceive and understand them.

Peter Fischli and David Weiss have always been great brakemen. They slowly and laboriously carve objects out of polyurethane that have a disarming resemblance to readymades, instead of simply picking them out of reality with the abovementioned speed of light. The artists have apparently adjusted to the ordinary speed of handcrafted work and come closer to life's sense of time. But there is a hitch: their deceleration is imperceptible from outside because the carved objects look exactly like actually selected readymades. Fischli/Weiss simulate readymades by hand—a procedure that inverts the conventional practice in our industrial age of simulating handcrafted work by machine.

There are certainly many reasons for this inversion. But one thing is clear: this strategy allows the artists to exhibit readymades without being exposed to the criticism that their work is not new, because making readymades by hand is new even, or rather especially, when no one notices it. Fischli/ Weiss thus sidestep the deceleration effect imposed on the speed of their art by the demand for novelty. They can quote anything they please from real life with uncensored serenity, as long as they go to the effort of replicating it by hand. The decelerated process of producing art, on one level, allows Fischli/Weiss to increase the speed of their art on another, much more important level—they do not have to follow Duchamp's advice and limit the number of readymades. And this increased velocity in turn gives the artists the privilege of enjoying things that would otherwise have been sacrificed to the censorship of innovation. This also applies to their videos of outings presented in the Swiss Pavilion at the 46th Venice Biennale, in 1995.

What deserves our attention? And what doesn't? Among the thousands and thousands of images with which we are bombarded, which ones shall we choose as valuable and which ones shall we discard as worthless? And according to what criteria? Fischli/Weiss are particularly vulnerable to this uncertainty in selecting images, because central to their long-time concern of the readymade are the criteria for selection. Images may be attractive, romantic, picturesque, gloomy, suggestive, or strange. But none of these qualities are acceptable criteria for the professional artist. Artists need new images that have been never be seen or shown before, and do not fit in any cubbyhole. They can let the images pass a mental review—which is a very speedy affair. But the uncertainty remains and paralyzes the determination to make a decision. If something is imaginable, then it can't be new; it is by definition trivial, dispensable. The speed of imagination runs headlong into a dead end, where it is consumed by the agony of making a choice. Fischli/Weiss step on the brakes just in time.

In their search for pictures, the artists drove through Zurich and its environs, or sometimes through more distant places and cities, filming things on their way. They stopped and got out, took walks, visited various places, watched and filmed what was going on, and drove back to Zurich again, filming the landscape on their way home. As a result, ninety-six hours of videographed material was shown in Venice on twelve different monitors: a real challenge for a visitor. Cars are fast, as Marinetti observed. But not as fast as the imagination and the gaze. Nor as fast as conventional film and video montage. While the speed of pseudo-readymade production was adjusted by Fischli/Weiss to the tempo of handcrafted manufacture, these video works are marked by a sense of time that evokes civilized leisure, unrestrained and contemplative enjoyment of time with no outside pressures, undefined and detached curiosity, relaxed recreation after work or on weekends. And once again, it is the increased speed of art that allows Fischli/Weiss to simulate the leisurely pace of unpretentious human existence.

Incidentally, the slow pace of the Fischli/Weiss excursion videos is not generated by artistically decelerating the tempo that now seems "normal" to us in films and videos, and that corresponds to our daily confrontation with the medium of television. Increasing or decreasing the tempo typical of television productions is currently the most common artistic device in the making of "art" films and videos. As a rule, a video or film production with artistic intent can be spotted immediately because time flows faster or slower than it does on television, or perhaps even in circles, through the constant repetition of certain scenes. But when Fischli/Weiss make videos of their outings, they are simulating the readymade sense of television time. Nor does the look of their pictures contradict the television viewer's conventional aesthetic expectations. There is nothing particularly "artistic" about the images; they are not distorted in any way, nor do they show any of the traits of "home movies" that often characterize art videos.

Instead, they cultivate the look of perfectly "normal" television aesthetics; in other words, precisely the look that current video art is trying to subvert in its quest for new images. The result of this strategy is again the effect of accelerated speed that characterizes the "production" of readymades. "Art" videos have to be short because it is an effort to invent, produce, and look at new pictures: every one of those "creative" video works involves a long, time-consuming, laborious, and difficult quest. But videos that act like television are relatively easy to produce and multiply. And they are easy to watch. This gives Fischli/Weiss a surplus of time, which means that they can produce a great deal within a relatively short period. This surplus time—not regained, as in Proust, but simply won—might in fact be read as the underlying theme of the excursion videos. The traditional aesthetics of the readymade, using objects and individual images, was never able to fully exploit the surplus of time because inevitably restricted exhibition space put a limit on speedy multiplication. Nonetheless, the idea of gaining time has always been an artistic concern. Warhol once said that any picture that takes more than five minutes to make is a bad picture. And Warhol was also the first one to really grasp the potential of film as a means of exploiting this surplus. His film *Empire* (1964) was the beginning of the development that has led to Fischli/Weiss's videos, because it was the first time that the difference between the investment of time by the artist and viewer was inverted. It used to be that the artist had to invest a great deal of time in creating his work, which the viewer was then able to see at one go, so time was apportioned in the viewer's favor but to the artist's disadvantage. And this

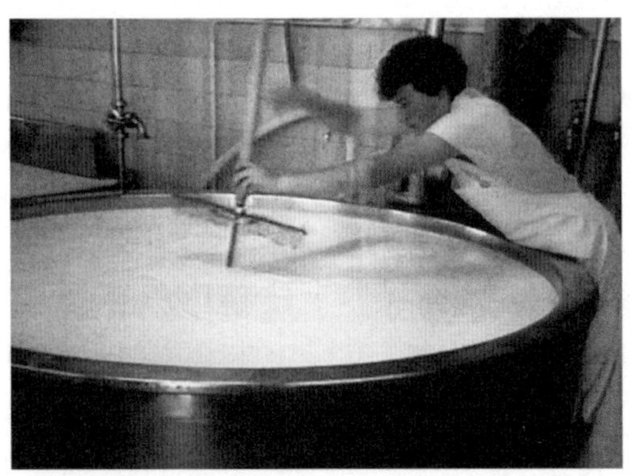

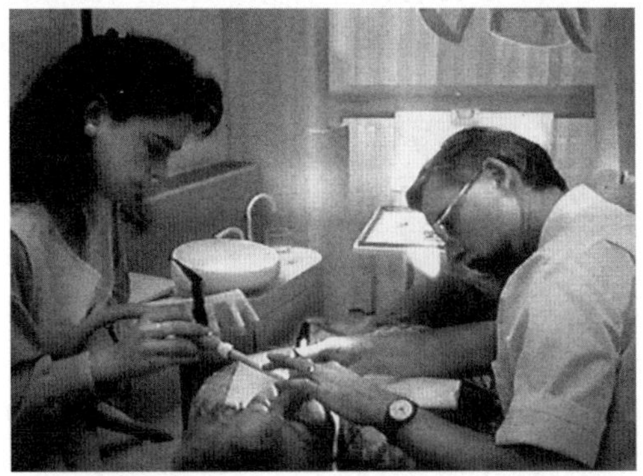

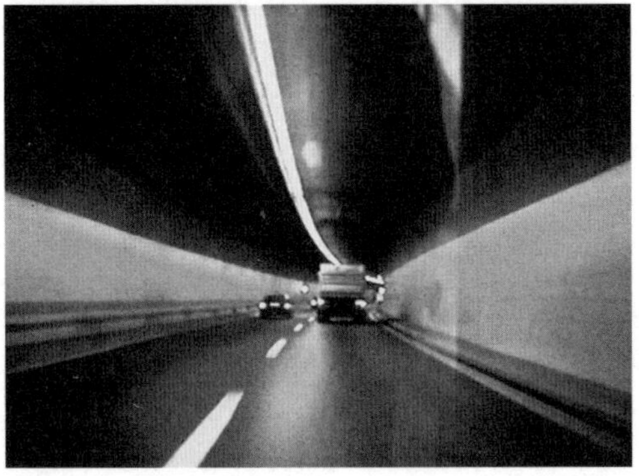

Peter Fischli and David Weiss, stills from
*Untitled (Venice Work)*, 1995

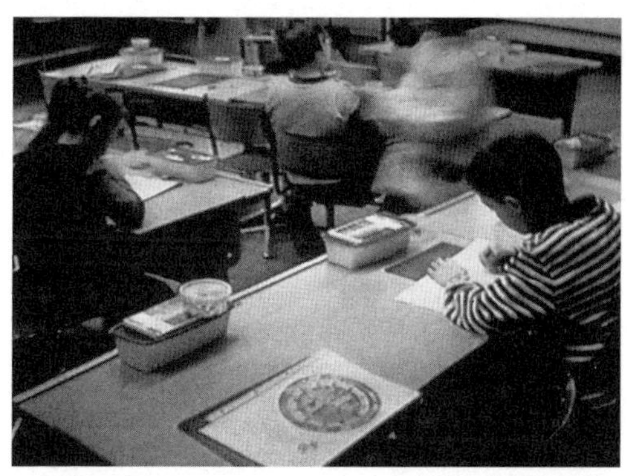

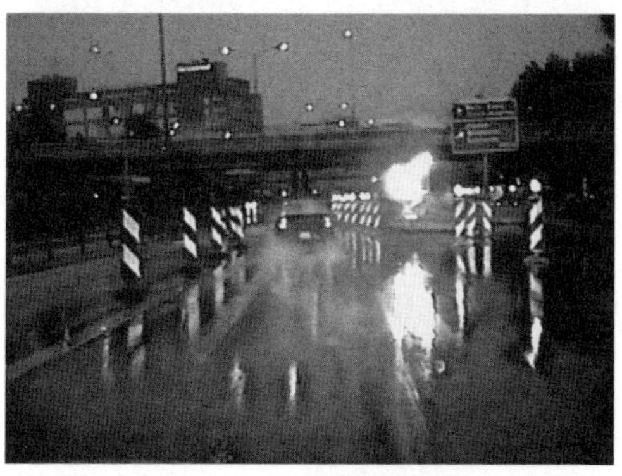

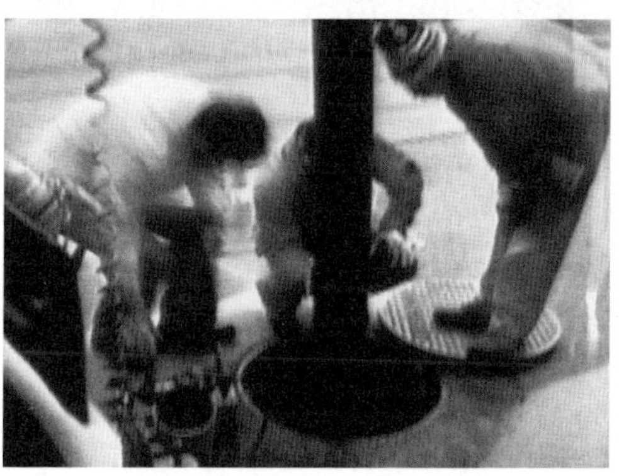

certainly still applies to art videos that generally take much longer to make than to watch. But *Empire* took exactly the same length of time to make as it does to watch. Viewers must now invest just as much time in the job of perception as the artists spend in the making of their works. Duchamp already observed that looking at something turns it into a work of art. And as so often happens, this privilege soon became a burden.

In Warhol's case, it is not necessary to watch the entire film in order to get the message. After a while the viewer realizes that there is just more of the same, which was basically Warhol's concession to a public accustomed to being able to take in a work of art if not at a glance, then at least within a reasonable length of time. Fischli/Weiss no longer make this concession. The outings recorded in their videos take them from one place to another and could continue anywhere. But the videos are anything but monotonous. In some cases they are even suspenseful and startling (an animal clinic), beautiful and poetic (mountain landscapes), strange (the army in the mountains, tanks, a techno party), or informative (milking cows, hunting)—but then again turn banal, pictures of the same old stuff. Where they belong, how important they are, what they mean—these questions can only be answered by surveying the entire enterprise, since Fischli/Weiss have embarked on a journey of discovery through traveling, whose stations acquire meaning only within the overarching context of the journey as a totality. But two problems arise. First, the artists, like all human beings, are finite and mortal, which means that they cannot obtain an all-encompassing view. Second, it is even harder for viewers to grasp the exhibited videos because, given the "normal" speed of their lives, there is no way that they will ever be able to catch up with all that the artists have seen and visited.

Television news reports have to be brief, and they have to make a statement that sounds complete in the time allotted to them. Fischli/Weiss have no such clear-cut ambitions. Their videos are simply an expression of the desire to go out and see if something interesting is happening. This attitude is, of course, out of the question in any professional investigation of an issue of public interest. But Fischli/Weiss show a vague, noncommittal interest in whatever comes their way—basically a recreational activity, a kind of hobby. It also solves the problem of establishing criteria for selection, because in our spare time we can devote ourselves to any number of things that are not subject to the censorship of relevance, significance, or innovation.

Now it is most unlikely that the average visitors, using their free time to come and look at the work of Fischli/Weiss in its entirety, would have a supply of time large enough to follow all the trips the artists took, at the same tempo and with undivided attention. Instead they will stop in front of a monitor for a while, and then move on to another one, the end result being that they will have seen only bits and pieces, fragments of the whole, and will be left wondering whether they have seen enough to grasp the overall project. The time relationship between the viewer and the work of Fischli/Weiss is therefore analogous to that between people and life in general. Structurally speaking, human beings are not endowed with enough time to see and understand the whole of life. Similarly, viewers cannot see and understand the whole work of Fischli/Weiss because the artists have used the surplus of time generated by the speed of contemporary art to put an invisible wall of time between their work and the viewers. It is of course conceivable that someone might actually take the time to watch everything Fischli/Weiss have done. It is theoretically possible. But a decision of that nature does not fit in with the conventional conditions of art reception that are still in effect today. Besides, the attempt to watch the entire piece would simply lead to its continuation on the part of the artists, since it is basically a work that can never be completed.

In their videos, Fischli/Weiss do not provide the closure that viewers traditionally expect. Artists are ordinarily expected to give a certain form to a messy and therefore frustrating reality so that it becomes at least visually consumable: even if an artwork is conceived as open-ended, it most often can still be grasped and identified at one glance. But in this case, we do not know what the final shape of the work is; perhaps it has a structure that will not surface unless we watch all the videos. The work in its entirety escapes not only the mental but also the physical faculties of the viewer: it is tiring. Perhaps the most appropriate way to take in this work would be to have the videos at home and watch them day after day as a substitute for daily television, or maybe even as a substitute for daily life.

The readymade procedure involves transporting items of daily life into the domain of the museum. Fischli/Weiss transfer the tempo of unpressured recreation to their professional lives. And in the process, they gain time, twice over. First, they have freed themselves from professional difficulties that steal time. And second, they have extended leisure time into working time without endangering their jobs. In our society this is a privilege reserved for artists. In return, artists generally feel obliged to show society a compressed and condensed version of what they have seen in all those hours of lonely observation. This is exactly what Fischli/Weiss do not want to do.

The difference may not seem very great, but it is decisive. It explains why the work of Fischli/Weiss, so harmless at first sight, is actually merciless. They force viewers to face their own shortage of time—the same situation that is so frustrating in "real life," the impossibility of taking in all the visual stimuli that present themselves. And this frustration happens precisely when viewers expect satisfaction from art. Art has broken many taboos in our century. And these violations have not only been visible, but have even enhanced the visibility of art. Now, in contrast, a movement is on the rise that is leading art away from visibility. Viewers are increasingly faced with works that withdraw from their gaze, sometimes in an even more radical way than life itself. Instead of making the invisible visible, which was once considered the traditional task of art, Fischli/Weiss have rendered something perfectly visible—namely, everyday Swiss life—invisible, because it is hidden away in the length of the videos. Thus, banality is becoming mysterious at a time when mystery has faded into banality.

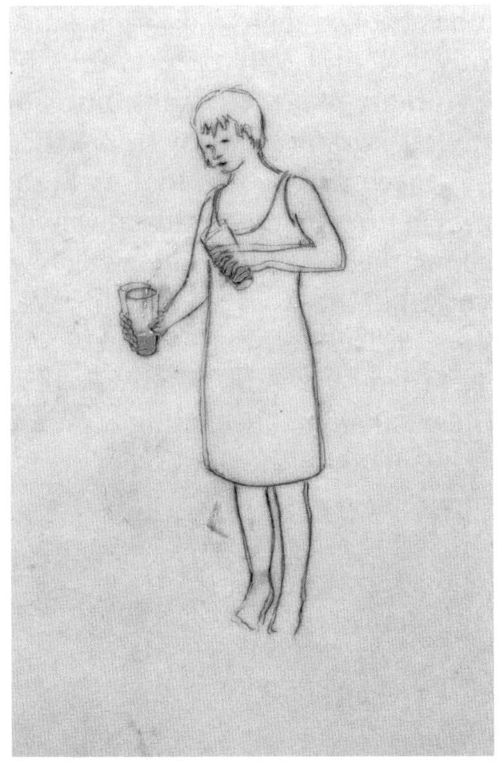

Francis Alÿs, still from *Song for Lupita*, 1998

11
Francis Alÿs
How to Do Time with Art

Like many other contemporary artists, Francis Alÿs works in different media, experimenting in various artistic and social fields and making art that is irreducible to a fixed meaning or message. In this text I will concentrate on the most contemporary part of Alÿs's work—namely, his videos. They are contemporary in at least two different but interconnected ways: they reflect in a very precise manner our present historical moment, but they also thematize, in a more general manner, the present as such, the presence of the present. Let us begin with this second, more general meaning of the word "present," which does not necessarily refer to our own present, our historical "here and now."

Under the conditions of our modern, technological, product-oriented civilization we tend to overlook the present. The dominating mood of modernity was aptly captured by the Obama campaign slogan: "Change we can believe in." And that in fact means: "Change, we should." Modern humankind wants to shape the future and overcome the past. Thus, the present is perceived primarily as a period of transition from the past to the future. This period often presents itself as a difficult time that puts obstacles in our way and slows down the realization of our projects. That is why the present is mostly resented, readily overlooked, and easily forgotten. The time that was invested in the realization of a certain project is accumulated—but at the same time obliterated, erased—by the result of this project. In the modern age, the loss of time in and through a product was compensated for by a historical narrative, which restored the lost time of its production. This narrative glorified the life of the artists, scientists, or revolutionaries who worked for the future. However, time disappears from historical memory in a much more radical way when this time is perceived as unproductive, wasted, meaningless. Such unproductive time becomes excluded from the historical narratives—and endangered with complete erasure.

That is precisely the moment when "time-based" art, including video art, intervenes. Time-based art is, in fact, art-based time. Traditional artworks (paintings, statues, etc.) are truly time-based because they are made in the expectation that perpetuity will be given to them by museums or important private collections. But time-based art is not based on time as a solid foundation or guaranteed perspective. It rather documents time that is in danger of being lost because of its unproductive character. Contemporary time-based art thematizes this unproductive, nonhistorical, suspended time by capturing and demonstrating activities that take place in time but do not lead to the creation of any definite product. And, even if these activities do lead to the emergence of such a product, they are shown as being separated from their result. They exemplify excessive time that is not completely absorbed by the historical process.

Let us consider Alÿs's looped animated film, *Song for Lupita* (1998). A woman pours water from one container to another, and back again—"pouring emptiness into the void," according to a Russian saying that is often applied to theoretical discourse. This activity has, by definition, no beginning and no end, and does not lead to any definite result or definite product. We are confronted here by a pure and repetitive waste of time—a secular ritual beyond any claim of magical power, beyond any religious tradition, beyond any established cultural convention.

One is reminded here of Camus's Sisyphus, a proto-contemporary artist whose aimless, senseless activity is a prototype of contemporary time-based art. For Camus, this nonproductive practice, this excess of time that is caught in the nonhistorical pattern of eternal repetition, constitutes the true image of what we call a "lifetime"—lifetime being irreducible to any "meaning," any "achievement," any historical relevance. The notion of repetition here is the central one. The inherent repetitiveness of Alÿs's video sharply distinguishes it from traditional narrative film and video but also from the happenings and performances of the 1960s. The documented activity is not a unique, isolated performance, an individual, authentic, original event that is taking place here and now. The repetitive gesture that is designed by Alÿs functions as a programmatically impersonal gesture—this animation can be repeated by any human being, then videotaped, then repeated again. Here, the living human being loses its difference from its media image. The opposition between living organism and dead mechanism is made irrelevant by the mechanical, repetitive, and nonpurposeful character of the documented gesture.

In his video *Politics of Rehearsal* (2005), Alÿs speaks about the time of rehearsal as a wasted, non-teleological time that does not lead to any result, endpoint, or climax. As an example, he offers a rehearsal of a striptease—in some sense, a rehearsal of a rehearsal, because the sexual desire provoked by the striptease remains unfulfilled. In the video, the rehearsal is accompanied by commentary by the critic Cuauhtémoc Medina, who interprets the rehearsal as the model of modernity that always remains an unfulfilled promise. The time of modernity is, for Medina, the time of permanent modernization that never really achieves its goals and never satisfies the desire of becoming truly modern. In this sense, the whole process of modernization begins

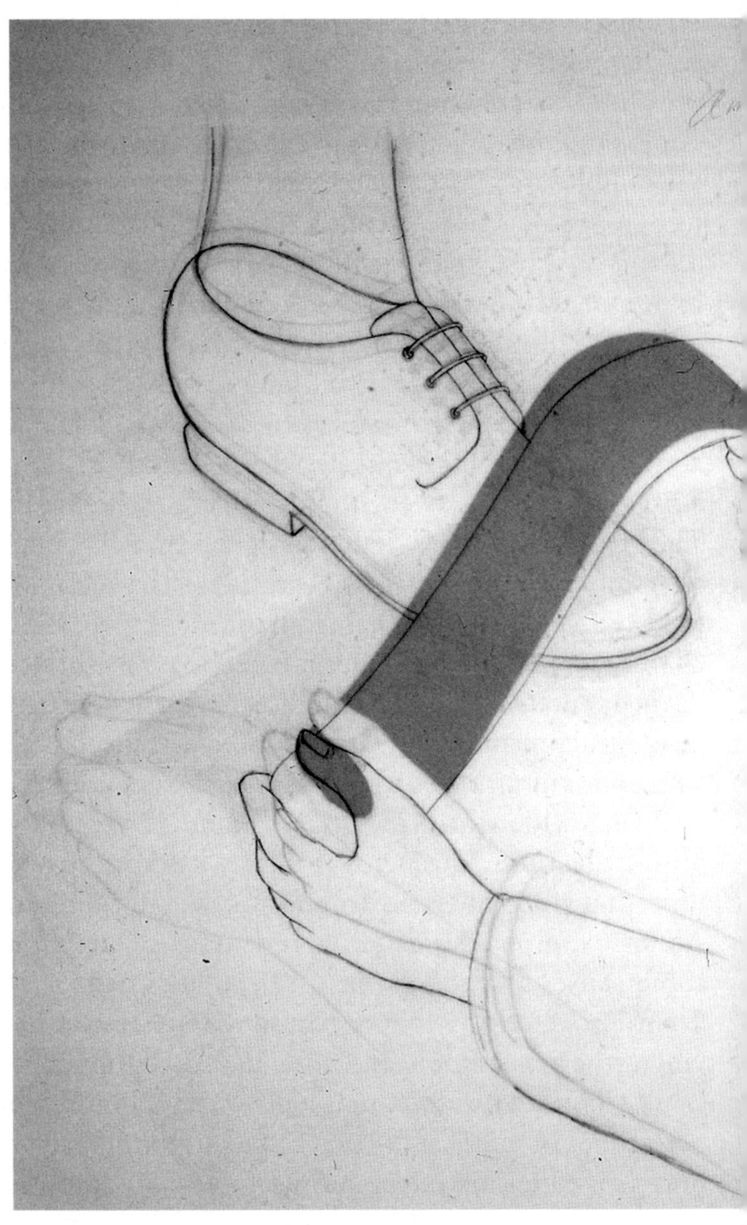

Francis Alÿs, still from *Bolero (Shoeshine Blues)*, 1999–2007

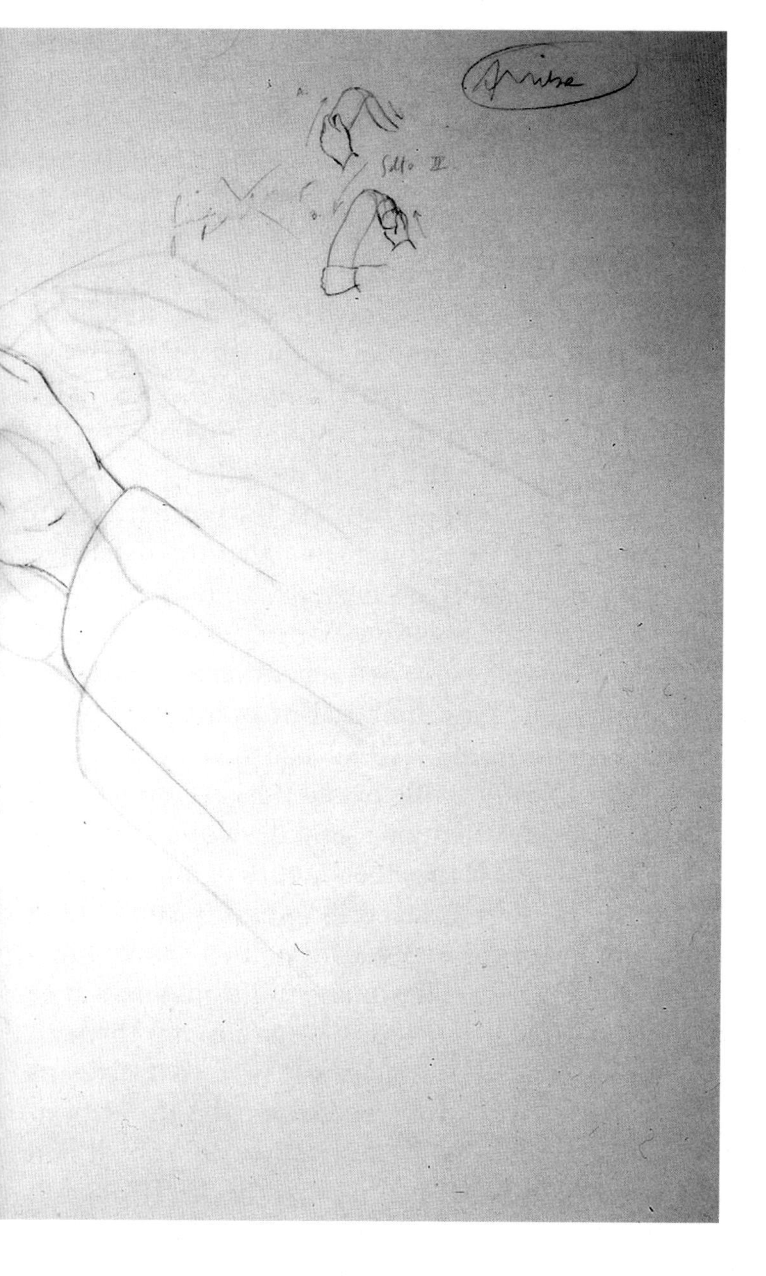
Salto II.

to be seen as wasted or excessive time that can and should be documented precisely because it never leads to any real result. In the looped animated film *Bolero (Shoeshine Blues)* (1999–2007), Alÿs demonstrates the activities of a shoe shiner as an example of work that does not produce any "value," in the Marxist sense of the word, because the time of cleaning cannot be accumulated in a product.

But precisely because such a wasted, suspended, and non-historical time cannot be accumulated and absorbed by its product, it can be repeated—impersonally, and potentially forever. Nietzsche had stated that the only possible way to think about infinity after the death of God, after the end of transcendence, is to envision eternity as the eternal return of the same. And Georges Bataille thematized the repetitive excess of time, its unproductive waste, as the only possibility to escape the modern ideology of progress. Certainly, both Nietzsche and Bataille perceived repetition as something naturally given and thus inescapable. But in his 1968 book *Difference and Repetition*, Gilles Deleuze speaks of literal repetition as being radically artificial and thus in conflict with everything natural, living, changing, and developing, including natural and moral law. Hence the practice of literal repetition can be seen as rupturing the continuity of historical life and creating a nonhistorical excess of time by means of art. Here is the point at which art becomes truly contemporary.

Indeed, one can argue that today we are living through precisely such a suspended nonhistorical time that gives us the opportunity to analyze and reconsider the projects of modernity. During modernity a "body of work" substituted the soul as a potentially immortal part of the self. Foucault famously gave the name "heterotopia" to the modern sites, like archives, museums, and libraries, in which time was accumulated instead of simply being lost. Politically, we can speak about modern utopias as post-historical spaces of accumulated time. Today, however, this guarantee of a future for the results of our work has lost plausibility. The museums have become sites of temporary exhibitions instead of spaces for permanent collections. The constant change in cultural trends and fashions makes any promise of a stable future for an artwork or a political project improbable. But the past is also perpetually rewritten—names and events appear and disappear, only to reappear and disappear again. The present has ceased to be a point of transition from the past to the future. Instead it has become a site of constant proliferation of historical narratives beyond individual grasp or control. Today, we remain stuck in the present. The loss of a reliable historical perspective generates the contemporary feeling of living through unproductive, wasted time. However, one can also perceive this wasted time positively as excessive time— the time that demonstrates our life as pure being-in-time beyond its utilization in the framework of modern economy and politics. Alÿs's videos do not treat our present as a unique historical moment, as an authentic event. Rather, they document the repetitive, nonhistorical character of a present that has lost its past and future. It is the present that was always already there and can be infinitely repeated.

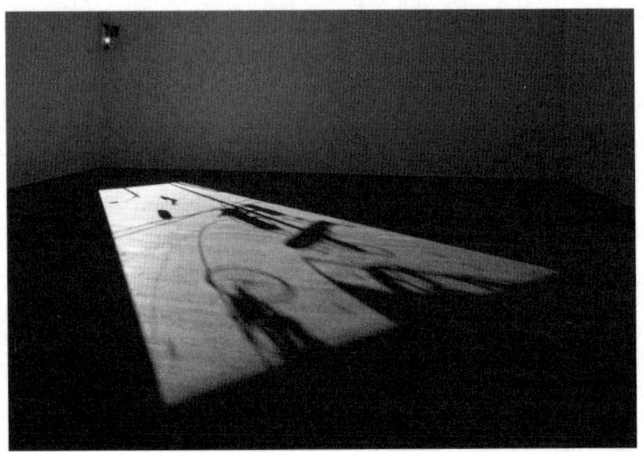

Paul Chan, *1st Light*, 2005

12
Paul Chan
Liberation in the Loop

In Plato's *Parmenides* one finds the following exchange between Parmenides and young Socrates. Parmenides asks: "Is there a form, itself by itself, of just, and beautiful, and good, and everything of that sort?" Socrates answers: "Yes." Parmenides then asks Socrates if he finds that not only human beings have a separate, ideal form, but also, as he says, "things that might seem absurd, like hair and mud and dirt, or anything else totally undignified and worthless." At that point, Socrates has to confess that questions of this kind trouble him too, but that he tries to avoid them so that he does not "fall into some pit of nonsense." To which Parmenides says: "That's because you are still young, Socrates, and philosophy has not yet gripped you, as in my opinion, it will in the future, once you begin to consider none of the cases beneath your notice."[1]

This passage came to mind the first time I watched the videos in Paul Chan's installation, *The 7 ~~Lights~~* (2005–7). In these videos, forms of the most ordinary objects are permanently moving upward, toward the heaven of pure ideas. And in the process of their ascension, they slowly begin to dissolve into a mass of fragments that appear so abstract that they are no longer identifiable as such. Thus, one can imagine the heavens being transformed by this slow yet interminable process into a kind of garbage pit—"some pit of nonsense," to use Plato's words. This pit would, in a somewhat paradoxical way, consist not of defunctionalized ordinary things themselves, but of their pure, abstract forms. Chan has insisted in various interviews on the importance that the word "light" is struck out in the title of the installation—like the word "being" in some of Derrida's texts. The light is understood here not as natural light—visually identifiable light having a certain equally identifiable natural source. Nor is it the light in which we see natural things. Rather, *light* is understood by Chan as metaphysical, one might say—as divine light that gives us the capability to imagine and see pure, ideal forms. This metaphysical, "other" light is the light of the Byzantine icons—light without a source of light. It is also the light of Malevich's Suprematist paintings, in which abstract geometric forms look as though they were caught by the eye of the painter during their slow movement up and to the right. Chan substitutes these pure geometric forms with "impure" trash-like forms from everyday life. And, at the same time, these impure forms are not moving up and to the right, but rather strictly upward, or up and to the left—opposite, in any case, to the vector of progress that we tend to imagine as pointing from left to right.

Indeed, one gets the impression that all of these pure forms of things, or souls of things, go strictly upward to escape the horizontal axis of progress—something that things themselves cannot escape. At least since Hegel we know that it is progress that makes things into things. In our civilization things are defined by their use. And their use is defined by the projects of biological survival, economic growth, political stability, social justice, and military security—projects of change and improvement that are directed toward the future. This radical subjection of all objects to the objectives of progress does not spare human beings, which, in the era of modernity, are regarded as things among other things— man is functionalized and instrumentalized, as is every other thing in the name of progress. It is precisely this modern and contemporary equation between humans and things that is reflected in Chan's *The 7 Lights*. The privileged position of humans vanishes and they escape the horizontal movement of the progress that enslaves them together with all other things—through the universal ascension of all forms, through the vertical movement that does not compromise the horizontal movement of history. And, of course, this form of escape is more difficult for humans than for the simple things of their everyday life, which is why in some of the videos human figures are seen falling down while the figures of the things are seen moving upward. The dissolution of these things through their free fall upward can look idyllic; the Dionysian dissolution of the human form implied by the same movement can look tragic.

The videos from *The 7 Lights* evoke cinematographic scenes of catastrophic explosions shown in slow motion, like the famous last sequence of Michelangelo Antonioni's 1970 film *Zabriskie Point*. Chan himself has spoken of the power of recession, which is the dark side of the power of progress as well as the chance to escape progress by suspending it.[2] One is reminded here of Walter Benjamin's famous interpretation of Paul Klee's *Angelus Novus* (1920), according to which the constant winds of progress propel "the angel of history [...] irresistibly into the future to which his back is turned" as he stares in terror at the ruins that the movement of progress leaves behind.[3] It is easy enough to imagine Chan as a contemporary *angelus novus*, recording the destruction that the wind of progress inflicts on the bodies of things. But this interpretation obviously contradicts the meditative, serene atmosphere of the installation. Here we are not witnessing the suffering of material bodies, but the ascension of their pure forms to the empty heaven of ideas. These forms move constantly upward as if a huge spiritual, antigravitational

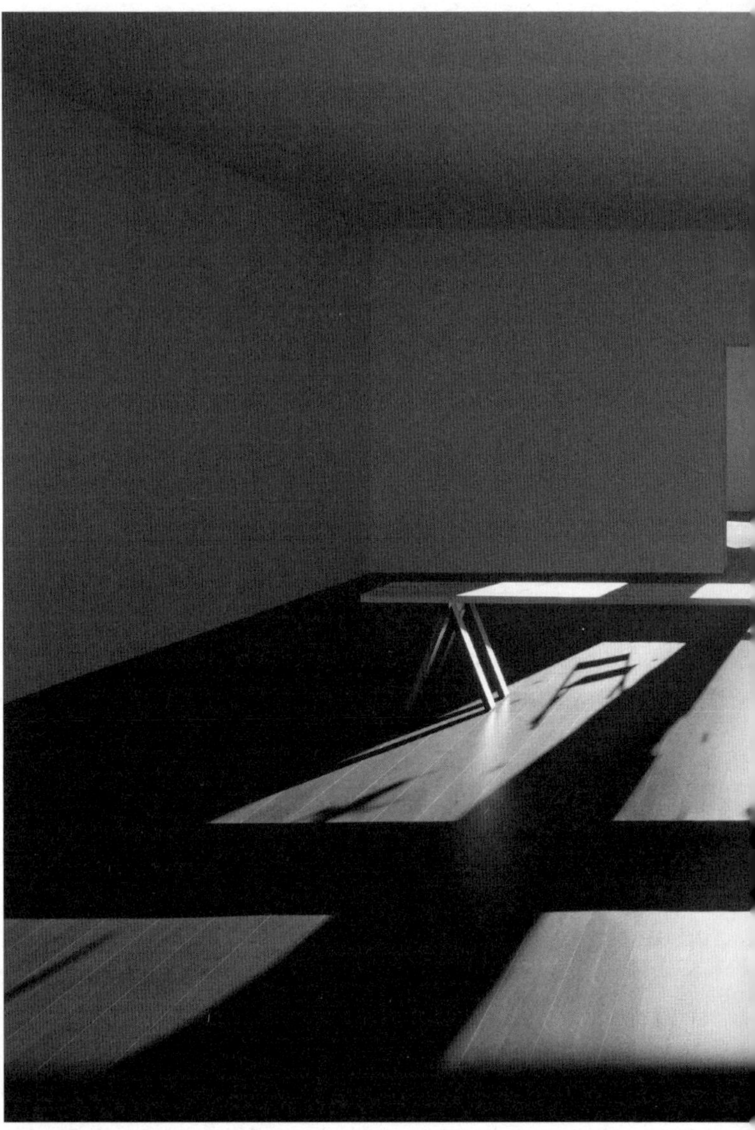

Paul Chan, *3rd Light*, 2006

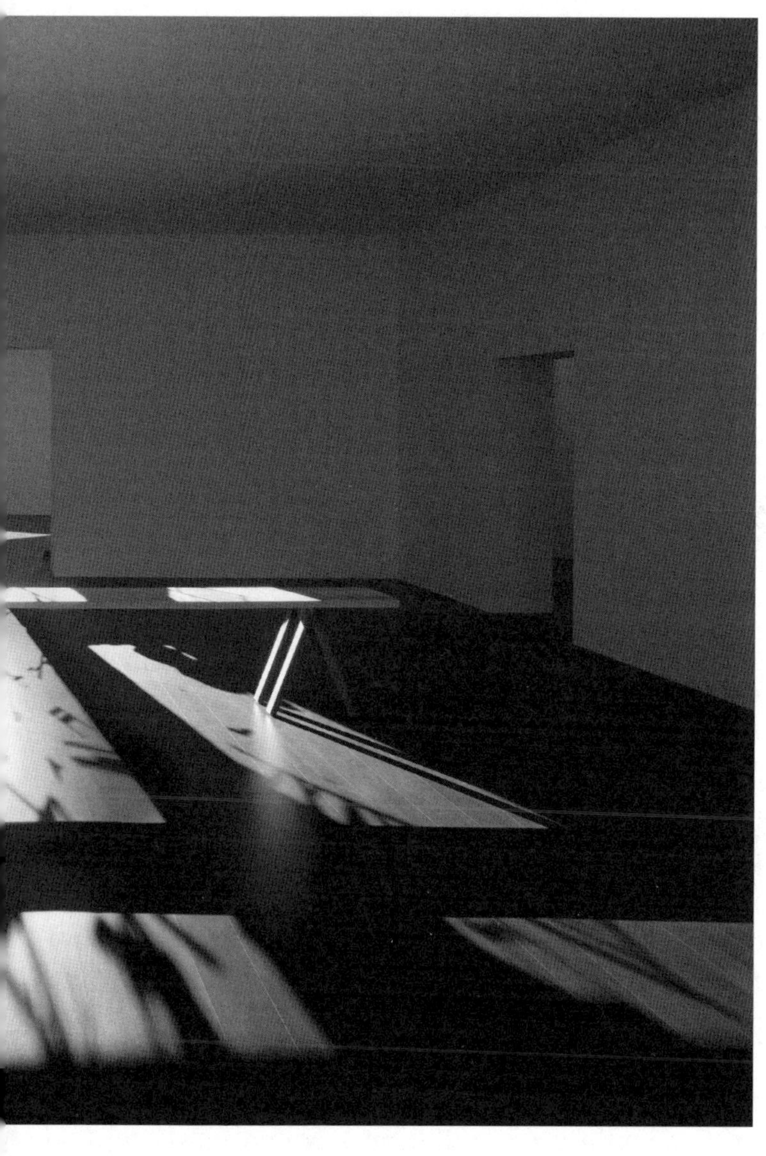

magnet has liberated them from their subjection to the law of utility, their enslavement by the power of progress, and set them free.

Nonetheless, these videos would merely function as another promise of radical liberation if they did not, at the same time, address the central characteristics of the medium itself as it is used in the context of the installation—video's movement in a loop. Traditional film is the most radical and spectacular embodiment of the linear concept of time. The filmic narrative inexorably moves from a beginning to an end—and all attempts by a range of experimental filmmakers to reverse or stop this linear progression have never really succeeded. Video inherited this compulsive progression along the axis of linear time. But when film and video made their way into installations they began to run in loops—and this totally changed their reception. There is a huge difference between looking at a film from beginning to end and looking at the same film (or video) in a loop, because the permanent return of the same in the latter radically destroys any illusion of linear time. The filmic narrative loses its power over the imagination if spectators know that all the elements of this narrative will keep returning to their field of attention. This makes the spectator feel like a Nietzschean Übermensch who has grasped the law of the eternal return of the same. Ordinarily, films and videos shown in art installations ignore this radical change of reception since their makers, being mere humans and unaware of the distinction, believe that their work can be presented as a unique event, seen from beginning to end.

Today, videos in an installation frequently attempt to reflect the conditions under which they are shown. This reflection necessarily takes the form of repetition inside the video's narrative—to remove the gap between its own narrative structure and the installational, looped repetition to which it is subjected. Now, there is nothing as repetitive as the act of liberation. Radical (self-)liberation means escape from any kind of instrumentalization, commodification, and utilization, which, in turn, excludes the possibility to inscribe the liberated thing in a narrative, for that would imply its renewed subjugation to the laws of cause and effect, or its renewed involvement in the horizontal movement of progress. Every liberation is a final liberation, and cannot be turned into a new beginning. Yet, at the same time, it is like any other liberation; the specificity of any particular action stems alone from its integration into some historical, horizontal process. The forms of slavery are different, but all the liberations are identical. And this is precisely what we see in Chan's videos. One thing is liberated after another—and every thing is taken directly to heaven (or to hell), away from the horizontal axis of universal history. And while the liberated things may be different, the act of liberating them is always the same. The videos present movement, but this movement is in itself a permanent repetition of the same act of liberation. In this sense, the gesture that constitutes movement in Chan's videos is repetitive long before it is looped. These videos demonstrate liberation as the eternal return of the same—liberation put into a loop.

Notes

1. Plato, *Parmenides*, in *Complete Works*, ed. John M. Cooper, trans. Mary Louise Gill and Paul Ryan (Indianapolis: Hackett Publishing, 1997), 364.
2. Paul Chan, "The Spirit of Recession," *October*, no. 129 (Summer 2009): 3–12.
3. Walter Benjamin, "On the Concept of History," trans. Harry Zohn, in *Selected Writings*, vol. 4, *1938–1940*, ed. Howard Eiland and Michael W. Jennings (Cambridge, MA: Belknap Press of Harvard University Press, 2003), 392.

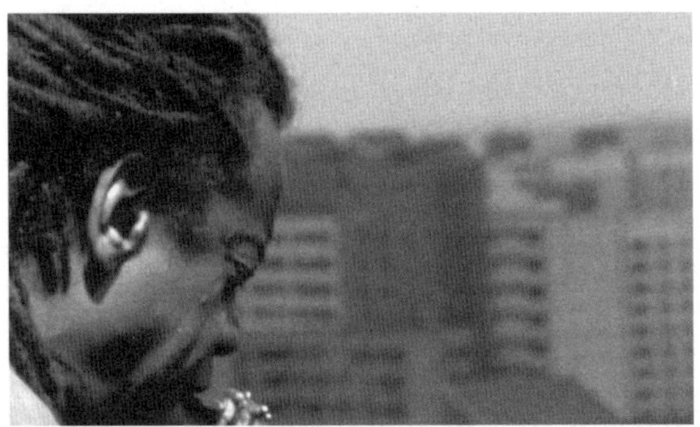

Anri Sala, still from *Long Sorrow*, 2005

13
Anri Sala
Scenes of Limited Subjectivity

At the end of the nineteenth century, writers and artists began to lose the language that they had shared with their audiences for many centuries. Religious beliefs became suspect, and national cultures looked obsolete due to technological revolution and political change. The familiar spoken, written, or visual languages turned into a set of dead conventions and empty formulas that had lost their meaning. As a result, these languages were supplanted by formalized structures and sound material. The historical avant-garde was an attempt to make art after the death and dissolution of the old language. Accordingly, it used two means of communication that had the aura of universality: mathematics, especially geometry, which legitimized collective submission under a commonly accepted order; and music, which infected the audience with fleeting moods, emotions, and passions. The radical movements of the historical avant-garde, such as Suprematism, Bauhaus, or De Stijl, took the way of geometric abstraction. The alternative program, to make all the arts "musical," had already been proclaimed in 1884 by Paul Verlaine in "The Art of Poetry":

> Let's hear the music first and foremost,
> And that means no more one-two-one-twos ...
> Something more vague instead, something lighter
> Dissolving in air, weightless as air.[1]

The program of turning the visual arts into a kind of painted music was also formulated by Wassily Kandinsky in *Concerning the Spiritual in Art* (1911). Kandinsky was especially inspired by the music of Arnold Schoenberg at the time: Kandinsky sought to liberate colors and forms from their representational function in traditional painting, just as Schoenberg liberated individual sounds from their submission to the melodic structure of traditional music.

The death of the old language at the beginning of modernity was, of course, not a single historical event. Rather, it started a series of such deaths: modern languages, such as the language of communism, also became old, and died time and again. Anri Sala shows the death of an old language in his video *Intervista (Finding the Words)* (1998) in which he and his mother watch old 16 mm footage of his mother speaking at an official party meeting in Albania. The soundtrack has disappeared. The language of official communist propaganda has died, and attempts to revive it fail: even after it becomes clear what his mother has actually said, the language in which she spoke remains a dead language—incomprehensible for Sala and for his mother herself.

To reestablish communication only two possibilities remain: geometry and music. In the video *Dammi i Colori* (2003) Sala shows an artistic action undertaken by Edi Rama. Upon becoming mayor of Tirana, Rama tried to transform the city by painting its facades in a neo-Constructivist, geometric way. The colors are bright; the design alludes to the time of early modernist utopian hopes. The geometric patterns and colors promise a new, happy life after years of communist gray. However, the people in the streets still seem depressed and occupied by their personal, everyday problems. The collective epiphany does not happen; everyday tristesse still dominates the mood. It seems that geometry does not work. Indeed, the modernist geometric architecture remains imposed from the outside. We have to live inside this architecture, but it does not manifest our subjectivity. Rather, it surrounds us and thus limits our ability to manifest the truth of our personal existence. Music, on the contrary, seems to give us a possibility to manifest our subjectivity—through its moods, its passions, its unique "living voice"—inside the objectified, alienated social space.

The conflict between standardized late modernist architecture and free-flowing "subjective" music is the topic of Sala's video *Long Sorrow* (2005). The title is a translation of the nickname that West Berlin residents gave to a huge building constructed in the neo-modernist style of the 1970s—*der lange Jammer. Jammer* can, in fact, be translated as "sorrow," but also as "complaint" (the verb *jammern* means "to complain"). In the video, the long complaint takes the form of a free jazz improvisation that—contrary to the standardized architecture—develops in an unpredictable, capricious, uncalculated manner. We are reminded of Verlaine: "Something more vague instead, something lighter / Dissolving in air, weightless as air." And, indeed, the body of the musician is shown as hanging in the air—outside the building, in the middle of nowhere. Here, as Theodor Adorno says, loneliness becomes a style.[2] Modernist architecture was created to let a new community of equals emerge, but instead it built a series of containers for lonely individuals. The long musical complaint gives this loneliness an artistic form. However, in his later works Sala begins to question the subjective status of the music itself. After all, music is also based on certain mathematical principles, and there is always repetition at the heart of every individual improvisation. Even in free jazz, all the variations refer to a theme and repeat it in a certain way.

To what degree music can function as a manifestation of free subjectivity is central to *Philosophy of New Music* (1946).

In his book, Adorno interprets Schoenberg's early pieces in which the composer attempted to manifest pure subjectivity through the unpredictable development of music in time—this living subjectivity, according to Adorno, was precisely such unique, haphazard events unfolding in time. Referring to traditional conventions of composition that used repetitive patterns, Adorno writes:

> Opposed to it, the integral organization of the artwork—today its only possible objectivity—is exactly the product of that subjectivity denounced by the music makers for what they call its haphazardness. Undoubtedly, the now-demolished conventions were not always external to music. Just as vital experiences were once sedimented in them, they in their way fulfilled a function. This function was organizational. Precisely this function, however, was taken over from them by an autonomous aesthetic subjectivity that aspired to organize the artwork in freedom, on its own terms.

He explains further:

> In music before Beethoven, with hardly an exception, variation was counted among the most superficial of technical procedures, a mere masking of identically preserved thematic material. Now, however, conjoined with development, variation serves the production of universal, concrete, non-schematic relationships. It undoubtedly continues to cling to its initial material, which Schoenberg called the "model"; all is identical, "the same." But the meaning of this identity is reflected as nonidentity. [...] By virtue of this nonidentity of identity the music achieves an absolutely new relationship to the time within which each work transpires. Music is no longer indifferent to time, for in time it is no longer arbitrarily repeated; rather, it is transformed.[3]

However, Adorno also states that the variations only *seem* to be truly subjective. In Adorno's argument, Schoenberg's twelve-tone music system demonstrates that the production of variations is a quasi-mechanical, mathematically ordered practice. It is through calculation that subjectivity comes to be produced. Here it can be mentioned that Kandinsky followed Schoenberg in believing that certain inner states of subjectivity—such as moods and emotions—could be produced in the soul of the listener or spectator in a calculated manner. That is why, according to Adorno, under the developed, modernist conditions reflected in Schoenberg's twelve-tone music, the new and subjective become possible only accidentally and in a limited scope. "The struggle between alienated objectivity and limited subjectivity is unresolved, and its irreconcilability is its truth."[4]

I am quoting Adorno at some length because I cannot imagine a better characterization of Sala's late work than the staging of this subtle struggle between alienated objectivity and limited subjectivity. Indeed, Sala's interest in music does not lead him to create videos that would be somehow "musical" in the sense meant by Verlaine or Kandinsky. Sala does not make music by visual means—he does not want his videos to be free-flowing and thus purely "subjective." Rather, these videos objectively document the production of subjectivity by means of music. They demonstrate not the repetitive pattern behind the subjective variations, but the impossibility of a perfect repetition. The variations are not planned, not consciously composed. These variations are uncalculated; they appear to be accidental, involuntary. The living bodies of the interpreters intervene in the musical composition in such a way that every musical performance becomes original and new—notwithstanding the "sameness" of the performed score. They emerge not on the level of composition but through the different interpretations of the same musical score. That is why the appearance of bodies in Sala's videos becomes central for the staging of the struggle between the identical and the nonidentical. Inhabiting neutral modern spaces and following the same musical scores, the bodies of

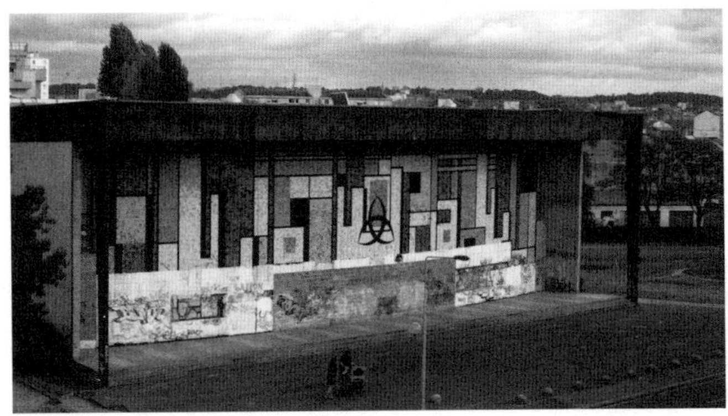

Anri Sala, still from *Le Clash*, 2010

performers remain partially unpredictable and "accidental," reflecting the unique event of their existence in time.

In this respect, Sala's video *Le Clash* (2010) is especially characteristic. Here, the melody of the song by the punk band the Clash, "Should I Stay or Should I Go?" (1981), is reproduced by a music box—an embodiment of the mechanical reproduction of sameness. We also see a wall covered by the late modernist geometric patterns that are reminiscent of the geometric patterns from *Dammi i Colori*—a promise of the utopian order that has already become obsolete. Indeed, it is the wall of the abandoned music hall in the Grand Parc of Bordeaux. In the video, the movement of the perforated strip of the barrel organ score that produces the sound can also be seen—with a geometric pattern reminiscent of the modernist pattern on the music hall's facade. The possibility of free, "subjective" variation seems here to be radically excluded. However, one sees a lone man walking around with the music box under his arm. The sound variations become substituted by the aimless, seemingly accidental wanderings of the man around the abandoned place of collective utopia. In Sala's video *Tlatelolco Clash* (2011), sixteen men and women are seen each inserting a perforated card into a barrel organ and turning the crank for the song to play. The segments of the same Clash song are heard in stochastic order—even as the melody remains the same. In these works Sala begins to thematize the silent score hidden behind the sound.

The correlation between the movements of the human body and variations of the same musical theme is the topic of Sala's *Ravel Ravel* (2013). Maurice Ravel's *Piano Concerto for the Left Hand in D Major* (1931) can be seen as a manifestation of extreme loneliness—the left hand becomes lonely if it cannot collaborate with the right hand. But Sala doubles this loneliness by juxtaposing the images of the left hands of two pianists and the sounds they produce. This doubled loneliness manifests in the differences between two performances of the same score, resulting in a persuasive example of the nonidentity of the identical. The identical score played by two different pianists manifests the irreducibility of their subjective, individual interpretations. This irreducibility is additionally thematized by the video images of the left hands of the two pianists: their movements also demonstrate the variations inside the same pattern.

Perhaps it is not accidental that Sala turned to Schoenberg's music in his recent work, *The Present Moment (in D)* (2014). Of course, the fact that Sala first presented his interpretation of Schoenberg's music in the hall of the Haus der Kunst in Munich is a powerful symbolic gesture in itself—the institution was initially built to present the official art of the Third Reich.[5] But more interesting is the way in which Sala subjected the musical material of Schoenberg's early piece *Transfigured Night*, op. 4 (1899) to a series of transformations. Namely, Schoenberg's music was modified by its inscription into the installation space. Schoenberg's sextet was broadcast through speakers installed in a series of arcs that led up to the screen at the end of the space—and each note was withheld until eleven others had sounded. This complicated procedure produced an effect that was similar to the twelve-tone system of late Schoenberg. Thus, Sala submitted the free, neo-Romantic, and Expressionist early music of Schoenberg to the discipline of calculated repetition that is characteristic of late Schoenberg. As Peter Szendy writes in the catalogue of the Haus der Kunst exhibition, "Yet it is indeed the principles of dodecaphonism that Anri folds over again onto a sextet that did not yet obey it, did not yet bend to it."[6] At the end of the *parcours* through the installation space all the notes are filtered out—but the D notes remain.

Szendy writes further, "The music is frozen in its movement; it seems to be nailed down, boiled to its own repetition."[7] Thus, the principle of variation—and with it, the epiphany of subjectivity—seems to be filtered out and completely substituted by repetition. However, the D note repetitions are subjected to the rhythm of the piece that brings variation into the length of the individual Ds. Most importantly, on the screen we see the movements of the musicians as they play their instruments, movements that never quite repeat one another. This piece by Sala could be seen as a subtle critique of Adorno's critical discourse. Even if a composer consciously tries to subject the production of variations to certain preconceived and strict rules, some uncontrollable, accidental, uncalculated variations remain possible.

Sala therefore documents scenes of limited subjectivity in his videos. The variations of the same—the nonidentity of the identical—constitute the field of possibilities in which subjectivity can manifest itself. But at the same time, these variations limit the scope of this manifestation. This is the principle of contemporary culture that Adorno anticipated. This principle can be easily interpreted in a way that denounces the subjective as an ideological illusion: behind the plurality of variations one discovers a hidden identity.

However, Sala demonstrates time and again that the same principle can be read in the opposite way: behind the illusion of the same he discovers a plurality of unpredictable and uncontrollable individual variations. One can see this strategy as an aftereffect of Sala's experience of a "totalitarian" past, which produced in him the desire to defend the individual and vital against the bureaucratic and mechanic. Here, Sala reacts to the more generally understood human condition. In the past, humans believed that their place was between gods and animals, but contemporary humans find their place between

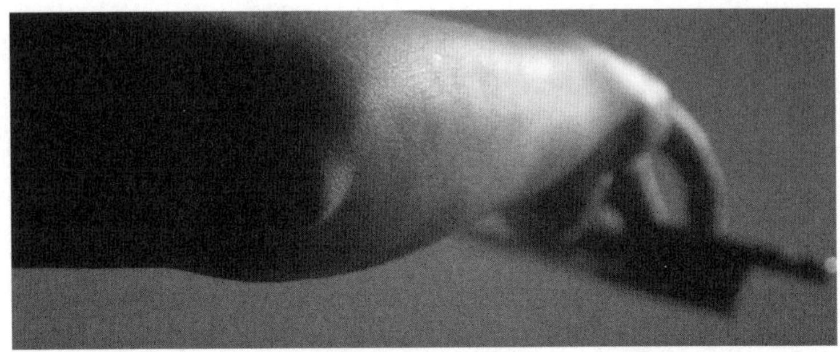

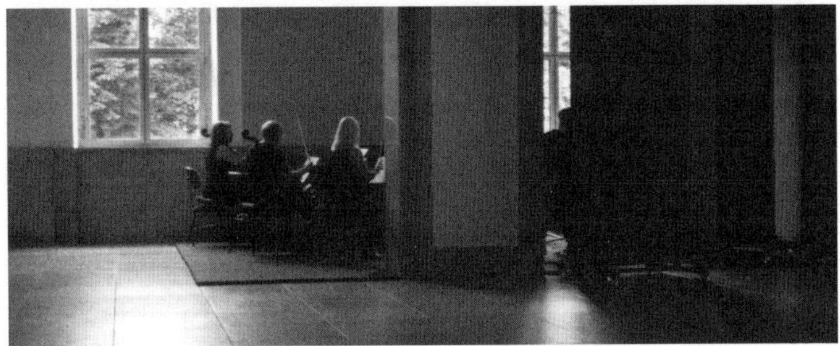

Anri Sala, stills from *The Present Moment (in D)*, 2014

animals and machines. Becoming an animal promises vitality, spontaneity, passion, and intensity—but also insecurity and mortality. Becoming a machine promises sustainability and even a kind of immortality—but also repetitiveness and boredom. Some authors and artists have tried to combine both positions: Deleuzian desiring-machines are the most obvious example of these attempts. Sala, on the contrary, underlines the tension between body and geometry, subjective variation and mechanical repetition. But in his works this tension never becomes explosive. It does not lead to a destruction of the apparatus of mechanical reproduction; rather, it leads to its destabilization and deconstruction. It is the interplay between the mechanical and the vital that offers the possibility of aesthetic pleasure.

Notes

1.  Paul Verlaine, "The Art of Poetry," in *Selected Poems*, trans. Martin Sorrell (Oxford: Oxford University Press, 1999), 123. "De la musique avant toute chose, / Et pour cela préfère l'Impair / Plus vague et plus soluble dans l'air, / Sans rien en lui qui pèse ou qui pose."
2.  Theodor W. Adorno, *Philosophy of New Music*, ed. and trans. Robert Hullot-Kentor (Minneapolis: University of Minnesota Press, 2006), 40.
3.  Ibid., 46–47.
4.  Ibid., 81.
5.  As is well known, modernist trends in art were condemned and forbidden by the Nazis who called them "degenerate." The most visible manifestation of this political agenda was the exhibition "Degenerate Art" that was shown in Munich in 1937, and Schoenberg was also considered by Nazi propaganda to be a degenerate composer.
6.  Peter Szendy, "The Bent Ear," in *Anri Sala: The Present Moment*, ed. Okwui Enwezor (Cologne: Verlag der Buchhandlung Walther König, 2015), 70.
7.  Ibid., 71.

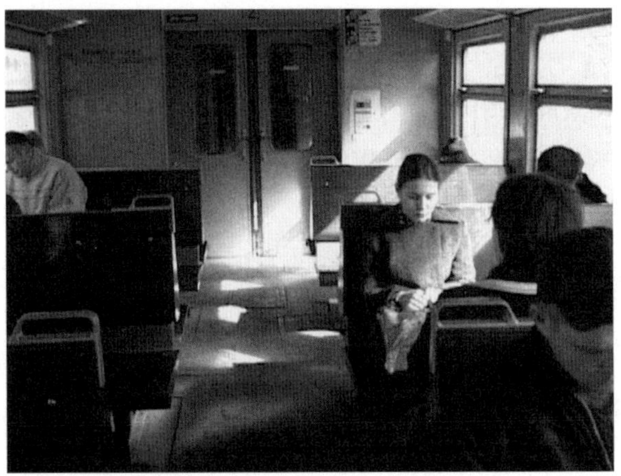

Olga Chernysheva, still from *The Train*, 2003

14
Olga Chernysheva
Looking for the Great Sunday


Contemporary art is heir to the great pictorial tradition of European art, from the Renaissance to nineteenth-century realism—and, at the same time, of the avant-garde's revolt against this tradition. Every contemporary artist has to find his or her own way to deal with this divided and divisive heritage. Olga Chernysheva is heir to the Russian version of this heritage—the critical, social-realist Russian art of the nineteenth century as well as the Russian avant-garde. Russian nineteenth-century realism was mostly produced by the Peredvizhniki (The Wanderers), a movement formed in 1870 by the artists who had broken with the academic tradition. Such a break also occurred in other places at that time. But in the case of the Peredvizhniki it was less a break with the form than with the content of academic art. The Peredvizhniki became interested in the life of ordinary people—of the "small man," as they said. That is why the movement remained highly esteemed during the Soviet period. The official socialist realism of the Soviet era was often criticized for viewing Soviet life through overly rosy spectacles, but at least the artists of socialist realism were still interested in the life of the ordinary working people.

Following the end of the Soviet Union, the celebration of the working class was replaced by the celebration of celebrity culture. Suddenly the country was inundated by images of the rich and glamorous. In this new visual context, Chernysheva's insistence on the continuation of the Russian and Soviet realist tradition and interest in the life of ordinary people can be read as a form of resistance to the glorification of this new social inequality. Her video *Tretyakovka* (2002), documenting a visit to the State Tretyakov Gallery, is a proclamation of her love of the art of the Peredvizhniki; the gallery has the largest and most important collection of nineteenth-century Russian realist art. At the same time, Chernysheva's interest in the realist tradition is not dictated by a desire to reveal the dark, unpleasant aspects of everyday experience that remain concealed by official propaganda or commercially oriented art. Chernysheva's art is critical, but not in the sense in which today's mainstream critical art functions. Chernysheva is not engaged in a political struggle or social critique. Rather, she is skeptical of certain claims and assumptions linked with her own profession and with her own social role, as well as with art in general and the figure of the artist in particular. Thus, Chernysheva does not simply depict ordinary people from a secure, unquestioned position of a professional artist, as traditional realism had. She rather looks for the moments of artistic behavior exhibited by people themselves.

Here, she is heir to the avant-garde tradition, especially of the Russian avant-garde tradition. I am not so much referring to Constructivism, which is most often associated with the notion of the Russian avant-garde, as the Proletcult and a number of other democratic trends in Russian art of the postrevolutionary period. Alexander Bogdanov and other leaders of the Proletcult did not try to impose their aesthetics on the population; they tried to offer common people an opportunity to become artists themselves—to write, paint, draw, etc. This anticipated the most radical movements of the 1960s. Several decades ago Joseph Beuys said that everybody has to become an artist. This requirement presupposes that, originally, "everybody" is not an artist—and has to be taught by a "true artist," like Beuys himself, how to do art.

For Chernysheva, like the Proletcult, everybody is always already an artist. As such, she is not interested in elevating ordinary people to the status of artists via her own artistic skills. Rather, she documents, in a seemingly neutral, objective manner, their attempts to aestheticize their own ordinary existence—to make art in the midst of life.

Chernysheva's art is different from that of her Russian and Soviet predecessors in one decisive aspect. Russian realist art, as well as that of the avant-garde and socialist realism, was predominantly interested in the subject of people at work. The social realism of the Peredyizhniki denounced the poor living and working conditions of the Russian population. The Russian avant-garde celebrated the creativity of the masses, the transformative power of industry, and agricultural labor that made ordinary work equal to artistic work. Let us quote some theoreticians of the Russian avant-garde—just to recall the historical background against which contemporary Russian art tries to makes itself visible.

In his programmatic book *Constructivism* (1922), Alexei Gan wrote: "Not to reflect, not to represent and not to interpret reality, but to really build and express the systematic tasks of the new class, the proletariat. [...] Especially now, when the proletarian revolution has been victorious, and its destructive, creative movement is progressing along the iron rails into culture, which is organized according to a grand plan of social production, everyone—the master of color and line, the builder of space-volume forms and the organizer of mass productions—must all become constructors in the general work of the arming and moving of the many-millioned human masses."[1] By contrast, Nikolai Tarabukin asserted, in his 1923 essay "From the Easel to the Machine," that the Constructivist artist could not play a formative role in the process of actual social production. Instead, his function was

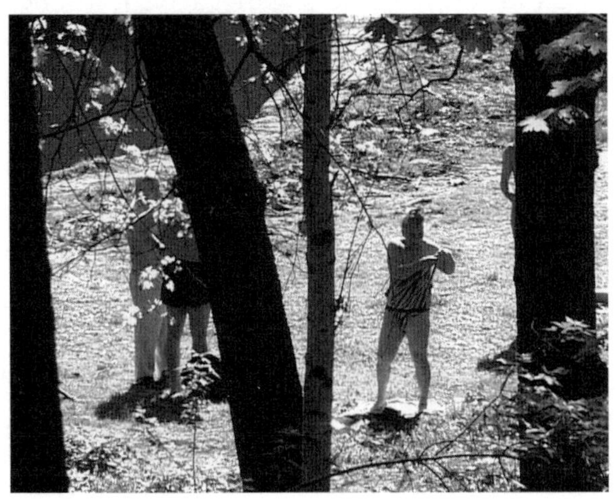

Olga Chernysheva, still from *Anonymous. Part 1 (Female Subject)*, 2004

that of a propagandist who defends and praises the beauty of industrial production, and opens the public's eyes to this beauty.[2] Socialist industry as a whole—without any additional artistic intervention—already reveals itself as good and beautiful because it is a result of the radical reduction of every kind of "unnecessary" luxury consumption, including that of the consuming classes themselves. Tarabukin writes further that communist society is already a nonobjective work of art because it has no goal beyond itself. In other words, the classical Russian avant-garde also came to the conclusion that art should cease to create and begin to document the creativity of the working masses. Here, ordinary people are celebrated only as working people. The same can be said about the Proletkult, which asked its working-class members to submit descriptions of their work. And the same can be said about socialist realism: it was interested in ordinary people, although only insofar as they functioned as builders of the new communist society. It was one's participation in collective work alone that redeemed the ordinary individual—that gave him or her the social dignity and right to be artistically represented.

Chernysheva, by contrast, shows the behavior of people during their free time, after working hours are over. She is the artist of Sunday—not of the workday. Here, one can also see a metaphor for the postcommunist mode of existence. The era of communism can be understood as a long working week. The postcommunist period presents itself as a long Sunday, a fulfilled promise—time for relaxation and consumption. Yet Sunday has, of course, a much longer history and deeper cultural meaning. Sunday signifies the only true liberation—not the liberation of work but, rather, liberation *from* work. Sunday means free time—time becoming free. But the freedom of time affects the ontological core of human existence. Man exists in time; if time becomes free, man is deeply endangered by this freedom. Sunday is therefore the most dangerous time for human life. In his 1932 treatise *Der Arbeiter* (The worker), Ernst Jünger describes a depressing and frightening impression that the Sunday crowd makes on its spectator—poorly dressed people, behaving in a vulgar fashion, undisciplined, disoriented, dully drifting through urban spaces.[3] In such a scenario Sunday can only induce one to impatiently wait until this unpleasant, disorganized human mass finally gets back to work and regains its pleasant appearance. But if Jünger describes the Sunday crowd as the most radical manifestation of kitsch, other authors of the period describe it as potentially dangerous. Mikhail Bakhtin, for instance, thematized the cruel, destructive sides of carnival, and Roger Caillois interpreted revolutions and wars as unexpected vacations from work—sudden eruptions of free time during regular working processes.[4] Indeed, every Sunday implies the possibility of a general strike that, according to Georges Sorel, is the highest form of violence.[5] This is why twentieth-century culture not only glorified the creative Working Man but also pronounced its utter dislike for the Sunday Man—the embodiment of free time.

This is also why different political regimes repeatedly tried to put free time under their control. Different religious rituals, including the traditional visit to church, as well as sports events and the theater, cinema, and museum, television and the Internet, shopping and other forms of consumption, are institutions for structuring and controlling free time. By contrast, the heroes of Chernysheva's videos are left to themselves. They fell out of the old socialist networks and do not have enough money to consume under the conditions of the new capitalist economy. They are thus left alone vis-à-vis their free time. And this is precisely the moment at which Chernysheva becomes interested in their fate—in their lonely and heroic attempts to put the monstrous powers of free time under their individual control. To domesticate free time. To challenge its destructive force. The heroes of Chernysheva's videos solve this problem by inventing and practicing their own private rituals. Good examples of this strategy are offered by the protagonists in the two parts of *Anonymous* (2004). A man takes all the time in the world to open a bottle of vodka. A woman needs the same amount of time to change her clothes. This is how these truly contemporary heroes "kill" free time—so that it will not kill them. Of course, we all always know that the only function of time is to kill us. But Sunday is a day on which we are directly confronted with this knowledge. This is why Sunday is an occasion for us to kill time.

Chernysheva is infinitely attentive and sympathetic to all these almost invisible but authentic artistic endeavors and struggles. The heroes of her videos engage in a kind of everyday art production by singing, dancing, exercising, or going sightseeing. And they are doing art without intending to and without any pretense of impressing anyone by what they are doing. The majority live in the lower strata of society, and it does not occur to them that what they are doing or feeling could be interpreted as a specific form of aesthetic experience. It is this unpretentious, sincere attitude toward themselves and their lives that fascinates Chernysheva in the first place. She recognizes fellow artists in these individuals—driven by the same inner impulses that drive her own art. These everyday artists do not try, and would not know how, to situate their art in the context of the contemporary art world, but they nonetheless remain artists. And perhaps precisely because of their modesty they seem to be genuinely true, authentic artists—unlike the busy crowd that populates today's art system.

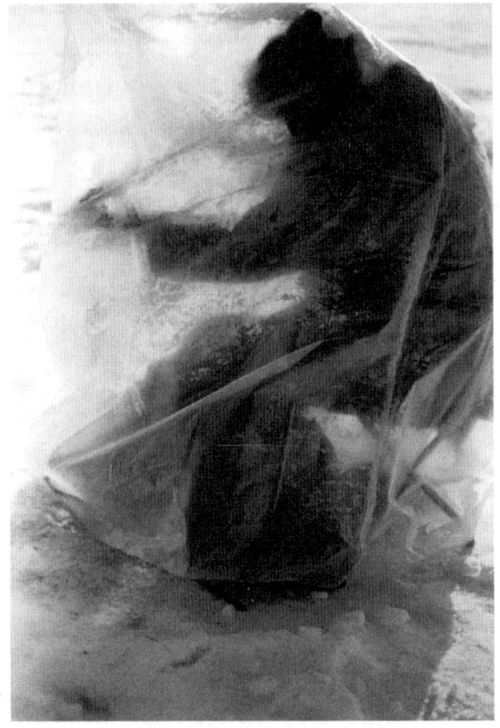

Olga Chernysheva, *Anabiosis. Fisherman-Plants,*
2000

Even so, the Sunday Man emerges not only on Sundays but any time working processes come to an end or a halt, or are interrupted. One of Chernysheva's videos, *The Train* (2003), presents people who have nothing in particular to do because they are sitting in the train and simply let themselves be transported by it. But Chernysheva became increasingly interested in documenting the lives of people whose work consists of doing nothing or almost nothing, like fishermen who spend hours on the ice without making a movement, or security guards who stand for hours in the same spot and just look around. Or the protagonist of the video *Trashman* (2011), who merely holds a bag and waits, at the end of every screening, for moviegoers to put their trash into his bag. Here the work becomes a specific form of killing time—not unlike the work of a contemporary artist.

Indeed, contemporary art—at least since Duchamp, and especially since the 1960s—abandoned the ideal of a dynamic, creative artist who produces like crazy. Artists became unwilling to constantly supply the art market with new commodities. The commodification of art undermines art's credibility, because artists begin to subject their art to the taste of the public and the requirements of the art market. Moreover, artists cannot compete with the mass production of commodities that inundate contemporary markets. As a result, many artists shift their attention from art products to the processes of artistic production. A visitor of museums or art spaces today is increasingly confronted with the documentation of artistic processes instead of traditional artworks. Often enough these processes have no beginning and no end—they are circular, repetitive. Such an artistic activity can be seen as a waste of time but, actually, it is a manifestation of the artist's subjectivity. The subjectivity exists only in time—it becomes obliterated in the final product of artistic work.

Throughout her art practice, Chernysheva thematizes this suspended, circular, repetitive time insofar as she captures and demonstrates activities that take place in time but do not lead to the creation of any definite product. Here we are confronted with instances of a pure and repetitive waste of time—with secular rituals beyond any claim of magic power, beyond any religious tradition, beyond any cultural convention. The heroes of Chernysheva's art almost always exist in a mode of expectation—of waiting for a chance, a surprise, a miracle. Her photographs show the half-frozen fishers waiting for a fish or bored bodyguards waiting for a crime. *Trashman* shows a man who is obviously waiting for "the gift" but only gets trash. And in *March* (2005) Chernysheva documents the juxtaposition of two repetitive, senseless welcome rituals: an old Soviet greeting and a new, post-Soviet, "capitalist" one. The spectator is reminded here of Albert Camus's Sisyphus and his aimless, repetitive activity. This nonproductive practice, this excess of time caught in a nonhistorical pattern of eternal repetition, constitutes for Camus the true image of what we call "lifetime"—lifetime being irreducible to any "meaning of life," any "life achievement," any historical relevance. Central here is the notion of repetition. The activities that attract Chernysheva's attention are repetitive per se, even before they are documented by a video that runs in a loop.

The depiction of these activities can be seen as a reflection on the medium of video and its conventions within an individual video itself. Chernysheva is one the few contemporary artists who not only work in the medium of video installation but who also have precisely grasped and practically implemented the specific aesthetics of the medium. Indeed, inside the video or film installation the film changes its mode of manifestation—and, accordingly, its inner structure. The film as an art form emerged in the epoch when European humanity believed in progress, when action was valued more than passive contemplation, when any movement forward was recognized as being much more important than the quiet repetition of the same. In contrast, a video installation is a place in which the film as such loses its historical perspective and is relieved of the burden of progress, replaced by the post-historical ritual of self-repetition. Within the framework of a video installation the film ceases to be narrative. Instead of demonstrating life in all its variations and dynamic developments, as has been done before, it unexpectedly becomes an ideal medium for revealing the repetitive rituality and regularity of life subsisting beneath all the claims for change and advancement.

In his time, Marshall McLuhan coined the phrase "the medium is the message." The success of any artistic project depends, first and foremost, on the extent to which the individual message of an artist coincides with the message of the medium used by the artist. Chernysheva's videos are spontaneously convincing and truly artistic inasmuch as they rest on a congruity between the medium and the message. Namely, they repeat their movement in the loop inside their own inner time of narration—so that here the medium reflects itself. And in many of Chernysheva's videos the image remains almost unchanged from the beginning to the end. Here the video reflects the fact that it is shown inside an artistic space in which we traditionally expect images to be unmoving, unchanging. In both parts of *Anonymous*, for example, each video represents a figure in a landscape—a topic that is quite common for a typical museum picture. The image remains practically the same throughout both videos. As a consequence, the viewer is able to react to these videos in a way that is similar to the way he or she responds to traditional pictures. If an exhibition visitor retreats from a particular

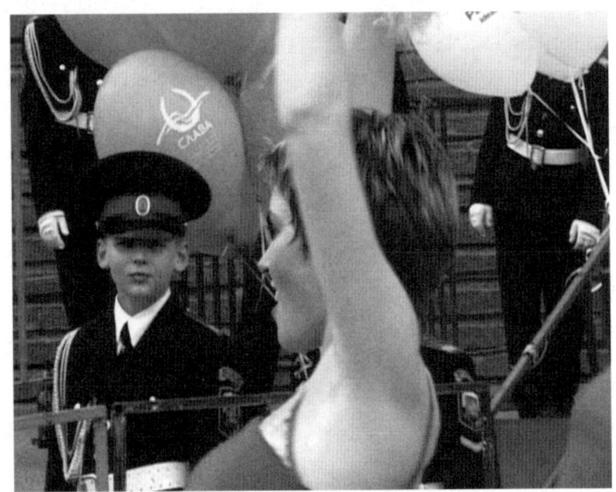

Olga Chernysheva, still from *March*, 2005

work for a while and then returns to it, he or she will find the characters approximately in the same places and doing the same things as when they were left. Even in the projections featuring movement, such as *The Train* or *Steamboat Dionysius* (2004), the scene of action remains stationary and easily recognizable. A video installation operates effectively only if it "installs" the movement and offers a compromise between the expectations of a moviegoer and those of an exhibition visitor. In her works, Chernysheva finds and displays this fragile balance between the motion of a film and the motionlessness of a traditional picture, a balance that best agrees with the nature of the medium of video installation.

Characters in Chernysheva's works are always involved in a continuous, reiterative, monotonous motion. Whatever such characters do—open a bottle of vodka, change clothes at a beach, or move through a train from front to rear and back again—it soon becomes clear that, in fact, they never start from a dead stop. Even their appearances indicate that they have once and forever fallen out of the dynamics of historical life and are doomed to eternally substitute each other in an endless circuit in a way that is hardly noticeable to others or to themselves. Such characters not only cannot, they do not *want* to keep pace with the movement of their epoch. They do not need the latest thing, or anything up-to-date, being quite satisfied with their participation in the cyclical time of eternal repetition. In other words, they are real-life people. Chernysheva is consistent in avoiding any elements of theatrical staging, as well as any claims of unconventionality or exoticism in the material she uses, or of a special originality, an exceptional "artistry" in her style. For her videos she uses a kind of documentary footage, which looks quite normal and trivial, even commonplace. The artist shoots the footage with her own camera as she walks along and observes people's behavior in everyday life. Such documentaries draw our attention to the aesthetics of the readymade.

Interesting for the spectator is not how the artist designed this or that image, but the image itself, and the criteria by which the image's material is selected. Such a refocusing of attention from artistic processing to selection, which is so typical for all contemporary art oriented to the present, with the lessons of Marcel Duchamp still fresh in mind, is attained by Chernysheva through her emphatically neutral, observational, documentary style of filming. The resulting materials, in terms of their stylistics, at first glance appear well suited to a TV news program devoted to the labor and leisure of our contemporaries. However, there is a great difference between a TV documentary and a documentary shown by Chernysheva in her video installations, which is most clearly evident in the aesthetic neutrality of the latter. A television report features, or at least is expected to feature, only urgent, red-hot news that interests today's general public and reflects current political or cultural situations. The contemporary mass media are solely interested in what is new and extraordinary.

Chernysheva's works, by contrast, present characters who live the most trivial lives and, therefore, never get a chance to appear on the news. Today, the context of contemporary art is the only one capable of documenting ordinary people's lives. Contemporary art makes it possible to represent things in the quotidian, things that otherwise would never have been elevated to the level of social visibility, things that are just ignored by the media. It is noteworthy that Chernysheva belongs to the very few contemporary Russian artists who adequately respond to this aesthetic, social, and political role of contemporary art in the current cultural and media context.

The interest in nonhistorical, ordinary forms of human existence grows during those historical periods when the social pressure requiring artists to act as fashion- and news-makers becomes especially irritating. In such periods it seems as if the real freedom lies not in the ability to make history but, rather, in the ability to be liberated from history—from the burden of historical work, from the obligation to make a next step. One aims at reaching the stage at which work and rest from work, *vita activa* and *vita contemplativa*, the working day and Sunday, coincide; when work is equated with nonwork—the Great Sunday that is extended to incorporate the entire working week.

Christianity understood this Great Sunday as paradise: in paradise it is still possible to do artistic work (such as singing) but not work in the worldly sense of this word. Of course, Christianity believed that this Great Sunday could be achieved only in the other world—beyond the grave. But Chernysheva went through the experience of communism and knows that an equivalence between work and nonwork can be realized on Earth. Accordingly, she continues to look for this equivalence in the postcommunist condition as well. In other words, Chernysheva looks for paradise on Earth. And she finds it where it is most unexpected—in non-teleological, nonproductive activity that is not oriented toward results. This activity seems to be frustrating to anyone who is trained to believe in creativity and productivity. Nevertheless, nonproductive, non-teleological, repetitive activity has a certain advantage over productive activity: non-teleological activity is potentially infinite, even eternal, because it can never come to an end, a result, a product. This infinite perspective is, actually, a source of happiness—not of frustration. Camus suggested that one had to see Sisyphus as a happy man. All the heroes in Chernysheva's videos are also happy people—in their own modest, subdued, nonspectacular way. They all live in the Great Sunday, which we can also enter if we want—or, rather, if we are capable of doing so.

Notes

1.   Alexei Gan, *Constructivism*, trans. Camilla Gray, in *Art in Theory, 1900–2000: An Anthology of Changing Ideas*, ed. Charles Harrison and Paul Wood (Oxford: Blackwell, 1993), 320 (translation modified).
2.   Nikolai Tarabukin, "From the Easel to the Machine," trans. Christina Lodder, in *Modern Art and Modernism: A Critical Anthology*, ed. Francis Frascina et al. (London: Harper & Row, 1982), 135–42.
3.   Ernst Jünger, *Der Arbeiter: Herrschaft und Gestalt* [The worker: Mastery and form] (Stuttgart: Klett-Cotta, 2007), 126ff.
4.   Mikhail Bakhtin, *Rabelais and His World*, trans. Hélène Iswolsky (Bloomington: Indiana University Press, 1994); Roger Caillois, *Man and the Sacred*, trans. Meyer Barash (Urbana: University of Illinois Press, 2001).
5.   Georges Sorel, *Reflections on Violence*, trans. T. E. Hulme and J. Roth (Mineola, NY: Dover Publications, 2004).

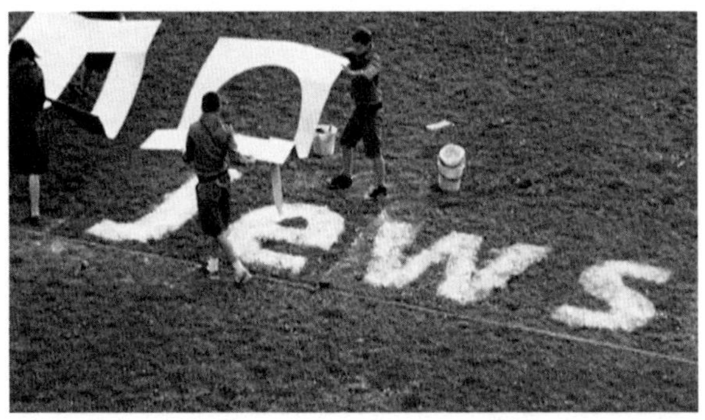

Yael Bartana, still from *Mary Koszmary* (*Nightmares*), 2007

15
Yael Bartana
Answering a Call

Yael Bartana's video trilogy, "And Europe Will Be Stunned," is indeed a stunning work of art. The effect that the work achieves cannot be explained by its subject alone—the return of Jews to Poland. A small diaspora of Israeli artists, writers, and other cultural workers has emerged recently in Europe, to no one's surprise. In the eyes of European public opinion this development has merely reaffirmed the tolerant, liberal character of the European Union and the validity of so-called European values. What makes Bartana's rendering of the Jewish repatriation of Poland a stunning event is the specific form that it takes: the Jews arrive not as isolated individuals ready to integrate themselves into the established European (in this case Polish) economic, political, and ideological order, but as a movement that practices its own way of life. And even more important: their ethos is collectivist. The return of the Jews symbolizes here not only—or even, not so much—a return of the repressed memories of the Shoah. To an even greater degree, the videos manifest the repressed lifestyle and aesthetics of socialism—the rejection of which was the historical precondition for the emergence of a contemporary Europe unified economically and politically. Indeed, the abolition of Soviet-style socialism in the countries of the former Eastern bloc laid the foundations for the European Union in its current form. Since some members of the European Union, such as Poland, are products of their (relatively recent) anticommunist revolutions, a certain anti-Sovietness is written into their social, political, and economic orders.

So Bartana's videos, abounding as they do with references to a communist and especially Soviet past, make a lasting impression. The red cravats that decorate the young listeners of Sławomir Sierakowski's speech in the first video, *Mary Koszmary* (*Nightmares*, 2007), are reminiscent of the red cravats of the Soviet pioneers. At the end of the trilogy—in *Zamach* (*Assassination*, 2011)—Sierakowski's funeral takes place in the Palace of Culture—a typical example of Stalinist architecture that was donated by Stalin as a "gift" to Poland after World War II, and which has since been regarded (and reviled) as a symbol of Soviet domination. The funeral ceremony itself is also redolent of the ceremonies practiced during the socialist era. The cult of leaders who sacrificed their lives for a communist future remained central to communist ideology for many decades. The last scenes of Bartana's trilogy imitate the carefully staged rituals of mass grief in the presence of the dead body of the leader, which are so familiar to those who witnessed them, either in person or on screen.

But it is the second of Bartana's videos that most explicitly references images belonging to a Soviet past. *Mur i wieża* (*Wall and Tower*, 2009) revives the aesthetics of early Soviet cinema and its dedication to the construction of a new socialist life and a new socialist man. The scenes of common work, common meals, and common recreation seem to have been directly lifted from Soviet films of the 1920s and '30s. This impression is only strengthened by the humble materials that are used in the building of their new life, and the absence of any contemporary machinery. Bartana's characters labor as if they are living in rural Russia after the October Revolution or, for that matter, in the Palestine of the same era. Their clothes also remind the viewer of socialist dress from the '20s and '30s—particularly as depicted in the photographs of Aleksandr Rodchenko and the films of Dziga Vertov. The whole process of constructing the settlement is shot from different angles to create dynamic imagery that is very much in the style of Rodchenko and Vertov. And these images suggest, just as they do in Vertov's documentaries, that the process of building a new life presupposes no hierarchy and almost no division of labor; that it is rather an egalitarian effort, a collective celebration of the building process that creates a characteristically desexualized camaraderie between men and women.

The result of this ecstatic unifying work seems to be rather modest: the small settlement looks a bit like a Stalinist labor camp and seems to be lost in the middle of nowhere. This nowhere is symbolized at the end of the film by another reference to Poland's past—the anonymous mass architecture of late socialism, examples of which can be seen behind the fragile structure of the settlement. The Jewish builders of the new future are depicted by Bartana as vital men and women, full of energy and hope. But the way in which they work is deeply anachronistic, belonging to a period of early industrialization, such as that of the Jewish collectivist agricultural projects in Palestine in the '20s and '30s. These young Jewish enthusiasts, with their socialist work ethics and primitive technology, seem to be lost not only in space but also in time. They build something resembling a cross between an Israeli kibbutz and a Soviet kolkhoz in the middle of postcommunist, postindustrial, postmodern Europe. They embody the collectivist and productivist enthusiasm of different socialist movements during the period between the two world wars, yet they live in our contemporary era of privatized endeavor and individual consumption.

Thus, one of the ambitions of this project seems to be not so much a return of the Jews to Poland but, rather,

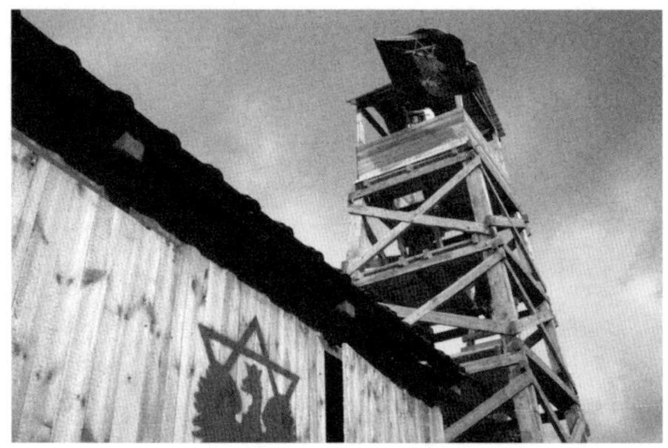

Yael Bartana, still from *Mur i wieża* (*Wall and Tower*), 2009

an attempt to return to the universalist roots of Zionism after many decades of crippling nationalism and provincialism. During the Cold War, Soviet Communism and Israeli Zionism were ideological and political enemies. The Cold War may now be over but neither ideology has emerged on the winning side of history. Today Zionism has a problematic reputation, and even within Israel the socialist roots of the movement have been mostly forgotten, and the kibbutzim essentially privatized. The posthumous reputation of the Soviet Union is equally poor, and inside Eastern Europe and Russia, communism remains an ostracized ideology. The recent history of both of these movements has made observers forgetful of their common roots in the socialist aspirations of a European intelligentsia and working class in the run-up to World War II. Bartana's video trilogy, in merging Zionist and Soviet imagery from the interwar period, reminds us of this shared history. The symbol of the Jewish Renaissance Movement in Poland (JRMiP), founded by Bartana, combines the Polish eagle and the Star of David—but, more importantly still, the color of the flag is red. It is interesting that this combination of kibbutz and kolkhoz, of Soviet ideology and Zionism, imagined so powerfully by Bartana, has a real historic precedent that has been largely forgotten.

In the late 1920s the USSR launched a call to Soviet and international Jewry to build a home for themselves on its territories. The Jewish Autonomous Region was founded in Birobidzhan—a region in Siberia on the Amur River, along the Sino-Soviet border. Launching the project in 1926, Mikhail Kalinin—then Chairman of the Central Executive Committee of the USSR—said that Jewish people had a task to secure their national identity and that this goal could only be realized by creating a compact agricultural population of at least several hundred thousands of Jews. In a speech,

Kalinin proposed Birobidzhan as a new Jewish homeland. A territory in the middle of the Siberian taiga arguably does not correspond to the historical image of Jews as intellectual deracinated city dwellers. But the Soviet ideologues hoped to use the Jewish settlements not only to economically transform Birobidzhan but also to transform the Jews themselves, through collective agricultural work, into new men. As Kalinin explained in a speech from 1934: "I think that the Jewish nationality of Birobidzhan will not be a nationality with the characteristics of the Jews of the ghettos of Poland, Lithuania, White Russia and even Ukraine, because it is already giving birth to socialist 'colonisers' of a free, rich land, to people with big fists and strong teeth, who will be the forebears of a new strong nationality within the family of Soviet peoples."[1]

This vision of Jews "with big fists and strong teeth" is not that distinct from the Zionist vision of a new race of "muscular Jews" emerging on Palestinian territory. It is no coincidence that one of the founders of the Zionist movement was Max Nordau, who became world renowned for his book *Entartung* (*Degeneration*, 1892), which was dedicated to the struggle against so-called degenerate art. The book later became the main source of inspiration for the infamous exhibition organized by the Nazis in Munich in 1937. Nordau, alongside other leaders of the early Zionist movement, also feared for the inappropriate professions and unhealthy lives that he felt Jews were leading in European cities, particularly Eastern European shtetls. It was not only the anti-Semitic press that perceived Jews to be physically weak, psychologically unstable, culturally underdeveloped, interested only in money, unfit for military training, etc., but also the founders of Zionism. Agricultural work and military service were encouraged by the Jewish renaissance in Palestine as a means to overcome the centuries of degeneration they felt had been inflicted on Jewish people under diasporic conditions.[2]

Soviet ideology of the 1920s and '30s also celebrated hard work, sport, military service, vitality, and youth. But of course this biopolitical renaissance was understood more in terms of class than race. New Soviet power wanted to overcome the degeneration of proletarian bodies that inevitably resulted from capitalist exploitation. The masses of poor Eastern European Jews seemed to be a perfect example of this exploitation. It is very telling that the communist and Zionist movements began to realize their shared goal of revitalizing Jewish bodies almost simultaneously. The Kibbutz Artzi federation was established in Palestine in 1927 and in 1936 they founded the Socialist League of Palestine; at the same time, the Soviet government launched the Jewish kolkhoz movement in Birobidzhan, and then founded the Jewish Autonomous Region.

It is clear that the Soviet powers felt in competition with the Israeli kibbutz movement. However, the Jewish kolkhozy in the USSR not only copied the kibbutz movement but also incorporated the internationalist claims of communism that the Zionist kibbutzim lacked. The Soviet ideologues hoped that this internationalism would give their project a global appeal, reaching out to Jews everywhere, including in Palestine. Accordingly, Soviet authorities began to collaborate with many international Jewish organizations in Europe, the United States, and Palestine to finance and organize the re-emigration of Jews into the Soviet Union. In the 1920s and '30s, around 1,500 foreign Jews (including a certain number of Jews from Palestine) joined thousands of Soviet Jews in emigrating to Birobidzhan. The Swiss architect Hannes Meyer—a former director of the Bauhaus in Dessau, a collaborator of El Lissitzky, and a dedicated communist—was commissioned to design the city of Birobidzhan, which was the administrative capital of the Jewish Autonomous Region. The formation of a new Jewish identity and the happy life of Jews in this region became a regular feature in the late avant-garde magazine *SSSR na stroike*. In one of the magazine's most widely known photographs, a Jew from Palestine is shown driving a tractor in Birobidzhan.

Especially interesting in this respect is the Soviet film *Iskateli schastya* (*Seekers of Happiness*, 1936), which depicts the early heroic period of organization of Jewish kolkhozy in Birobidzhan. The film was an attempt to demonstrate the creation of a new kind of socialist Jew—hardworking, collectivist, healthy—through their participation in agricultural labor. At the heart of the film's narrative is a Jewish family that emigrates in 1928 from "abroad"—journeying from an unnamed land, which is "warm" and with "fresh air," but where there are "no jobs." The place they have come from is unmistakably Palestine.

The family is made up of old Dvoira, her three children (two daughters and a son who represents the new "muscular Jew") and Pinya, a husband to one of the daughters, who embodies the stereotype of degenerate Jewish diaspora: weak, work-shy, and obsessed with money. At the end of the film Pinya commits a crime and tries to flee to China before getting arrested by Soviet security forces. His fellow Jews, meanwhile, find relative success, and the film ends in a celebration of their new socialist homeland. The parallels to the Zionist ideal are manifold. However, there is one crucial difference: Jews here are not opposed by the indigenous Russian population. They did not arrive uninvited; they were called—and answered this call. Their colonization of Birobidzhan was needed and valued, so they were never in conflict with their surroundings. The factual history of Jews in Birobidzhan is, of course, rather different. At the end of the '30s, and again at the end of the '40s, there were concerted attempts to suppress the cultural identity of the Jewish population. The number of Jewish people in Birobidzhan never exceeded forty thousand; today, the Jewish Autonomous Region still exists as a part of the Russian Federation, although its Jewish population has diminished to some four thousand.

The Jewish colonization of Birobidzhan has an uncanny relevance to the JRMiP. As in Bartana's trilogy, the Jewish colonization of Birobidzhan was an answer to a call. In both instances the coming Jews built a closed, collectivist community. And in both cases the socialist work ethic that contributes to the creation of the "new Jews" is documented in photographic and film images that are heavily influenced by the aesthetic of the Soviet avant-garde. The merging of Zionist and communist symbolism in Bartana's trilogy arguably reflects an attempt by the artist to return to their common (progressive, atheist, activist) roots—and to liberate the Zionist project from the ethnic separatism that has crippled and destroyed its former utopian appeal. The socialist dream corresponds to the traditional Jewish hope to transcend ethnic isolation through cosmopolitanism and universalism, while at the same time avoiding complete cultural assimilation. Bartana attempts to revive this hope through her project for a Jewish renaissance in Poland and through the revival of socialist idealism and aesthetics—a form of Zionism that does not need to be connected to Zion, to the blood and soil of Jewish ancestry, nor does it need to obsess over a return to origins, but instead crafts a place for the Jews in the middle of a nowhere that is at the same time a somewhere where others are amenable to the project. It is no accident that at the end of the trilogy the representatives of the new generation speak a shared language, English, while

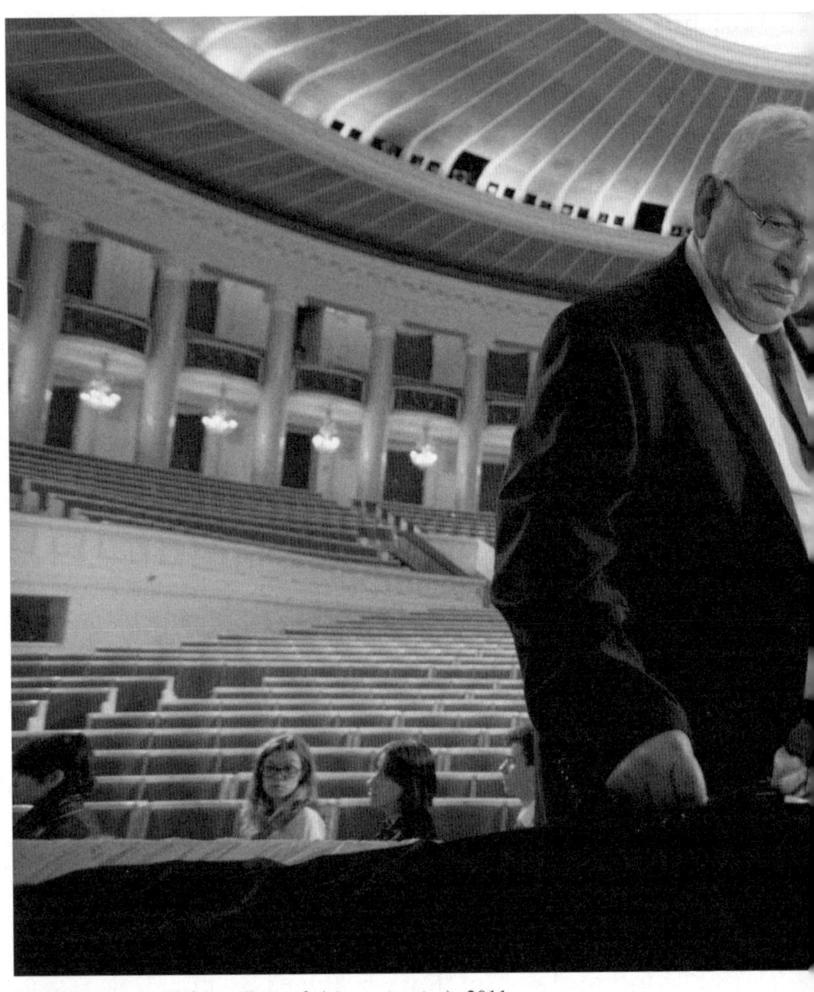

Yael Bartana, still from *Zamach* (*Assassination*), 2011

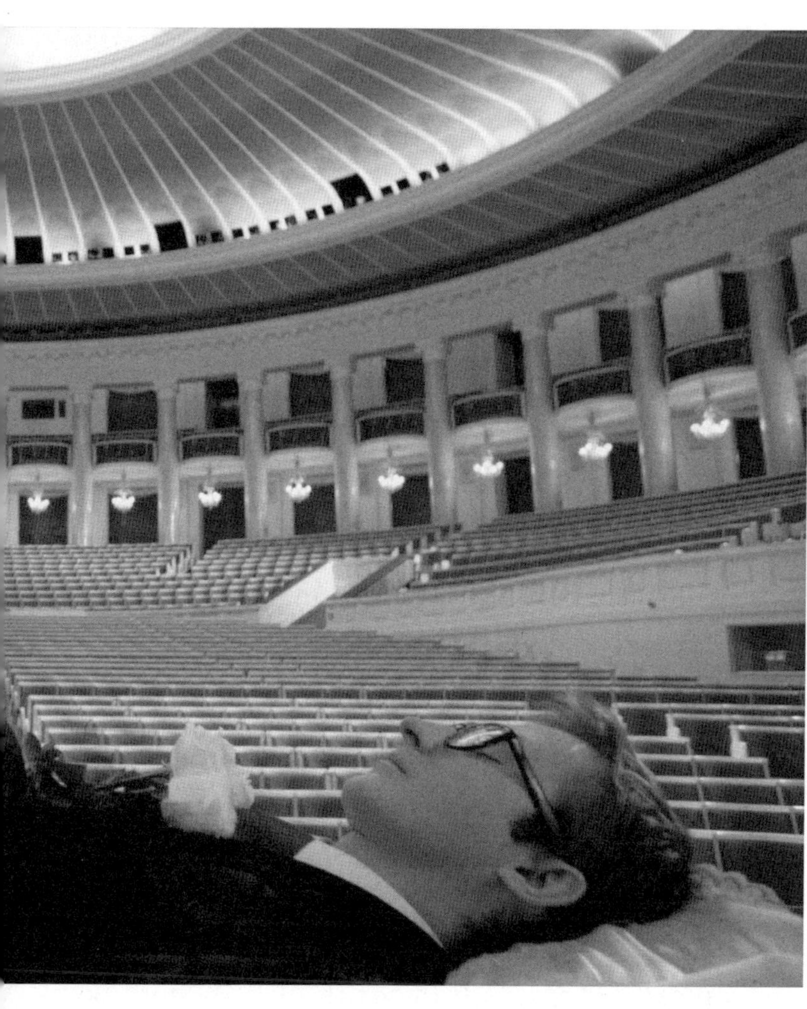

those representing an older generation speak in a number of different tongues, including Polish, German, and Hebrew. We watch an ultimate synthesis between the two old foes of the Cold War, a socialist dream formulated in the universal language of our time—English.

The idea of answering a call has an important place in Jewish history. Beginning with Abraham, the Jews understood themselves as a people answering a call—of God, of reason, of a better future. But Bartana does not conceal her skepticism toward this new call; indeed, the JRMiP and the expectation of another Jewish revival is colored by a degree of irony. In some respects, Bartana's trilogy reminds me of Sots art in the 1970s and '80s. At that time, in the middle of late socialist tristesse, certain Russian artists revived the aesthetics of Stalinist socialist realism. What was their goal? In part, their ironic reminder of former enthusiasms was intended to jar the contemporary mood of disillusionment. Sots art also operated by "defamiliarizing" the symbolism of communism, placing images outside of their familiar context in order to expose the mechanisms of the Soviet propaganda machine. The combination of Soviet and Western visual idioms, which was experienced as a violation of the Cold War division between these two cultures, had an absurdist, stunning effect. Two works by Alexander Kosolapov—*Sashok! Do You Want Any Tea?* (1975) and *Lenin Coca-Cola* (1982) serve as good examples: here the pictorial language of official Soviet ideology is used in a very private context and in the framework of a Western commercial advertisement. Similarly, when an Israeli settlement is built in Poland instead of Palestine it becomes "defamiliarized"—its absurdity is made even more apparent when infused by anachronistic images from Soviet history. In this sense, Bartana's trilogy might be described as an example of

"Zion art," as she simultaneously ironizes and aestheticizes the obsolete pathos of the Zionist project.

However, we know well enough that in our current cultural climate, to ironize a cultural phenomenon is also to revive it, to release its hidden possibilities. Ironization is rejuvenation. In "And Europe Will Be Stunned," an anachronistic, ideologically mobilized Jewish youth builds (again) a utopian project in the middle of nowhere. But utopia is, by definition, located nowhere, and its time is, by definition, anachronistic (out of time) or even "achronistic" (without time). If the call had not been made in the "real" world, it could be launched in a different, hypothetical one—the fact that Jewish renaissance movements have not been historically successful does not mean that the idea is logically impossible. Thus Bartana's project may be utopian, but it is not fantastical. The world that Bartana constructs for us is certainly anachronistic and consequently melancholic, but it is not as depressing as our current world.

Notes

1. Cited in *USSR in Construction*, nos. 3–4 (1935).
2. Todd Samuel Presner, *Muscular Judaism: The Jewish Body and the Politics of Regeneration* (London: Routledge, 2007), 2.

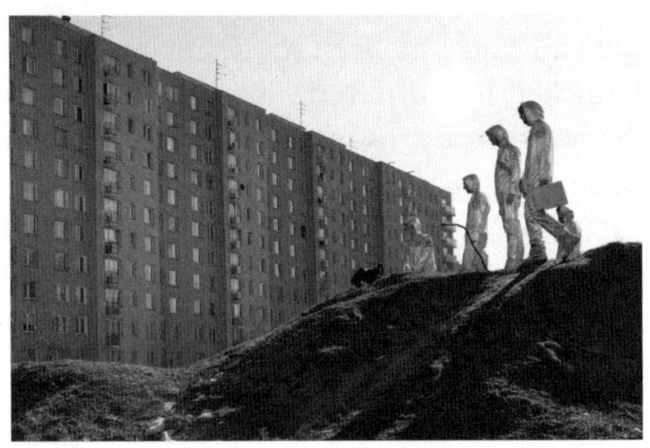

Paweł Althamer, *Common Task, Bródno District in Warsaw*, 2008

16
Paweł Althamer
Soul = Design


The decline of the Roman Empire was accompanied by the emergence of syncretic religious teachings combining Neoplatonic philosophy, Hebraic and Christian gnosis, Eastern spiritual teachings, and pagan rituals. Before the civilization's collapse, the contradictions between the different religious and philosophical schools began to seem less relevant than their similarities—similarities that were imposed by common cultural, social, and political contexts on the verge of disappearance. I was reminded of this historical period when I saw documentation of Paweł Althamer's project *Common Task* (2008–ongoing). The project creates a syncretism of socialist and capitalist utopias in a fascinating, truly postmodern fashion, revealing the deep similarities between these two dominating and seemingly contradictory utopias of the nineteenth and twentieth centuries. The project opens up the possibility of a smooth transition, without losing common ground, from a socialist utopia to a capitalist one. This shift surely corresponds to the transition that Poland made from a socialist reality to a capitalist one. But it is much easier to change our reality than it is to change a dream. *Common Task* attempts to light the way for this much harder conversion by building a bridge between the dreams of socialist and capitalist utopias.

The socialist component of the project is more or less obvious. A group of people, mostly Althamer's neighbors in Bródno (a lower-middle-class neighborhood in Warsaw), clothed in matching golden costumes resembling astronaut jumpsuits, are brought to different places on Earth (initially Brussels, followed by Brasília, Munich, and Mali) where they impress local populations by traveling around and sightseeing in procession.[1] This group represents the "golden humankind" from post-socialist Poland that arrives in the capitalist West to manifest equality for all its members.[2] At the same time, communist humankind is also presented here as a tourist group curious about the wonders of the West as well as non-Western cultures. Even if the golden group is clothed in worker jumpsuits, the members do not work. They enjoy their free leisure time.

In our contemporary world, being a tourist means having money. Otherwise, it is necessary to work in the places through which one travels—as the majority of Polish emigrants to the West do. But the representatives of golden humankind do not have money; rather, they *are* money. In our culture, gold is associated with wealth and money. Here, humankind becomes a currency and an individual man becomes a currency unit. The members of Althamer's golden group are "living currency"—although not in the way meant by Pierre Klossowski, since they do not offer any use value.[3] This is precisely the point where the communist dream slips into the capitalist dream. Communist humankind was imagined by Kazimir Malevich as white, or maybe even black, but never golden. Further, all the other utopian projects of the communist-inspired artistic avant-garde exclude the color gold, which refers not so much to the communist future as to a past golden age. However, to become money, rather than simply having money, is the actual utopia of capitalism.

At first glance, the golden humankind looks as though it is simultaneously a visualization and radicalization of the central notion of neoliberalism: human capital. The utopian dimension of neoliberal theories of human capital was extensively analyzed by Michel Foucault in his lectures from the late '70s on the "birth of biopolitics."[4] Human beings cease to be seen merely as a workforce sold on the capitalist market; rather, individuals become owners of nonalienated sets of qualities, capabilities, and skills that are partially hereditary and innate and partially produced by education and care (primarily by one's own parents). In other words, an original investment is made by nature itself. The word "talent" expresses this relationship between nature and investment well enough—talent being a gift from nature and at the same time a certain sum of money. The utopian dimension of the neoliberal notion of human capital becomes clear because due to this notion everybody becomes a "capitalist." Each person's participation in the economy thus becomes the investment of one's own human capital and therefore loses its character of alienated and alienating work. The human becomes a value in itself. Even more importantly, the notion of human capital, as Foucault describes it, erases the opposition between consumer and producer—an opposition that bears the danger of tearing the human apart under the condition of capitalism, in which man is simultaneously functioning as both producer and consumer. Foucault indicates that in terms of human capital, the consumer becomes a producer—the consumer produces his or her own satisfaction—consequently enabling his or her human own capital to grow.[5] In this sense, it really is possible to work as a tourist, because the work increases one's own human capital.

So the neoliberal utopia seems to be perfect—except it has one fundamental flaw. The neoliberal notion of human capital can be used—and is de facto used—as a means for the legitimization of economic, social, and political inequality as allegedly dictated by nature. The distribution of natural

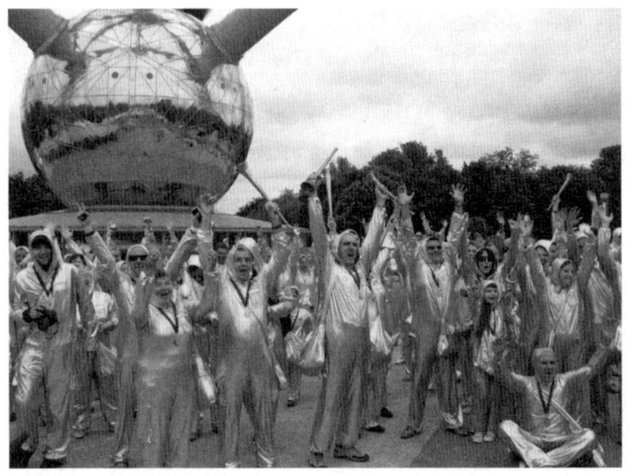

Paweł Althamer, *Common Task, Brussels*, 2009

gifts among human bodies is, indeed, unequal, and so is a society built on the concept of human capital. However, our understanding of utopia is intimately connected to the ideal of universal equality. And the golden humankind, as presented in Althamer's project, is obviously also a society in which every human has the same value—as a unit of the same currency. So is it possible to say that the ideal of universal equality, as expressed through Althamer's project, has communist origins? This is doubtful. In fact, the neoliberal notion of human capital is not very different from the standard understanding of the human under the conditions of communist society. According to the socialist tradition, communist society is defined by the principle: from each according to his/her ability, to each according to his/her needs. It is obvious that the notion of human capital is at the core of this definition of communism because production and consumption are both regulated by the natural gifts that constitute an individual's human nature. Thus, one can argue that the inequality characteristic of the socialist states will not necessarily disappear in the communist stage of their development because different natural gifts will also then require and dictate different modes of social participation.

At the beginning of the '70s, Joseph Beuys was inspired by the idea of human capital, and tried to reunite capitalist and socialist utopias on this common ground. In the lectures he gave in Achberg from 1974 to 1978, published under the title *Kunst = Kapital* (Art = capital), Beuys argues that all economic activity should be understood as creative practice so that everybody consequently should be perceived as an artist.[6] The "expanded notion of art" (*erweiterter Kunstbegriff*) would then coincide with the "expanded notion of economy" (*erweiterter Ökonomiebegriff*). Beuys tries to overcome the inequality that, for him, is symbolized by the difference between creative artistic work and noncreative alienated work. For Beuys, to say that everybody is an artist means introducing universal equality by mobilizing aspects of everyone's human capital that remain hidden and inactivated under standard market conditions. Beuys indicates that Duchamp had already seen and revealed the identification between regular work and art, but was unable to draw all the necessary consequences from the discovery.[7] However, during the discussions that followed the lectures, it became clear that Beuys's attempt to overcome social and economic inequality by erasing the difference between artistic and nonartistic activity was not sufficiently effective. The reason is simple enough: according to Beuys, a human being is creative because nature gave him or her initial human capital—the capacity to be creative. Therefore, art practice remains dependent on nature, and we return to the unequal distribution of natural gifts. A human should be able to apply his or her creative ability, but this ability is distributed by nature in an unequal way.[8] At the end of these lengthy discussions, Beuys confessed that he did not know how to deal with laziness and an unwillingness to be creative. In other words, the concept of human capital alone, be it capitalist or socialist, does not provide us with the possibility of establishing universal equality and eliminating our dependency on the unequal distribution of natural talents.

This is why, in looking for a secure basis for universal equality, Althamer turns to the past rather than the future. To create a syncretic socialist and capitalist utopia of equal human capital, he recurs to the old syncretic religious teachings combining Catholicism, Theosophy, and Buddhism. Although human bodies are diverse and unequally gifted, immortal souls are equal. Immortality equals immortality; an immortal being equals all other immortal beings. The

Christian concept of equality in terms of everyone's relationship to God was based on the belief in the immortality of the human soul—the equal immortality of all human souls. This is the belief that Althamer returns to time and again in his interviews and artworks—even if the immortality of the soul is thought to be independent of all Christian promises of redemption. In a conversation with Artur Żmijewski, Althamer says, "A sense of timelessness and non-mortality accompanies me at all times. I have no fear of death. [...] I myself feel immortal. In the context of today's world, this is madness, but I say what I'm thinking and feeling."[9] In some interviews, Althamer also discusses the possibility of the separation of the soul from the body as well as body exchange. Specifically, he speaks about dreams in which his soul occupies different bodies.[10] Substituting his own body with a body that is fictional and artificially produced, but similarly mortal and instable, is a recurrent topic in his artistic production. In fact, his first major work for his graduation project at the Academy of Fine Arts in Warsaw consisted in the production of an artificial double of his own body—a double that was presented together with a video showing the artist running away and disappearing.[11]

Althamer treats the immortal soul as an exchange value of the body: a general equivalent that allows one body to be exchanged with another. In other words, the soul functions here as gold, as currency. The currency is immortal because it is purely abstract. As the Marxian theory of commodity fetishism reminds us, the price of the object cannot be found in the object itself or deduced from a specific, "natural" characteristic of the object—the exchange value is perfectly artificial. It is a supplement, and not an integral part of an object, which is why every object can become a commodity— i.e., be substituted by another object of the same value.

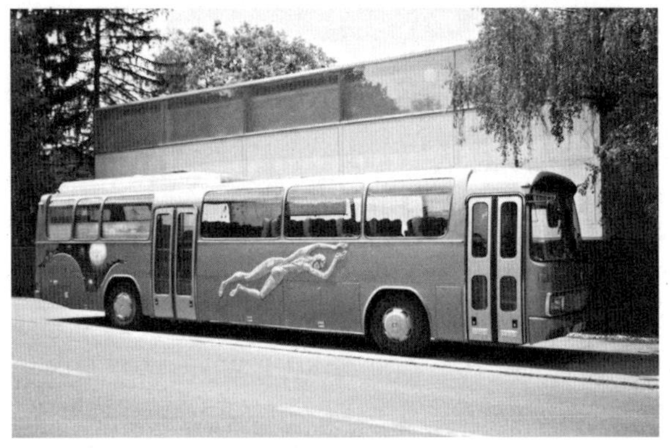

Paweł Althamer, *Common Task, Munich/Sammlung Goetz*, 2012

After the death of God and the demise of traditional European metaphysics, one of art's goals (combined with technology and economics) is now to create equality among humankind: an artificial equality based on the universal exchange value of human bodies. At the end of the nineteenth century, Nikolai Fedorov, a Russian philosopher who did not believe in the immortality of the soul but wanted equality for all, developed a project to substitute all past and present mortal human bodies with new, artificially produced immortal bodies by technological and artistic means, to compensate politically and artistically for the unequal distribution of natural gifts (coincidentally, his project was also called "Common Task").[12] However, Althamer is interested not in the immortality of individual bodies, but in the possibility of substituting one body with another and the stability of exchange value that makes such a substitution possible. It is here that the "golden standard" becomes important. The golden humankind is an embodiment and living guarantee of the stability of human exchange value notwithstanding any financial or ecological crisis.

It becomes obvious that the golden humankind demonstrated by Althamer represents not so much the future or past of mortal humankind but an eternity in which future and past coincide. The golden humankind is the collection of human souls that have materialized and become the golden equivalent for exchange that allows every existing human to be substituted by any other human—for example, socialist humankind by capitalist humankind, and vice versa. The fact that the bodies of the golden humankind are Polish bodies is purely accidental. The universality of the golden group is manifested not by their bodies but by the gold uniforms that cover their bodies. The immortal inner self is manifested by the external golden garment. Soul becomes a uniform. This transformation could be seen as strange or even disturbing, but it is actually the most interesting aspect of the work. The substitution of the soul by cloth is the oldest possible religious practice. All the theories of aura are based on the assumption that a body is clothed in its soul—the soul becoming visible like a luminous cloth. This understanding of the spiritual as auratic also informs Walter Benjamin's definition of the artwork's originality (its soul, so to speak), as the "here and now" into which the artwork is inscribed. We also know that medieval icon painters covered the naked bodies of their protagonists with clothes not only out of prudishness, but also because painting and sculpture do not have any other means to indicate the represented person's place in the spiritual, social, or political hierarchy. Similarly, the artists of socialist realism presented their models clothed because it was the only way to indicate their social class.

In other words, soul equals cloth because they are both artificial supplements of the human body. They indicate the hierarchies and cultural differences among the human bodies that they cover. To introduce a uniform instead of having the diversity of clothes means to introduce universal equality. Here, bodies are exchanged but the uniform remains—analogous to the exchange of bodies as mortal physical containers of an individual immortal soul. Ernst Jünger believed that the military uniform is immortal—even if the bodies that fill the uniform die and become exchanged.[13] The diversity of clothing produced by the fashion industry signifies mortality and death. The uniform, however, not only refers to immortality, but also actually produces immortality. Thus the opposition of diversity and inequality, on the one hand, and equality and uniformity, on the other, ceases to be a metaphysical problem, and becomes an issue for design. Beuys said that art equals capital. But that was not enough. Althamer goes further and demonstrates that soul equals design. To obtain this result, it is necessary to go through not only capitalist but also socialist life experiences.

Notes

1. Stach Szabłowski, "The Shaman in the Space Suit of His Own Body," in *Paweł Althamer*, ed. Ingvild Goetz et al. (Ostfildern: Hatje Cantz, 2012), 114.
2. Claire Bishop, "Something for Everyone: The Art of Paweł Althamer," *Artforum*, February 2011, 175–81.
3. Pierre Klossowski, *La monnaie vivante* (Paris: Rivages, 1997).
4. Michel Foucault, *The Birth of Biopolitics: Lectures at the Collège de France, 1978–79*, ed. Michel Senellart, trans. Graham Burchell (New York: Palgrave Macmillan, 2008), 215ff.
5. Ibid., 226.
6. See Joseph Beuys, *Kunst = Kapital: Achberger Vorträge* (Achberg: FIU-Verlag, 1992).
7. Ibid., 91.
8. Ibid., 112ff.
9. Paweł Althamer, in "The Song of a Skin Bag: Interview with Artur Đmijewski, 1997," in *Paweł Althamer* (London: Phaidon Press, 2011), 137.
10 Goetz et al., *Paweł Althamer* (2012), 66.
11. Bonnefantenmuseum, ed., *Paweł Althamer: The Vincent Award, 2004* (Ostfildern: Hatje Cantz, 2004), 100–101.
12. Nikolai Fedorov, *What Was Man Created For?*, trans. Elizabeth Koutaissoff and Marilyn Minto (New York: Hyperion Books, 1990).
13. Ernst Jünger, *Der Arbeiter: Herrschaft und Gestalt* [The worker: Mastery and form] (Stuttgart: Klett-Cotta, 1982), 152ff.

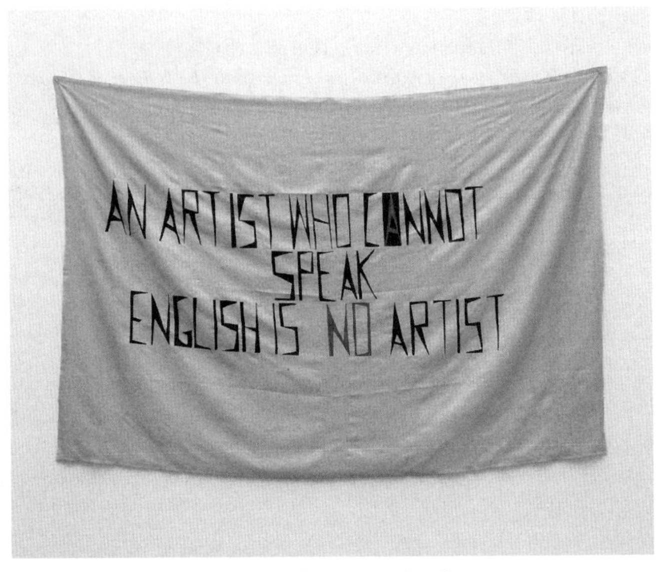


Mladen Stilinović, *An Artist Who Cannot Speak
English Is No Artist*, 1992

17
Mladen Stilinović
Poetics of Entropy

The modern/contemporary subject tends to react to a "system" with a desire to change it, undermine its order, or escape its control. At the same time, the dominant system seems almost omnipotent, because the technology at its disposal is incommensurate with the forces and capabilities of an individual. Thus, the fight against the system appears lost from the beginning. That is why the modern subject is so often described as the subject of an impossible desire, or rather of a desire for the impossible—a desire doomed to frustration. An individual seems condemned to a state of ontological solitude without any chance for help from the outside: God is dead and the forces of nature are already under technological control. However, all systems, including modern and contemporary systems of control, are subject to forces of entropy. Modern technology is immune to divine intervention, but not to the fatigue of the materials of which it consists. Entropic processes permanently undermine every system, dissolving it into material chaos. The forces of entropy operate mostly underneath the surface of the world. Their workings remain unobserved and they sap energy from the system and render it unstable. Only after the system collapses into chaos does it become clear that it was the forces of entropy that undermined it—and without any conscious, heroic effort by the subject.

The modern/contemporary artist is a collaborator in this entropy. Every genuinely modern/contemporary artwork stages the processes of entropy within itself. Every such artwork operates by deforming and dissolving traditional artistic forms. In this way, an artwork gives to its spectator a promise that the system controlling this spectator's individual fate will also be undermined by entropic forces and will eventually dissolve. However, the collaboration between art and entropy is highly ambiguous. By consciously staging the working of entropic forces, art gives them a certain form. And by giving them a form, art reinscribes them into the existing system, or at least opens a way to build a new system upon a new foundation. Indeed, it is always hard to say what it is that actually provokes our anger: the stability of the system, or, on the contrary, the slow decline of the system, its loss of vitality, energy, and efficiency. Accordingly, it is hard to say what the modern subject really wants when it starts a revolt against the system: Does he or she want the dissolution of this system and every other system together with it? Or instead, the establishment of a new, more vital, energetic, efficient system?

We know that modern artists often protested against dominant artistic forms, accusing them of being old or even dead—while at the same time proclaiming their own art as living and vital. The same can be said about the neo-avant-garde artists of the 1960s and '70s—it is never quite clear what they really want: the breakup of the system or its revitalization. To use the language of Walter Benjamin from his 1921 essay "Critique of Violence," the modern/contemporary subject of artistic as well as political violence hesitates between "divine violence"—or, one can say, entropic violence that has no beginning and no end—and "mythical violence"—i.e., the desire to instrumentalize violence with the goal of establishing a new, revitalized, reinforced order.[1] From today's perspective, one can say that only very few artists of the twentieth century resisted the seduction of the "new order" and remained faithful to their union with the forces of entropy and anarchy. One of these very few artists is undoubtedly Mladen Stilinović.

Stilinović's art has an obvious critical edge. But, for example, his critical reactions to the ideological language of the Socialist Federal Republic of Yugoslavia were not meant to propose an improved ideology; he did not confront the official message with his own. Rather, the artist demonstrated that this official message had de facto become a zero message. The ritualistic language in which this message was formulated and distributed had already been long subjected to the forces of entropy, and all that remained were words on paper and sounds in the air. Language became a material object that could be fragmented, displaced, and reduced to zero. Stilinović operated with the language of the official ideology as the neo-avant-garde artists operated with traditional paintings and sculptures. For them, a painting was simply a canvas covered with paint, sculpture was an object in space, and so forth. Stilinović expanded this strategy to encompass all cultural and ideological phenomena that he had to deal with. The party slogans were simply combinations of words—and words can be combined with other words. Written words are simply combinations of lines—and can be combined with other combinations of lines.

A political authority guarantees the stability of certain modes of speech, forms of behavior, images, and rituals. But these are all material objects and processes. And so the "spiritual," ideological authority is not able to stabilize them, to guard them against the forces of entropy, against their dissolution in material flow, their fragmentation and recombination with other material elements of this flow. These are the forces that Stilinović stages in his works. All the elements of these works—whether text, painting, drawing, or

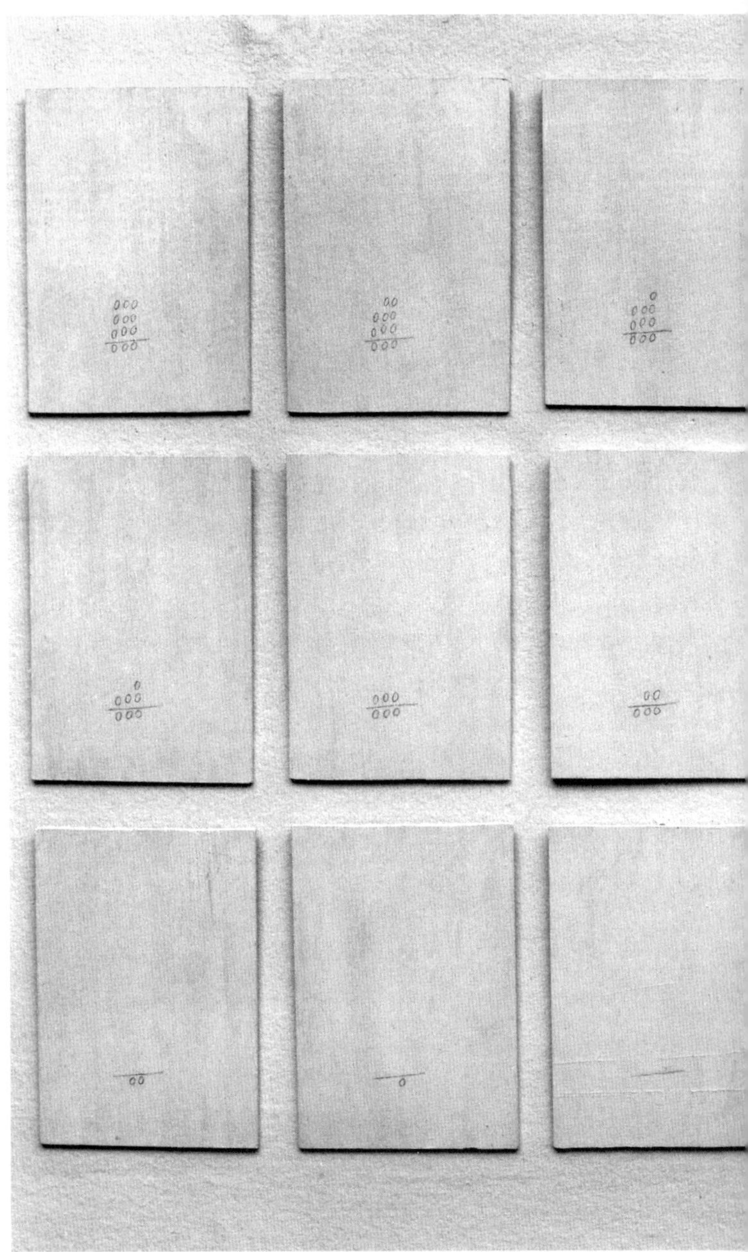

Mladen Stilinović, *Subtraction of Zeros*, 1993

film—seem to be included in this flow. They all seem to drift, shift, slip, and stumble into new combinations, contexts, and situations. No effort. No revolt. Rather, they let things go, and they move and slide in different directions—beyond the control of a political or cultural authority. The artist rejects any attempt to give this drift toward anarchy and chaos any definite direction, to let it culminate in any new order. Socialism collapses. Capitalism triumphs. But the process of entropy goes on. Stilinović now demystifies money as he had demystified party language earlier. After all, money is also merely images, signs among other signs. They are also made up of material components; their forms can also be destabilized. A room remains a room—be it an exhibition space, a bank, or an office of the party committee. And an image remains a combination of colors and forms, be it a portrait of a leader, a currency unit, or a combination of both.

This shifting and sliding of images and signs on the blank surface of nothingness is a strong reminder of the Suprematist art of Kazimir Malevich. Malevich also rejected any attempt to interpret his art as a foundation for a new order. In Malevich's Suprematist paintings, geometric forms drift and slide in a way that is more deconstructive than constructive. Unlike Mondrian's paintings or the geometric constructions of the Bauhaus, Malevich's Suprematism does not create a stable geometric order that can serve as a starting point for ordering architecture, living space, and society in general. Not accidentally, Malevich was extremely skeptical about the possibility of building any new utopian order.

In 1919 Malevich wrote "God Is Not Cast Down," in which he criticized Russian Constructivist artists for submitting their art to the goal of creating a new socialist state.[2] Malevich saw the communist project as a repetition of the Christian project but in a new, technological form. Christians wanted to enter paradise, he wrote, by achieving inner spiritual perfection through permanent self-improvement, through working on their souls. Communists wanted to enter the radiant future by perfecting the material conditions of human existence, by turning the whole world into a factory. However, Malevich did not see any substantial difference between the church and the factory: both wanted perfection, and both were unable to achieve it because the material world is permanently subjected to the forces of entropy. So Malevich proposed that the artist relax, that the artist give up the ambition of shaping the permanent flow of the material world. Instead, Malevich preached laziness and inaction, which were supposed to release entropic forces that had true revolutionary power.

The references to Malevich's Suprematism remain noticeable throughout the whole of Stilinović's work. Malevich was not seduced by the enthusiasm for life building in postrevolutionary Russia—and neither did Stilinović allow himself to be carried away by the enthusiasm for the post-socialist democratic/capitalist opening. His distance from the neoliberal utopia that replaced the communist utopia was, of course, not dictated by any "ostalgia"—conservative nostalgia for the old socialist order. Almost immediately after the establishment of the new capitalist order, Stilinović began to ironize it in a way analogous to his ironization of the old socialist order. No aspect of the new utopia was spared—from the power of money to knowledge of the English language as a precondition for an individual's functioning in the new economy. The statement proclaimed by Stilinović's work *An Artist Who Cannot Speak English Is No Artist* (1992) became so famous precisely because of its matter-of-fact character. Malevich, like many other representatives of the early avant-garde, was not ready to submit his artistic practice to ideological control by the new socialist powers. Stilinović demonstrates his unwillingness to accept the new rules of the game and submit his own work to evaluation by the international art market. Thus, even if the social and political orders that were rejected and ironized by both artists are not identical—and even opposed to each other—the contemporary gesture of rejection as such repeats the avant-garde gesture. However, this repetition of the avant-garde gesture is not the same as a repetition of avant-garde form.

Art, as I stated above, consciously stages unconscious entropic processes—and thus gives them a certain form. This form becomes solidified, petrified, and canonized by time. Malevich is no exception. Malevich investigated and deconstructed the high artistic canon of the past and laid bare its geometric basis—culminating in *Black Square* (1915), which demonstrated the formal geometric structure of any standard painted image consisting of a rectangular canvas and a frame. The geometric forms that Malevich used in his own Suprematist paintings referred to Platonic ideas, to the Western philosophical and artistic tradition of the mathematization and geometrization of nature. These forms suggested a higher, "cosmic" level of reality toward which the imagination of the spectator was to soar. Stilinović, on the contrary, takes all possible fragments and bits of everyday reality, language, documentation, propaganda, and so forth, and lets them drift and slide on the blank Suprematist surface. The celebration of the reality of everyday life was a common feature of many artistic practices and philosophical discourses of the 1960s and '70s. But Stilinović's transportation of the everyday into the Suprematist heaven of pure ideas is not only a celebration of the quotidian. Rather, the texture of everyday life demonstrates itself as porous and fragmented—having gaps that a Suprematist nothingness can slip through.

Stilinović's para-Suprematist images remind me of the technological garbage that currently circulates in the cosmic space around the earth. The dissolved fragments of the everyday technological world enter the stage of their eternal return—and fill the heaven of our contemporary civilization. Now, Stilinović is obviously completely consumed by art and cares even less than Malevich did about what other people think. So he is not afraid to bring his own artistic method to the point of absurdity. Indeed, Stilinović combines certain positivism and realism with an acceptance of, and even delight in, absurdity.

This delight in absurdity is a part of the heritage of Dada and early Surrealism. But Stilinović also radicalizes the Dadaist and Surrealist approach. His photographic series *Artist at Work* (1978) is a good example of this. This work reminds me of a passage from the first "Manifesto of Surrealism" (1924) by André Breton: "A story is told according to which Saint-Pol-Roux, in times gone by, used to have a notice posted on the door of his manor house in Camaret, every evening before he went to sleep, which read: THE POET IS WORKING."[3] Breton shares the perception of the poet as working during sleep because he believes that true poetry and art consist of the production of dreams. During sleep, our imagination becomes liberated from all the restraints and obligations imposed on it by our everyday mode of existence. Here the poetic dream is opposed to prosaic reality. And so it is important that, going to sleep, the poet closes the door behind him—to prevent the free flow of his imagination from being disturbed by the intrusion of everyday reality and the gaze of others.

However, Stilinović allows himself to be photographed during sleep. Instead of poetic dreaming, we are presented with a prosaic image of a sleeping body. The sleeping artist

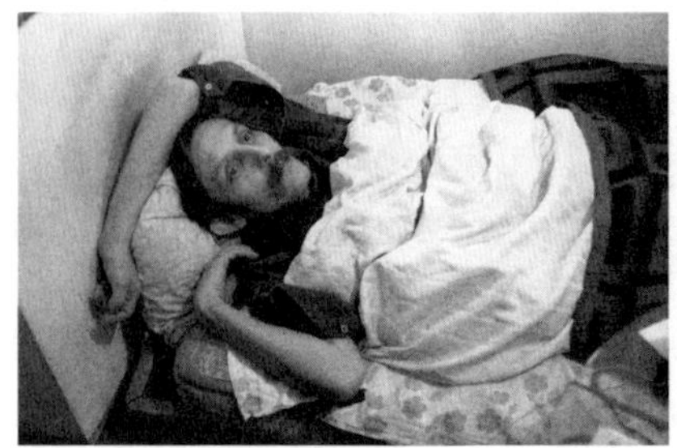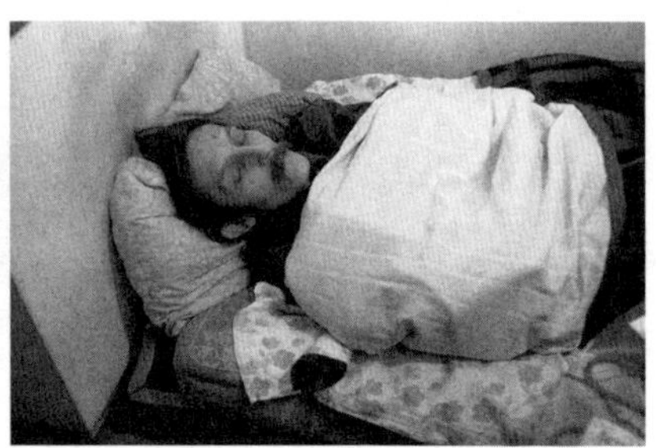

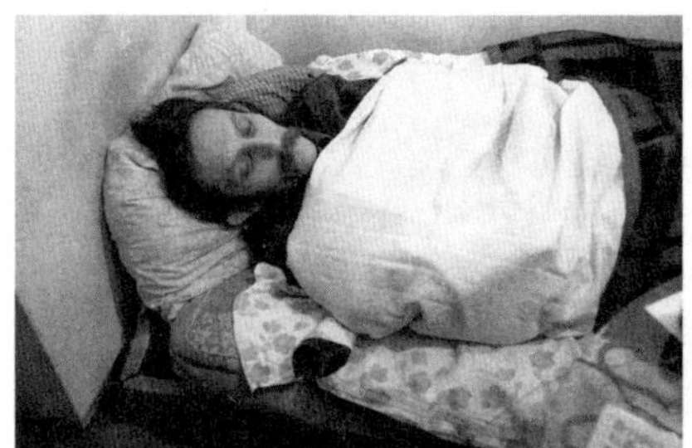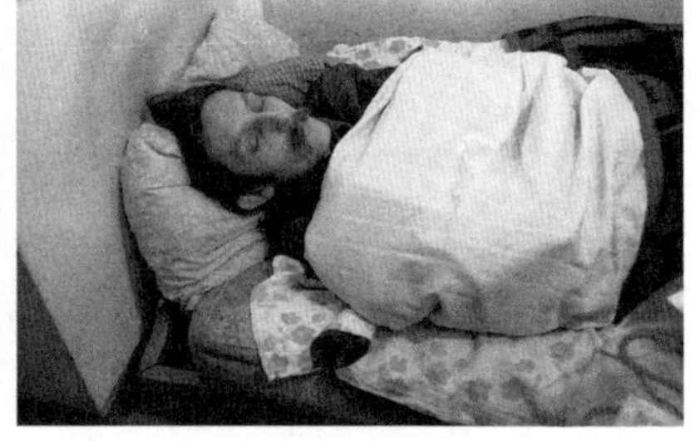

Mladen Stilinović, *Artist at Work*, 1978

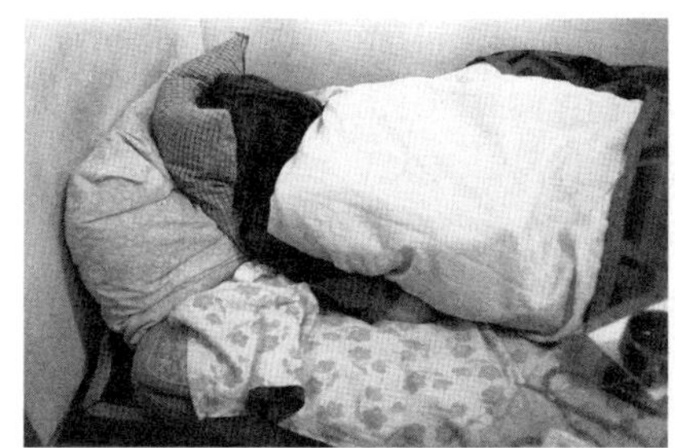
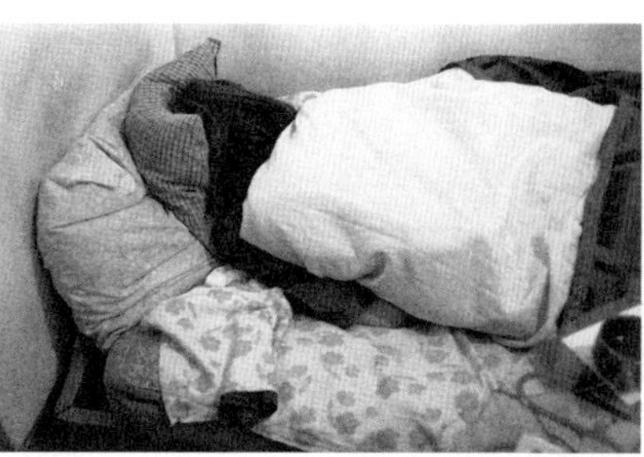
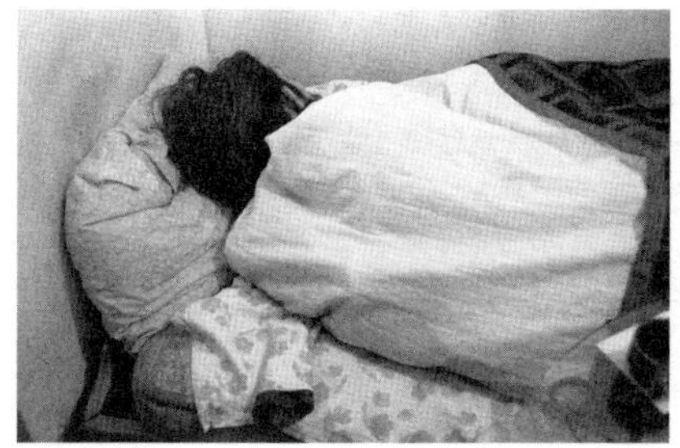
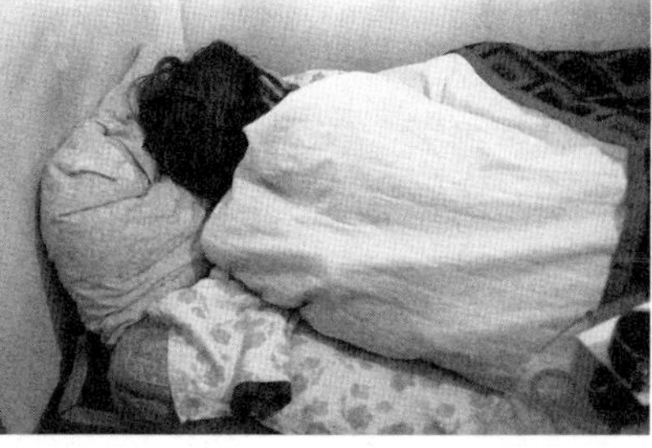

here is not a poet who forgets the world, flying from it into a poetic dream, thus escaping the gaze of others. Rather, the artist completely delivers up his body to the gaze of spectators, unprotected and uncontrolled. In sleep, one loses the ability to manipulate, direct, and seduce the gaze of the spectator. Stilinović's sleeping artist reminds one more of *Sleep* (1963) by Andy Warhol than of Breton's sleeping poet. Presenting a sleeping body instead of a poetic dream, Warhol asserts once more the final victory of positivism and everyday life over "metaphysics" and "spirituality." But in Warhol's video, the sleeping man is an actor and not the artist himself. Warhol does not relinquish but rather strengthens his manipulative, controlling position of authority. When the artist sleeps, he lets the life around him and in him flow without control—thereby creating beyond work. Thus, the artist undermines the obligation to work—the true common ground between ideologies of capitalism and communism. It is this obligation to work that our everyday life depends upon.

Indeed, the power of the everyday was not regarded as seriously in the socialist East as it was in the capitalist West. Of course, communist ideology was a materialist and atheist one. However, under the conditions of socialism, everyday life was subjected to ideological definition and interpretation to a degree that reminded one of medieval Europe. Each everyday decision was analyzed and justified in ideological terms: Does this decision serve the cause of building the socialist future? Does this decision conform to Marxism and its ideological principles? Here, indeed, the idea of every seemingly small and insignificant everyday thing was separated from the thing itself—and submitted to ideological scrutiny. Thus, the socialist subject always mediated between two worlds: an ideological world and a world of everyday survival.

The rejection of official ideology did not abolish the ideological, spiritual, utopian world altogether but rather transformed it into blank nothingness. This nothingness is not simply an absence of ideology; it is a space of ideological freedom that should not be identified with freedom from ideology. It is this space of freedom that came to be endangered after the end of socialism. The victory of Western positivism meant the abolishment of this blank space of ideological, subjective, inner freedom that was so familiar to Eastern European dissident artists and thinkers. Instead, the post-socialist subject became the slave of the everyday—like his or her Western counterpart. That is why the art of Stilinović is so different from the art of many of his Western contemporaries and colleagues. It is different because it continues to celebrate the experience of radical spiritual freedom. And this freedom dissolves not only ideology, but also any familiar social space—allowing nothingness to permeate our everyday world.

Notes

1. Walter Benjamin, "Critique of Violence," in *Reflections*, ed. Peter Demetz, trans. Edmund Jephcott (New York: Schocken Books, 1986), 277–300.
2. Kazimir Malevich, "God Is Not Cast Down," in *Essays on Art, 1915–1933*, vol. 1, ed. Troels Andersen, trans. Xenia Glowacki-Prus and Arnold McMillin (London: Rapp and Whiting, 1971), 188–223.
3. André Breton, "Manifesto of Surrealism," in *Manifestoes of Surrealism*, trans. Richard Seaver and Helen R. Lane (Ann Arbor: University of Michigan Press, 1969), 14.

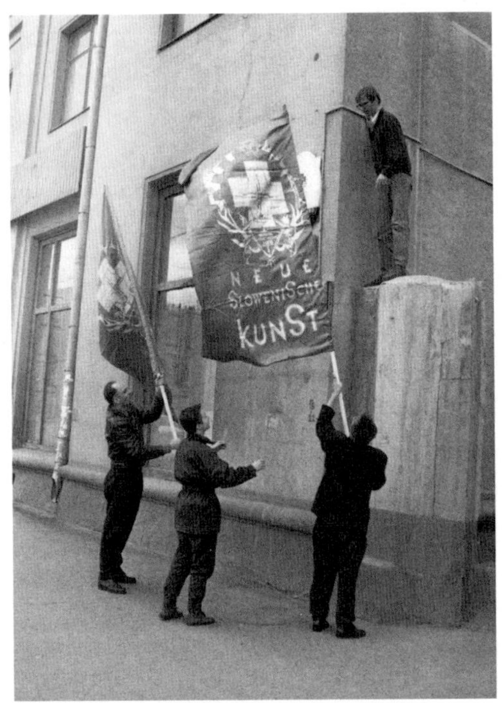


NSK Embassy Moscow, 1992

18
IRWIN
From Hybrid Socialism to Universal State

Over the past three decades, the group IRWIN, as a part of the NSK (Neue Slowenische Kunst) has dominated the Slovenian art scene, influencing many artistic practices throughout Eastern Europe. The art practice of IRWIN seems at first glance to be a specific version of postmodernism; indeed, IRWIN artists combine quotations from different artistic periods, styles, and movements in a way that is typical of postmodern art of the 1980s and '90s. However, IRWIN's practice is different from Western postmodernism in many decisive respects.

Western postmodernism was a reaction against the modernist canon—against the emergence of a new type of salon and the establishment of normative rules for the production and appreciation of art. In other words, postmodernism was a reaction against the academization of modernism. Indeed, in the mid-1970s the modernist canon dominated Western art museums, institutions of art education, the art market, art history, and art criticism. The goal of postmodernism was to rehabilitate everything that was repressed and excluded by this canon: a certain type of figuration (Italian Transavanguardia, German Neo-Expressionism), photography, cinema, performance, and so on. The same can be said of architectural postmodernism, which was directed against the modernist architectural canon, and of literary postmodernism, which rehabilitated literary trash of all kinds. Postmodernism privileged reproduction over production, secondariness over originality, anonymity over individuality.

However, Western postmodernism also had its own utopian dimension. Postmodernism dreamed of infinite flows of desire and information and of a "hive mind" or "crowd mind" that had the power to undermine every attempt to control and secure the meaning of individual signs: all these signs were supposed to be turned into empty, free-floating signifiers. Thus, even if Western postmodernism, in all its different forms, was a reaction to late modernist formalism, it inherited a formalist attitude toward signs and images. All artistic forms were understood as zero forms devoid of any specific content or meaning. According to postmodernist dogma, all content and meaning were permanently deconstructed by the anonymous processes of reproduction and dissemination. The only way to give meaning to art forms was to use them artistically in the here and now—the meaning of any particular form being totally dependent on its contextual use. And because all art forms were understood as empty—mere form without content—every individual artist had a right to combine and recombine them in every possible way. Thus the famous "death of the author" was easily combined with the proclamation of unlimited artistic freedom and the vocabulary of forms inherited from the various artistic movements of the twentieth century. However, all these combinations and recombinations became, in the end, as empty as their individual parts.

The emergence of this type of postmodernism was not possible in Yugoslavia, nor anywhere else in Eastern Europe, because the conditions under which art was practiced there were completely different. First of all: the modernist canon was never established, formalized, and institutionalized in Eastern Europe to the same degree that it was in the West. Even if modernist trends were permitted in some Eastern European countries—or even welcomed, as in Yugoslavia—

they did not have the same normative power as in the West. (Here I mean the normative power supported by art institutions with an international reach, big money, and so on.) But most importantly, art in general, and modernist art in particular, was never totally depoliticized like it was in the West. In Eastern European countries public space remained controlled: the postmodern vision of the totally free, potentially infinite flow of signs could never take hold there. Signs were not free-floating but politically charged—and the art forms that circulated in the same space were also politically charged. They were never experienced as empty signs that could obtain meaning only through their individual artistic use.

Living in a Communist country one still felt a close connection to the artistic practices of the early avant-garde. For a late socialist subject, the black square of Malevich was not merely a self-referential image that initiated the international zero-style of geometric abstraction; rather the black square, as well as other images from the early Russian avant-garde, signified the beginning of the communist era, with all its utopian aspirations. Similarly, older realist images didn't function as politically innocent representations of landscapes or city scenes, but symbolized the national tradition that was partially denied and partially ideologically reinterpreted by the regime. The same can be said about socialist realism and art under the Nazi regime. And the same can be said about late modernist art, which was experienced not as a production of empty signifiers, but as a commitment to an orientation toward Western cultural values. In other words, every use of this vocabulary of images manifested not the creative freedom of an individual artist, but a certain political stance within the sociopolitical field in which this artist lived. Thus, under socialist conditions the artist could not, in the Western postmodern manner, operate freely with empty art forms understood as language without content. Using a Heideggerian phrase, under socialism *die Sprache spricht* (language speaks): the forms used by the artist are always already ideologically charged. Their combinations are also ideologically charged—and so these combinations have their own message, which not merely undermines but rather over-determines any subjective artistic message.

Socialist and Post-socialist Hybridity

When Heidegger says *die Sprache spricht*, he means that it is the community, the nation, that speaks through the artist, because any language is basically always a national language. This is precisely the point at which the artistic strategies of IRWIN and other late and post-socialist artists emerge. Historical communism produced a broken national identity in Eastern European countries. Communist ideology was and still is universalist and internationalist—in every country its worst enemy was local nationalism, which was regularly characterized as "bourgeois nationalism." However, at the same time, historical communism was defined by Stalin's theory to build "socialism in one country." From the beginning it became clear that the program of socialism in one country would lead to the rebirth of nationalism—and in a certain way, it did. The socialist camp began to split along national lines: after Soviet Communism there was Yugoslav Communism, Chinese Communism, Albanian Communism, and so on—up to the Euro-communism of the Communist parties in Italy and France. However, these national communisms remained committed to a universalist message. In a certain way, this was already prefigured by the Stalinist definition of socialist realism: socialist in content and realist (in fact, national) in form. This definition presupposed, of course, that the socialist content remained identical throughout the different national forms. However, the national form began to shape and thus fragment the socialist content. But this fragmentation did not produce a simple return to traditional national cultures—understood as specific, even idiosyncratic ways of life. Every particular communism had a claim to represent the universal and authentic truth of communism—interpreting the communists of other countries as "revisionists." Here, the analogy with Christianity is obvious, as the latter was also split along national lines during the Reformation and religious wars. Yugoslavia understood its own national version of socialism as transnational—first of all, because Yugoslavia was a union of several national republics, but also because Yugoslavia was an important member of the Non-Aligned Movement. Thus, late socialist and post-socialist national identity could not be taken for granted. Accordingly, the language, including the visual language, that artists were supposed to use was not given but reconstructed. Now let us consider what such a project of reconstruction actually means.

The goal of national reconstruction was explicitly formulated by the IRWIN group at the beginning of its activities. It's no accident that the term "retro-avant-garde" has been used to characterize the practice of IRWIN and, more generally, NSK. "Avant-garde" here is basically Constructivism. Reconstruction is the construction of the past for the future, and at the same time the construction of the future as work on the past. Retrospectively, one can say that IRWIN and NSK did this work of reconstruction better than any other Eastern European artists or artist groups. There are different possible explanations for this. It may have been because Slovenian identity was broken at different places and along different lines;

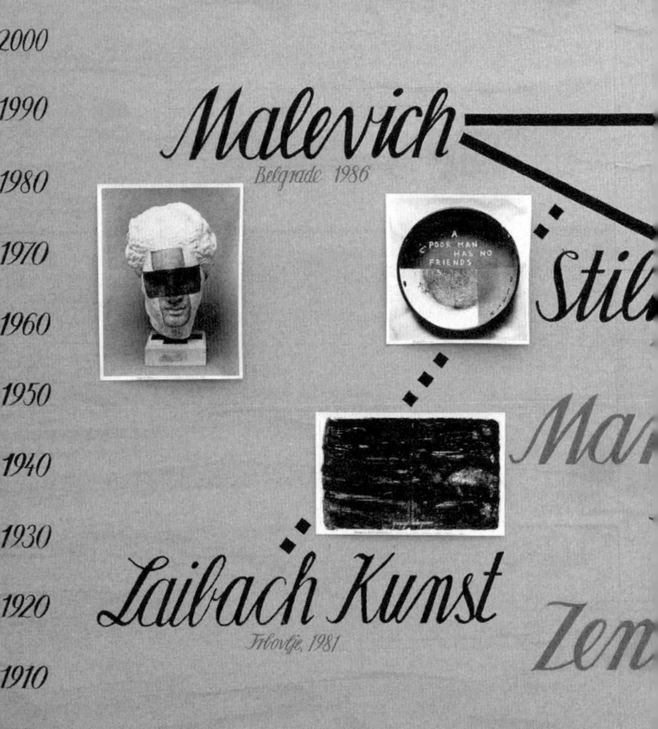


IRWIN, *Retroavantgarde*, 1996

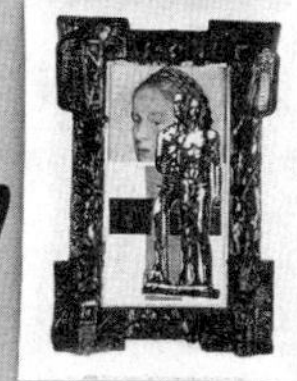

*ntgarde*

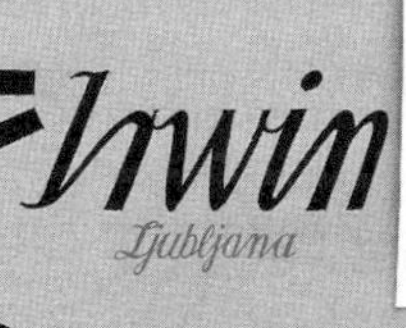Irwin
*Ljubljana*

*Dimitrijević*
*Sarajevo*

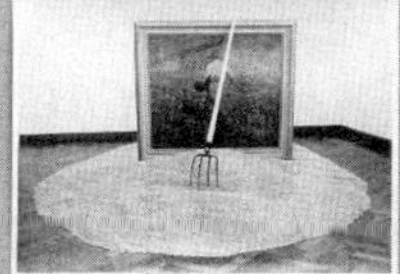

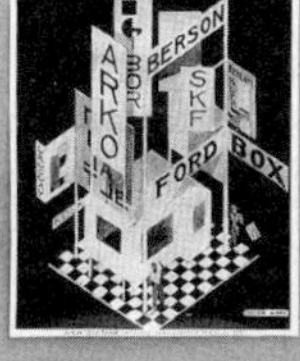

                                                

there was not only the socialist Yugoslavian past, but also the Nazi past, which could not simply be ignored, and which was related to a more traditional German part of Slovenian identity. It may have also resulted from the fact that the level of theoretical reflection and philosophical awareness was much higher in Slovenia than in other late and post-socialist countries. Whatever the reason, the IRWIN group found a better solution to the problem of broken identity than many other artists and art theoreticians—it was, in fact, the only possible solution. Like any true solution, it was very simple. Instead of trying to repair a broken identity, IRWIN integrated into it the forces that were supposed to have broken it: the radical avant-garde, socialist realism, and Nazism. All the forces that had denied a separate identity to Slovenian art were interpreted by IRWIN and NSK as forces that had modernized this identity. A certain combination of the revolutionary Russian avant-garde, socialist realism, and Nazi art thus became, retroactively, the image of the Slovenian avant-garde. Could one say that this Slovenian avant-garde never existed, that it was simply a later invention, a construction of the NSK? Yes and no. Yes, because all these phenomena were imposed on Slovenian cultural identity and not historically produced by it. And no, because even if all these ideological and artistic attitudes came from abroad, their particular combination was characteristic only of Slovenia. So it is enough to reevaluate this combination, to perceive it as authentic, an integral part of the genuine historical fate of the Slovenian nation instead of imposed from outside, to be able to reconstruct and not merely construct the Slovenian avant-garde as a part of Slovenian cultural identity. And that is precisely what NSK did.

In this way IRWIN substantially expanded the field of art forms available to artists living under the standard conditions of postmodernity. At first glance, this seems paradoxical, because IRWIN has operated in the relatively closed late and postcommunist ideological space. But this expansion of artistic vocabulary has its explanation. Indeed, the free and allegedly unlimited play of empty, or rather floating signifiers of postmodernism was based on its own rules of exclusion and censorship. The ideologically motivated art of socialist realism and the Nazis was excluded from this play of signifiers. The explanation for this is simple enough. Emptying art forms of their content brought up moral issues, and the content of socialist realism and Nazi art seemed too toxic, too contagious to be completely removed through the operation of aesthetic purification. This is why the Shoah and other crimes of the twentieth century were proclaimed to be "unrepresentable." If the related images were allowed to join the multitude of modern art forms, one feared that they would in turn be deconstructed and emptied, and would begin to function as pure aesthetic objects. In this way their toxic, contagious character (which will never really go away) would become neglected—and thus, these images could slowly infect the whole field of modern art forms. This anxiety regarding the infection of aesthetic form by ideological content is so strong that images from socialist realism and the Nazis are still excluded from the contemporary system of art representation. Here we have a pretty strong form of censorship. But the same form of censorship also has weak versions. For example, when I traveled across the United States I saw a lot of artworks from the period of the New Deal with explicitly progressive political and ideological content. These artworks (mostly murals, especially those by Thomas Hart Benton) are hardly represented in standard American art history—one struggles to find catalogues or books about them.

For IRWIN, this ideological, toxic character of art forms referring to totalitarian regimes was not such a problem—the group saw all art forms as ideological and toxic to the same degree. For IRWIN, art forms are not empty signifiers—and thus they had no reason to suppress certain images as ideological. The group thus shows that if we accept that all signs are ideological to the same degree, we become much freer in our choice of artistic forms and means than if we believe that signs can or must be empty. The remobilization of signs from the early avant-garde as well as totalitarian art was used by IRWIN to give more energy to their project of reconstructing Slovenian national cultural identity. "Retro-avant-garde" here means not only the reenactment of certain avant-garde attitudes and gestures, but also—and maybe primarily—the influx of avant-garde energies into IRWIN's artistic practice. The general mood of postmodernity was a certain melancholy after the end of the love affair with utopia. However, the project of reconstructing Slovenian national identity required some utopian energy—energy that IRWIN got from the sources of radical modernity.

It can be asked, of course, whether we need national cultural identities at all today—whether broken or unbroken, simple or hybrid. Is it not better to swim in anonymous flows of information and operate globally? Yes, today we live in the age of globalization and the Internet. Both are effects of the end of the Cold War and the erasure of the ideological divide between the West and the East. However, instead of producing the infinite flows of desire and information that were supposed to undermine and ultimately kill the modernist subject of self-reflection and self-control, the Internet has delivered an almost unlimited power to algorithmically organize surveillance and control. The cultural aspect of globalization also hasn't turned out the way many people initially expected. In fact, contemporary globalization is the direct opposite of the modern ideal of internationalism and universality. The world of globalization is not a world of international solidarity or shared cultural values. Nor is globalization the realm of the anonymous "crowd mind," as it was celebrated by postmodernism. Rather, it is the world of global competition of everybody against everybody. This competition pushes the participating subject to mobilize his or her own human capital. And human capital—as described, for example, by Michel Foucault—is primarily the cultural heritage that is mediated by the family and milieu in which an individual grows up. That is why the contemporary logic of globalization, unlike modernist internationalization and universalization, leads to cultural conservatism and an insistence on one's own cultural identity. The combination of globalization and extreme cultural conservatism defines the politics and art of our time.

My Western colleagues ask me from time to time: How are the Russian and Eastern European artists doing—did they already move on from communist and postcommunist times? This question actually means: Have they already forgotten the repressions and traumas of communism and become what they always were—Polish, Slovenian, or Russian? From this perspective, for Eastern European artists to move on means, in fact, to go back—back to a national cultural identity before it was allegedly repressed and distorted by communism. Here, of course, the question emerges of how far they have to go back to be able to rediscover and reappropriate their own cultural capital. Obviously, Russians have to go back to at least 1916. Maybe to 1913. This means that on the way to postcommunist normalization and globalization they have to abandon and subtract almost the whole twentieth century from their cultural capital. The situation of other post-socialist countries is not so dire—they have to go back merely to the period before World War II. But they still lose several decades—and, in terms of cultural capital, this is not such a negligible amount of time.

Thus, today the old line between the West and the East reemerges in a different form. The West is not supposed to subtract certain periods of its history from its cultural capital (maybe the only exclusion here is the German art of the Nazi era). This produces obvious inequality in the conditions of cultural accumulation and capitalization. However, on the level of official cultural policy, this Western point of view has also been adopted by Eastern European countries. This culturally conservative discourse currently dominates the public scene in Russia. But also in Eastern Europe, communism is understood mostly as a mere interruption, interval, or delay in the so-called normal development of these countries—a delay that, once it was over, left no traces other than a certain appetite to "make up for lost time" and build capitalism of the Western variety. The project of building capitalism through the erasure of the leftovers of communism is reminiscent of the well-known politics of erasing the leftovers of capitalism with the goal of building communism.

One can say that this is the anticommunist perspective on the phenomenon of Eastern European "real socialism." However, Western leftist intellectuals share this perspective, even if it is for different reasons. When it came to the Soviet Union, Western intellectuals were convinced that they understood Marxism much better than Russians did—and this insight was enough for them to see the entirety of Soviet culture as a historical mistake. For them, any further investigation of Soviet culture made no sense because it was clear from the beginning that this culture was based on an interpretation of Marxism that was simply wrong (dogmatic, primitive, and so forth). State socialism of the Soviet variety was seen as a perversion and a betrayal of the communist ideal, a totalitarian dictatorship that was more a parody of communism than its true fulfillment. Thus, from the position of the Western Left, real socialism also looks like a mere delay—this time, a delay in the development of the communist ideal. There is a consensus among the Left and the Right in the West that the Eastern European communist experiment should be forgotten. Both Left and Right reject "historical communism," or "national communism," or "communism in one country," because it offers a peculiar mixture of national traditions and the universalist communist project. The conservatives hate communism for contaminating the national traditions that they want to purify from everything communist. And the neo-communists want, on the contrary, to remove all the elements of Russianness, Chineseness, and so on, to restore the communist ideal in its absolute purity.

Indeed, Stalin's project of building socialism in one country led to the hybridization of communism and nationalism—and thus to a folklorization of communism and the artistic avant-garde. By folklorization I mean the integration of communist ideology and avant-garde art into networks of legends and myths that constitute the historical memory of a particular people, or rather a particular nation. Socialist revolutions inscribed political utopias and the artistic avant-garde into the mass culture of the countries in which these revolutions took place, to a degree that was unthinkable for Western countries. For a contemporary post-Soviet citizen there is no basic difference between Malevich's black square, Mayakovski's yellow shirt, Lissitzky's red wedge beating the whites, and jokes about Chapaev and Pet'ka.

The emergence of this new folklore, or kitsch, was diagnosed by Clement Greenberg in his 1939 essay "Avant-Garde and Kitsch." At the end of this essay, Greenberg formulates the hope that the avant-garde will be saved by inter-

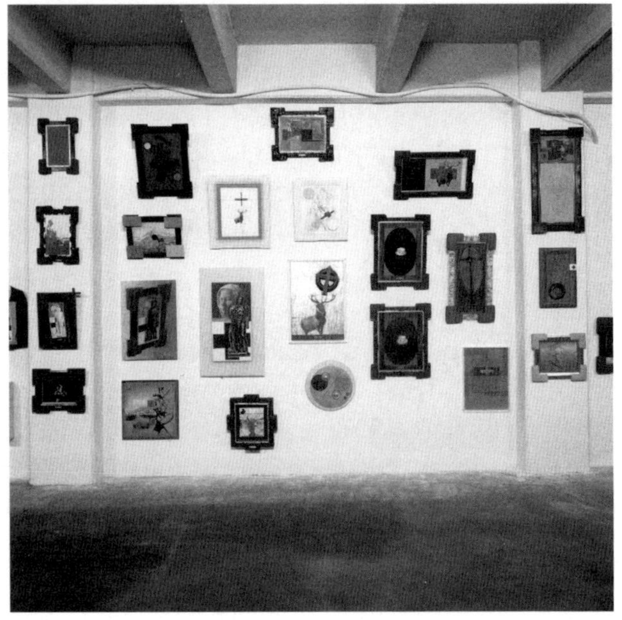

IRWIN, *Was ist Kunst*, 2005

national socialism—i.e., Trotskyism. André Breton, in his manifesto-like 1935 text "On the Time When the Surrealists Were Right," takes a similar position. He quotes the naive-sounding letters about loving one's mother and respecting one's parents published in the newspaper *Komsomolskaya Pravda* as a reason for his final break with the Soviet Union. (Obviously, these letters were kitsch for him.)

However, it is precisely this socialist and post-socialist folklore, or kitsch—this mixture of communist tradition and national cultural identity—that is used as material by many contemporary Russian and Eastern European artists. IRWIN is an especially good example here because they practice the folklorization of the avant-garde in a very systematic and conscious manner, combining avant-garde images with heavy traditional-looking frames, placing them together with mounted deer heads and thus referring to the atmosphere of a provincial stube, and so forth. One speaks of modern antiquarianism; IRWIN make modern folklore.

It is possible to find other examples of the folklorization of modernity all across Eastern Europe. The use—or better yet, the production—of folklore is a Romantic tradition. Romanticism, at the beginning of the nineteenth century, was a reaction to the collapse of the universalism of the Enlightenment and the failure of the French Revolution. Romantic poetry and art, with their mixture of desire and horror, the beautiful and the sublime, were manifestations of nostalgia for revolutionary times. Our time—the time after the end of the great universalist projects and secular utopias of the twentieth century—is very much reminiscent of the nineteenth century: it is dominated by the same combination of open markets, nationalism, and cultural conservatism. Under these conditions, it is only art that can maintain the memory of the hybrid national communisms of an earlier time. And it is precisely this memory that constitutes the main cultural capital of contemporary Eastern European artists and writers.


## The NSK State

This memory is, among many other things, a memory of a communist internationalism that was formulated in opposition to the project of globalization, which was understood as the creation of open global markets—the process of economic globalization initially started and, as stated above, was partially realized already in the nineteenth century. At that time—or even earlier, in the eighteenth century—the correlative project of a world culture emerged in which all national cultures would be included and dissolved. This vision of world culture is, of course, a fascinating one. However, the question remains: Can this vision be realized by the power of open markets alone? Of course, cultural products, like all other cultural commodities, have become globally accessible. But cultural products are not consumed like other commodities. If I consume bread, it disappears after I eat it. If I buy a car, it becomes my property and can be used— and also ruined—by only me. However, cultural products are consumed in such a way that they do not disappear in the act of consumption. Thus, they need archives to be preserved—libraries, museums, universities. Open markets are not able to create and sustain such cultural institutions—this is a task, historically and today, for national states. Art and culture in general function today in this ambivalent situation: they are globalized as commodities but remain preserved as parts of national cultural heritage. There are no international museums, libraries, or universities. Of course, one can argue that the Internet is such an international archive—and this is partially true. But the Internet is based on the following simple principle: it answers the questions that you ask it. The Internet does not give you information that you do not want to know. And people usually ask for information they are taught to ask for. In this sense, the Internet cannot substitute for national educational institutions. What's more, it is in private hands—and thus reflects the cultural identity of the American corporations that have control over it. IRWIN's answer to this situation was the creation of the NSK state. Here we have the rehabilitation, or the artistic reenactment, of the Hegelian/Marxist idea of a universal state, which in the nineteenth century was already opposed to the capitalist vision of globalization.

One of the books that seemed to capture the mood of the early 1990s was Francis Fukuyama's *The End of History and the Last Man* (1992). This book was mostly interpreted as a celebration of the victory of the West over historical communism and the impossibility of further social change. In fact, the book was not celebratory; it was rather pessimistic ("the last man"). The figure of the end of history was initially formulated by Alexandre Kojève in his lectures on Hegel's *Phenomenology of Spirit*, which he gave at the École pratique des hautes études in Paris from 1933 to 1939. These were regularly attended by intellectuals such as Georges Bataille, Jacques Lacan, André Breton, Maurice Merleau-Ponty, and Raymond Aron. The transcripts of Kojève's lectures circulated in Parisian intellectual circles and were widely read, notably by Jean-Paul Sartre and Albert Camus. Leo Strauss (whom Fukuyama studied under) admired Kojève, but believed that Kojève described the end of history too optimistically—due to the influence of Marx and his historical optimism. Strauss followed Nietzsche in believing that the post-historical mode of existence is the realm of the last

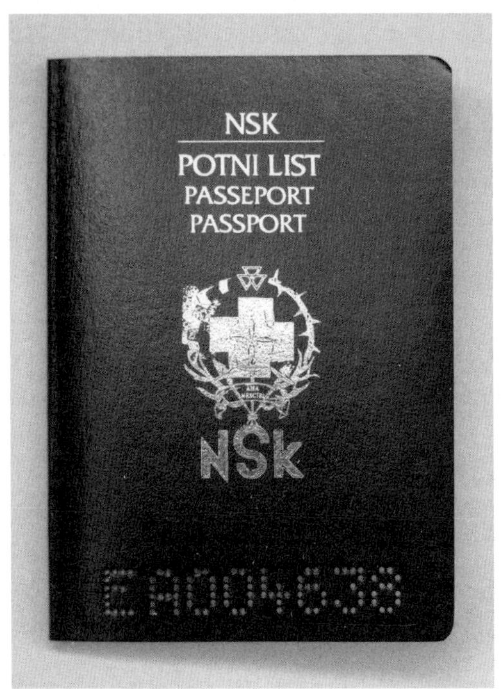


NSK Passport, 1993

man, the realm of decay and decline. Actually, at the end of his life Kojève also became much more skeptical about the post-historical condition. Fukuyama shares this pessimistic viewpoint and follows Kojève very closely in his interpretation of history and its end. However, he misses the central point in Kojèvian discourse. For Kojève, the end of history is marked by the emergence of a universal and homogeneous state. The end of history means political and not merely economic globalization. So from the Kojèvian point of view we are not yet at the end of history. The universal state remains utopian—it has to be implemented, but still hasn't been yet.

The NSK state is precisely such a utopian universal state, built on the territory of art. What the artists practice here is a kind of Romantic bureaucracy—the artist becomes a bureaucrat, a clerk of the nonexistent universal state. In his 1927 work *La trahison des clercs*, Julien Benda aptly described the ethos of post-Hegelian modern bureaucracy. He named its members "clerks." The word "clerk" is often translated as "intellectual," but in fact, Benda sees the intellectual as a traitor of the clerk's ethos, because the intellectual prefers the universality of his or her ideas to the duty of universal service. The true clerk does not commit him- or herself to any particular worldview—even to the most universalist one. The clerk, rather, serves others by helping them to realize their own particular ideas and goals. Benda saw the clerk primarily as a functionary, an administrator in the framework of the enlightened democratic state ruled by law. Today, even if the state is internally organized in the most universalist way, it remains a national state. Its clerks, notwithstanding their universalist ethos, are necessarily embedded in the apparatuses of power that pursue particular national interests. This embeddedness is one of the reasons why the traditional clerk ethos, as described by Benda, has become utopian.

It can be argued that the contemporary art world tries to compensate for the lack of a universal state. One has to remember that Kojève was not only a follower of Hegel but also a nephew of and commentator on Kandinsky. Indeed, there is an inner affinity between the modern state and modern art: both believe in the predominance of form over content. The modern state is a form—a beautiful form. The true bureaucrat—or true "clerk"—serves this form before he loves it, because his thinking is formalistic through and through. The bureaucrat who serves not the form but the "content," be it the content of his own desires or the desires of others, is a corrupt, bad bureaucrat. The same can be said about the modernist artist: he serves the form and tries to avoid corrupting it through his personal psychology or through external influences, motives, interests, and goals. As stated above, conceptual and even postmodern art inherits this service to pure form. Of course, the artist, a bureaucrat as well, cannot be completely immune to corruption through content of different kinds. But both see their profession as an attempt to resist this corruption and to serve the beautiful form of art or the state as selflessly as possible. This concerns not only the creation but also the presentation of art in public space—the task where art and politics necessarily collaborate.

The figure of the independent curator is especially interesting in this respect. Earlier curators were appointed by the state. Today, so-called international curators appoint themselves. In their curatorial practice they navigate between many private, institutional, and local interests, but their goal is to create an image of international art. They act as appointees of a nonexistent universal state. The contemporary international curator is a Romantic bureaucrat. NSK creates not merely a curatorial program but a Romantic state in which every participant—every curator or writer or artist—becomes a bureaucrat, one who is responsible for the well-being of the state, selfless and conscious of his or her social duties. This artistic appropriation of the state and state bureaucracy seems paradoxical because the artist is supposed to be an anarchist. But anarchy and institutional critique are good when there are art institutions. In Eastern European countries, though, art institutions are not very strong—and the art market is not especially powerful. Artists in this situation have to create art institutions themselves—together with the state, which is theoretically responsible for maintaining these institutions. Here again the artists of IRWIN demonstrate their precise grasp of the current cultural and political situation. They announce the era in which all people will become citizens of their state—or of any other universal state.

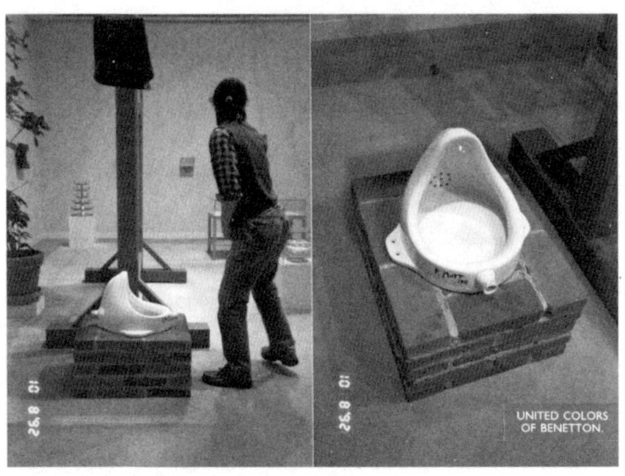


Inga Svala Thorsdottir and Wu Shanzhuan, *Bird Before Peace 'An Appreciation'*, 1992/93

19
Inga Svala Thorsdottir and Wu Shanzhuan
The Right (of Humans and Things) to Become Extra-ordinary

Inga Svala Thorsdottir and Wu Shanzhuan's manifesto and series of works titled *Thing's Right(s)*, a revision of the 1948 Universal Declaration of Human Rights, cuts to the core of the Western cultural tradition—to the relationship between art und human rights, the French Revolution and aesthetic contemplation, the privileging of men and privileging of artworks.[1] I would like to use this intervention by Thorsdottir and Wu into the Western art tradition as a starting point of my text. This intervention has the character of a protest, a contestation. Its primary target is the readymade practice as it was introduced by Marcel Duchamp. Duchamp's art became a target for Thorsdottir and Wu's artistic actions early enough: in 1992, as the first collaboration with Thorsdottir, Wu pissed into one of the urinals signed by Duchamp that was on display in the Moderna Museet in Stockholm. The title of the work was *An Appreciation.*

One could say it was also a violent reaction. But it was obviously a reaction against a certain kind of violence that was applied by Duchamp himself to the things that were taken out of their original everyday context and then, under the name of "readymades," moved into the space of the art museum. One can say that Duchamp's artistic decisions have (unjustly) privileged certain things in relationship to other things: for example, a particular urinal in relationship to all the other urinals. Indeed, even if some art theorists argued that the readymade practice erased the border between museographed art and ordinary reality, or between artworks and ordinary things, the selection of a particular urinal (or several particular urinals) has not emancipated its brethren that remained on their accustomed places inside lavatories all around the world. However, this is not the main objection that Thorsdottir and Wu have with the ready-made practice. For the artists, the true "appreciation" of a thing is precisely the use of this thing. According to this view, Duchamp insulted the urinal by forbidding its use. Thorsdottir and Wu's reaction to Duchamp's gesture reminds us of the opposition between "ritual value" and "exhibition value" that was introduced by Walter Benjamin. Indeed, the usual use of the urinal can be understood as a kind of ritual that is negated and destroyed by the defunctionalization of the urinal in the exhibition space.

The act of violence that removes an object from its immediate context of everyday use, isolates it, and prevents it from being plunged back into the flow of the quotidian has its historical roots in the violence of the French Revolution and its ideology of human rights. Indeed, our contemporary notion of art has its roots in the decisions that were taken by the French revolutionary government concerning the objects that it inherited from the ancien régime. The change of a regime—especially such a radical change as was introduced by the French Revolution—is usually accompanied by a wave of iconoclasm. One could watch these waves in the cases of Protestantism, La Conquista, or recently after the fall of the socialist regimes in Eastern Europe. The French revolutionaries took a different course: instead of destroying sacral and profane objects belonging to the ancien régime, they defunctionalized them—or, in other words, aestheticized them. The French revolution turned the things of the old regime into what we call today art—i.e., into an object not of use but of pure contemplation. This violent, revolutionary act of the aestheticization of the old regime created art as we know it today.

The revolutionary origin of modern aesthetics was conceptualized by Immanuel Kant in *Critique of the Power of Judgment*, written in 1790. Toward the beginning of his text Kant refers (albeit indirectly) to the political context of his time. He writes: "If someone asks me whether I find the palace that I see before me beautiful, I may well say that I do not like that sort of thing [...] in true Rousseauesque style I might even vilify the vanity of the great who waste the sweat of the people on such superfluous thing. [...] All of this might be conceded to me and approved; but that is not what is at the issue here. [...] One must not be in the least biased in favor of the existence of the thing, but must be entirely indifferent in this respect in order to play the judge in matters of taste."[2] Kant does not like the palace as a representation of wealth and power. However, he is ready to accept the palace as aestheticized, which actually means defunctionalized, made nonexistent for all practical purposes—reduced to pure form. Since the French Revolution, artworks began to be understood as defunctionalized and publicly exhibited things of a past reality. This understanding of art determines artistic strategies up until today. One can say that Duchamp and other artists of the readymade expanded this strategy to include its own contemporaneity: this contemporaneity was seen by them as already past, a disappearing reality that can be easily reduced to pure form. And as pure form it became unusable. The fact that the artworks are not used means that they have their goal not outside, but inside themselves. In this sense, artworks are "humanized" things: they have a "soul" that makes them autonomous. The modern humanist ethics is based on the requirement that man can never be a means, only a goal. In this sense, artworks are treated like men among things. But one can also say that men are treated like artworks among animals. Here one can see a deep and decisive connection between the autonomy of things and their form. Things become protected artworks when they are perceived only as "forms" and not as usable objects—and animals become protected from use when they have a human form. Thus, speaking about the rights of things, Thorsdottir and Wu point to the core of the problem—the connection between art and humanism. But what, actually, is a thing?

According to Martin Heidegger, only an artwork can manifest itself as a thing. In his essay "The Origin of the Work of Art" (1935–36), Heidegger writes that we originally encounter all things as "tools." In other words, we always perceive them as objects of possible use—and thus overlook precisely their thingness. Art alone is able to demonstrate to us the thingness of things by taking them out of the context of their ordinary use. Thus Heidegger writes: "Nothing can be discovered about the thingly aspect of the work until the pure standing-in-itself of the work has clearly shown itself. But is the work in itself ever accessible? In order for this to happen it would be necessary to remove the work from all relation to anything other than itself in order to let it stand on its own and for itself alone."[3] But if our ability to experience the work of art "on its own and for itself alone" depends on the decision to remove it "from all relation to anything other than itself," such a decision must in some way be unfounded and unprecedented. Heidegger writes: "The setting-into-work of truth thrusts up the extra-ordinary (*das Ungeheure*) while thrusting down the ordinary, and what one takes to be such. The truth that opens itself in the work can never be verified or derived from what went before. In its exclusive reality, what went before is refuted by the work. What art founds, therefore, can never be compensated and made good in terms of what is present and available for use. The founding is an overflowing, a bestowal."[4] And at another point: "The more essentially this thrust comes into the open, the stranger and more solitary the work becomes."[5]

What presents itself in these passages as a mere description is evidently a normative proposition: the work of art cannot be understood in terms of the past; it breaks with the habits of perception. Though Heidegger himself did not have particularly "progressive" artistic taste, and evidently stuck with moderate expressionism, his theory of art nonetheless privileged a radical, avant-garde, innovative art by encouraging the artist to present the decidedly "extra-ordinary." The extra-ordinary here is obviously not merely a historical innovation, but the extraction of the artwork from the ordinary. Here Heidegger seems to speak a language that is very similar to the language of Duchamp: we can see the urinal as a thing only if we remove it from everyday use. Or, the urinal becomes a thing only after it has become an artwork. Before that it was merely a tool. In other words, to expand human rights, as understood by the French Revolution, to the realm of things means to defunctionalize them—so that these things can be only contemplated but not used. Under such a presupposition to speak about the right of things means to turn the whole of ordinary life into an artwork or a museum space, or to completely destroy it. That is the actual problem that Thorsdottir and Wu address with *Thing's Right(s)*. But before we come back to this problem let us discuss the following question: Is the art system the place that guarantees things their thingness—by completely relieving them from their role of tools?

Heidegger was famously more than skeptical about the role of the art system. He writes: "Well, then, the works themselves are located and hang in collections and exhibitions.

But are they themselves, in this context, are they the works they are, or are they, rather, objects of the art business? […] Official agencies assume responsibility for the care and maintenance of the works. Art connoisseurs and critics busy themselves with them. The art dealer looks after the market. The art-historical researcher turns the works into the objects of a science. But in all this many-sided activity do we ever encounter the work itself?"[6] The answer, of course, is no. Paradoxically, the art system turns the artworks back into tools—their thingness is overlooked again. For Heidegger, the artwork is an event that takes place in the "clearance of Being." However, entering this clearance, this opening of Being, the artist immediately sees its closure. Of course, the art system is not a supermarket. When I buy a thing in a supermarket I can use it as I please—I can even destroy it. But I cannot freely use or destroy a work of art—I cannot "enslave" it, turn it into a tool instead of keeping its status as a goal. Such a behavior would be judged as barbaric by contemporary society.

Nevertheless, I can use an artwork as a sign of power and wealth. Even if the art system negates the ordinary use value of a thing, it keeps its exchange value intact. From the Marxist point of view (as formulated in the first volume of Marx's *Capital*), art can be seen as the ultimate stage of "commodity fetishism," and the readymade practice as the final triumph of exchange value over use value: the moment at which a ready-made ceases to remain as a pure object of contemplation and begins to circulate inside the globalized art world, the soul of the thing is substituted by its price. Thus, the actual accusation directed against the art system is this: the art system uses art as art—whereas art should not be used in any way, including as art. It is precisely this use of art as art that has produced so much criticism and negative reaction recently against the art system all over the world. The Heideggerian return to the truth of art as an opening of the world seems increasingly improbable in our days. So the answer to the use of art as art is mostly: the use of art as nonart. Art becomes politicized and subjected to "good" social goals.

However, in *Thing's Right(s)*, Thorsdottir and Wu offer a different way of dealing with the same problem: the aestheticization of the use of things as such. Or, in other words, the aestheticization of ordinary life in its totality. In the context of the reflection on the relationship between the aestheticization of politics and the politicization of aesthetics, undertaken in the epilogue to "The Work of Art in the Age of Mechanical Reproduction" (1936), Walter Benjamin critiques the aestheticization of politics as the Fascist project par excellence. Namely, Benjamin interprets the aestheticization of life, including politics, as a proclamation of the war of art against life, and summarizes the Fascist political program by the words: *Fiat ars—pereat mundus*. Benjamin writes further that Fascism is the fulfillment of the *l'art pour l'art* movement.[7]

Benjamin comes to this conclusion because he still understands art as pure contemplation beyond any use. In that case the aestheticization of the totality of everyday life would indeed amount to stopping and destroying it. However, the aestheticization of the use value of things changes this equation in the most radical way. Wu has the experience of Chinese communism behind him—in other words, he has experienced a total aestheticization of reality to a degree that Western artists never have. And one should not forget: economically speaking, communism is nothing other than victory of use value over exchange value. Under the conditions of communism, the market, including the art market, gets abolished. And that means that communism starts with the exchange value of things reduced to a zero level. The use value that

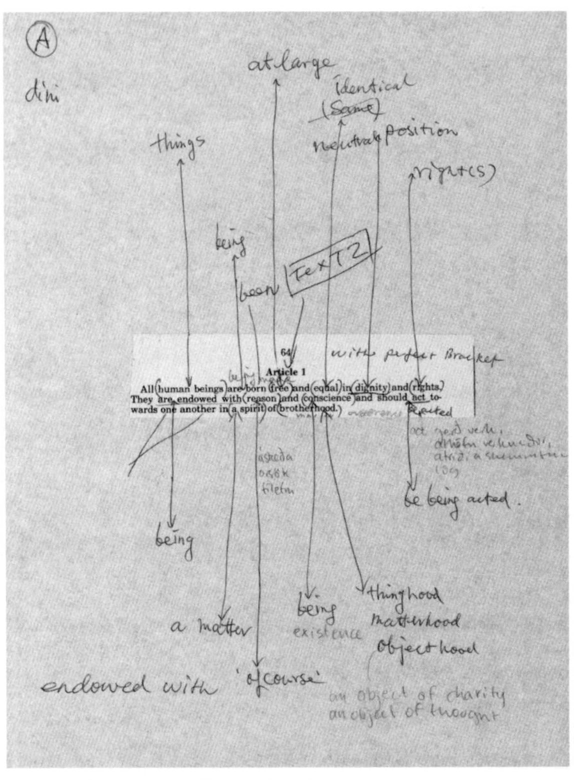

Inga Svala Thorsdottir and Wu Shanzhuan,
*Thing's Right(s)*, 1995; Article 1

earlier depended on the exchange value becomes artistically reinvented or even newly invented. Here, the ordinary itself becomes extra-ordinary—and thus, according to Heidegger, a work of art.

This constructivist character of communist society—when all things become reduced to zero and then reinvented together with their use—finds its correspondence in Suprematist, or Constructivist, art practices, as well as reductionist practices of postwar and more recent art. Not accidentally, Thorsdottir practices the pulverization of things in her own art. Her pulverization practice reminded me of a project to burn all existing artworks, proposed by Kazimir Malevich in 1919. At that time the new Soviet government feared that the old Russian museums and art collections would be destroyed by civil war and the general collapse of state institutions and the economy. The Communist Party responded by trying to secure and save these collections. In his text "On the Museum," Malevich protested against this pro-museum policy of Soviet power by calling on the state to not intervene on behalf of the old art collections because their destruction could open the path to true, living art.[8] Malevich proposes not to keep or save things of the past that have to go, but to let them go without sentimentality and remorse. To let the dead bury their dead. And at the same time Malevich professes his love for the new objects of ordinary use as belonging to the creation of the new world. In other words, it is the reduction to dust (or pulverization) of the old things along with the destruction of their exchange value that opens the way for new things to have a new use value.

Here one can see the difference between the French Revolution and the Communist Revolution. The French Revolution will establish human rights but it is, indeed, not interested in the rights of things. In other words, it wants to regulate the relationship among men—but not the relationships among things. That is why the French Revolution remained stuck halfway: it liberated ordinary life, but did not artistically transform or reinvent it.

When Heidegger speaks about the ability of art to show the truth of things, he means that their truth lies in their ordinary use. As an example, Heidegger cites a pair of worn-out shoes presented by Van Gogh in one of his paintings. Heidegger assumes that these shoes are so radically used that they have no exchange value any more—only use value. But the painting itself obviously has an exchange value. And a new pair of shoes, not yet worn-out, would have an exchange value too—at least in the society in which Heidegger lived. The interesting aspect of communist society is that a new pair of shoes only has a use value—and no exchange value. Thus, this pair of shoes does not need to wait to become worn-out, unwanted, or unsellable on the market in order to become aestheticized by Van Gogh and/or Heidegger. In a communist society the rule of the use value is total (what isn't usable is forbidden; who doesn't work doesn't eat) and includes things and humans alike. It is this experience of the total artwork based on use value that Thorsdottir and Wu conceptualize in *Thing's Right(s)*.

However, the total does not mean totalitarian here. The use of things is total—but it remains undetermined. Wu writes: "I believe art is a silent ocean. [...] It is a static, formless empty box—it must accept absolutely anything, absolutely anyone, and it is destined never to be full. Its strength is in nothingness."[9] Related to this notion of art, Wu's concept of the "deficit (red) character"—that words or characters do not have one single meaning—and his idea that "methodology of presentation precedes the existence of a concept,"[10] remind me of the elegant theory that was formulated by

Claude Lévi-Strauss as he tried to conceptualize the notion of mana that was used by Marcel Mauss in *The Gift* (1925).

The term mana that Mauss uses derives from the relatively closed orbit of Polynesian culture. Mana can be understood as an exchange value of a thing that is given as a gift. However, it is of crucial importance to Mauss's theory of mana that the character of this exchange value changes over time. At first, the mana within the gift is always benign, but later it necessarily begins to exert a negative effect on its new owner—because its connection to the gift-giver begins to be forgotten. Good mana is guaranteed as long as the strangeness of the gift has not been forgotten. The inevitable domestication of the gift later on not only leads to the loss of positive mana, but also to the rise of negative mana. We might say that as soon as the sign of the new and strange becomes part of the familiar surroundings, it becomes a locus of negative powers and feelings. We encounter this phenomenon as the cycle of fashion: those who dress themselves according to the latest fashion appear hip and attractive, yet nothing is more detrimental to one's image than last year's fashion. Decades-old fashion, by contrast, might signify "return," and thus acquire positive mana and become attractive again. Fashion, in fact, is nothing other than a particular form of the economy of symbolic exchange, which forces all people to exchange their signs constantly in order for these signs to appear forever strange.

Mauss's use of the term mana was criticized by many commentators because its use seemed too dependent on Polynesian mythology. The most radical, most profound, and, at the same time, most theoretically important critique was formulated by Lévi-Strauss. Contrary to most critics, however, Lévi-Strauss did not want to abandon the term, but sought to endow it with a more precise definition. According

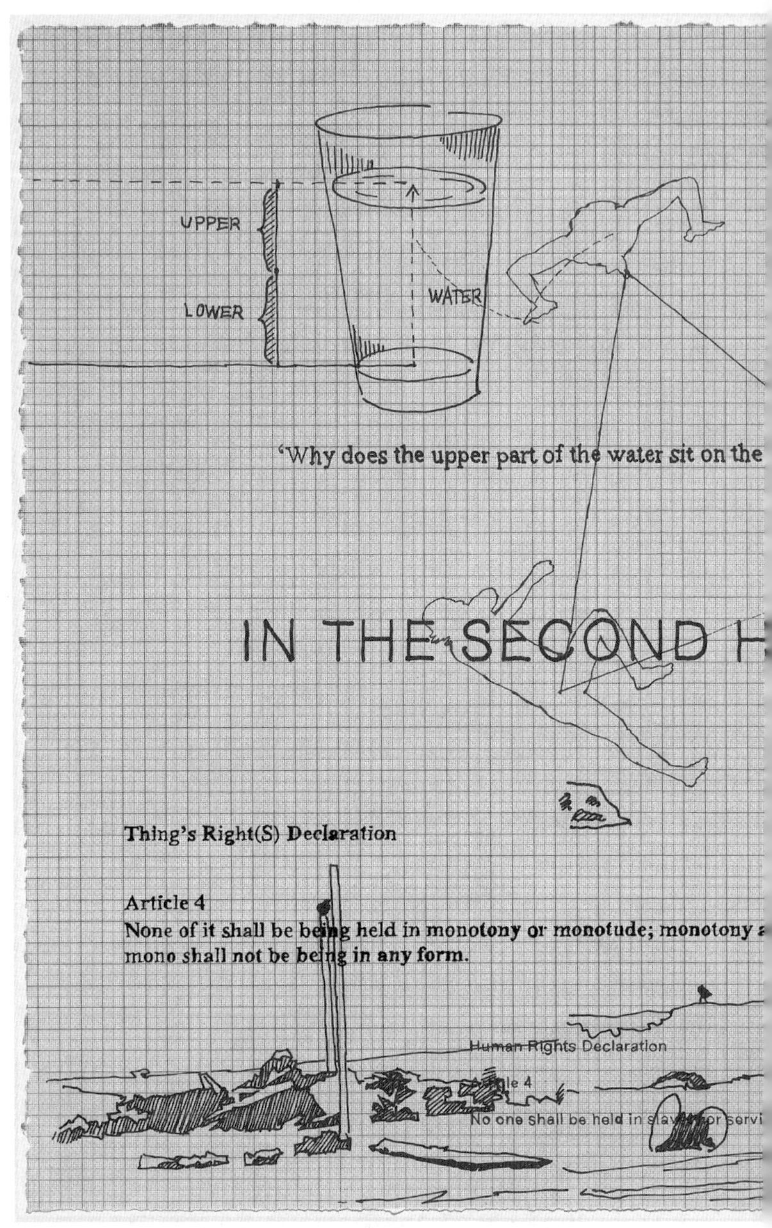


Inga Svala Thorsdottir and Wu Shanzhuan, *Thing's Right(s) Declaration Article 4*, 2013

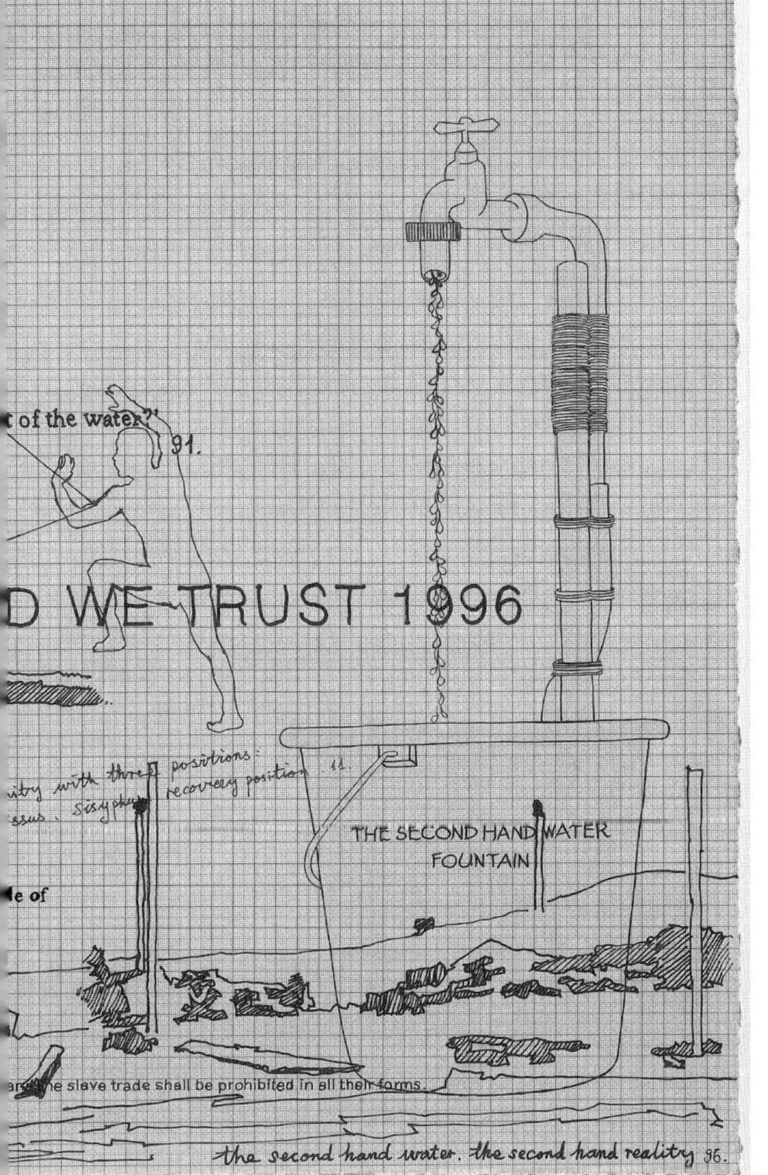
of the water?"
91.
D WE TRUST 1996
ity with three positions:
recovery position 11.
Sisyphus
THE SECOND HAND WATER
FOUNTAIN
e of
the slave trade shall be prohibited in all their forms.
the second hand water, the second hand reality 96.

to Lévi-Strauss, mana does not belong to the order of reality, but solely to the order of signs. He assumes that at a certain point in time the entire universe suddenly experienced a revolution of signification, and became saturated with signs. Prior to this big bang of signification, there was no meaning at all in the world; afterward, there was only meaning. All things instantly became signs or, rather, signifiers, which ever since have each been waiting for their signified. So the world after the big bang of signification offers us an infinite number of signifiers, yet we do not know what they mean—they are signifiers without signifieds. We only know *that* they signify. The progress of thinking, says Lévi-Strauss, consists in "the work of equalising of the signifier to fit the signified"; that is, in the gradual filling of empty signifiers with particular meanings, with signifieds.

Yet the progress of thinking is very slow as well as always finite and partial. Although it takes place "inside a totality which is closed and complementary to itself," or, to use Wu's words, inside a box, it can never completely fill the infinite number of empty signifiers with signifieds, because every labor of thought is carried out in a finite lifetime. The basic condition of man in the world—understood as a world of signification—thus consists in the fact that the human always has far too many signs at his disposal to which he cannot assign meaning: "There is always a non-equivalence or 'inadequation' between the two [the signifier and the signified], a non-fit and overspill which divine understanding alone can soak up; this generates a signifier-surfeit relative to the signifieds to which it can be fitted."  Hence there always remains a "supplementary ration" of signifiers without signifieds that marks the difference between the infinite divine and our finite human reason—a difference humans must somehow cope with. According to Lévi-Strauss, mana is nothing else but the name for this surplus of empty signifiers that have no concrete meaning. Mana is the "floating signifier" that represents the entire infinite surplus of signifiers, and that is "the disability of all finite thought (but also the surety of all art, all poetry, every mythic and aesthetic invention), even though scientific knowledge is capable, if not of staunching it, at least of controlling it partially." Hence, mana is "a *zero symbolic value*, that is, a sign marking the necessity of a supplementary symbolic content."[11]

But what are these signifiers without a signified? Using the language proposed by Thorsdottir and Wu, one can say that they are deficit things waiting for use—and this status of waiting is precisely the mana that makes them attractive and potentially poetic. The communist revolution can be interpreted as a version of the revolution of signification that Lévi-Strauss speaks of. It creates an ocean of floating things/signs that are waiting for use. Human beings are laborers who ascribe meaning to them. This is a poetic, artistic job. But it is not the only artistic job possible. Another job is precisely to thematize the floating character of things and signs—and the impossibility of its complete domestication and familiarization. Things and signs have the right to remain forever floating, foreign, strange—and fascinating. It seems to me that this right to be strange and extra-ordinary is what *Thing's Right(s)* is aiming at. Let us be reminded of some of these rights. Every individual thing, in particular, "has the right(s) to be active being, at large and existence (being) of object" (Article 3), and "None of it shall be being held in monotony or monotude; monotony and trade of mono shall not be being in any form" (Article 4). Here, monotony is equated with slavery. Things should be used—but in dynamic, unexpected, extra-ordinary ways. Only then would the aestheticization of life mean not its destruction, but its artistic reinvention. The only true human right and the only true right of things is the right to become extra-ordinary.

Notes

1.  Thorsdottir and Wu started writing the Thing's Right(s) Declaration in the early 1990s; the first English version was published on the occasion of their show "Thing's Right(s) – Cuxhaven 1999," Cuxhavener Kunstverein, 1999. It has since been published in Chinese, Sanskrit, Hindi, Swedish, Malay, and Tamil, on the occasion of different exhibitions.
2.  Immanuel Kant, *Critique of the Power of Judgment*, ed. Paul Guyer, trans. Paul Guyer and Eric Matthews (Cambridge: Cambridge University Press, 2000), 90–91.
3.  Martin Heidegger, "The Origin of the Work of Art," in *Off the Beaten Track*, ed. and trans. Julian Young and Kenneth Haynes (Cambridge: Cambridge University Press, 2002), 19.
4.  Ibid., 47.
5.  Ibid., 40.
6.  Ibid., 19.
7.  Walter Benjamin, epilogue to "The Work of Art in the Age of Mechanical Reproduction," in *Illuminations*, ed. Hannah Arendt, trans. Harry Zohn (New York: Schocken Books, 2007), 241–42.
8.  Kazimir Malevich, "On the Museum," in *Essays on Art, 1915–1933*, vol. 1, ed. Troels Andersen, trans. Xenia Glowacki-Prus and Arnold McMillin (London: Rapp & Whiting, 1971), 68–72.
9.  Cited in Qiu Zhijie, "Introduction: Wu's Question or the Questioning of Wu," in *Wu Shanzhuan: Red Humor International*, ed. Susan Acret and Jasper Lau Kin Wah (Hong Kong: Asia Art Archive, 2005), 25.
10.  Ibid., 24ff., 27.
11.  Claude Lévi-Strauss, *Introduction to the Work of Marcel Mauss*, trans. Felicity Baker (London: Routledge & Kegan Paul, 1987), 61–63 (italics in original).

# Acknowledgments

Texts reprinted with the kind permission of
the publishers and rights holders.

"Kandinsky's Bauhaus." Translated from the German by Nicholas Grindell. *frieze d/e*, September/October 2013, 92–99.

"Marcel Duchamp's Absolute Art." In "100 Years of Readymade," special issue, *Mousse*, December 2012–January 2013, 86–89.

"The Inner Life of a Can of Preserves." In *Manzoni*, edited by Germano Celant, 46–53. Milan: Electa, 2007. Exhibition catalogue.

"In Search of Suspended Time." In *Cast a Cold Eye: The Late Work of Andy Warhol*, translated from the German by Catherine Schelbert, 29–37. New York: Gagosian Gallery, 2006.

"Simulated Readymades by Peter Fischli/David Weiss." Translated from the German by Catherine Schelbert. *Parkett*, nos. 40/41 (1994): 24–39.

"The Case of Thomas Schütte." In *Robert Lehman Lectures on Contemporary Art No. 3*, edited by Lynne Cooke, Karen Kelly, and Bettina Funcke, 139–56. New York: Dia Art Foundation, 2004. © Dia Art Foundation, New York.

"The Archive of Ashes." In *Concert for Buchenwald*, translated from the German by Matthew Partridge, 33–42. Zurich: Scalo, 2000. Exhibition catalogue.

"A Self-Collector." In *Martin Honert: Catalogue Raisonné, 1982–2003*, translated from the German by Steven Lindberg, unpaginated. Cologne: Verlag der Buchhandlung Walther König, 2004. Exhibition catalogue.

"Life without Shadows." In *Jeff Wall*, translated from the German by Shaun Whiteside, 58–67. London: Phaidon Press, 1996.

"The Speed of Art." In *Peter Fischli, David Weiss*, edited by Bice Curiger, Patrick Frey, and Boris Groys, translated from the German by Catherine Schelbert, 53–61. Baden: Lars Müller Publishers, 1995. In collaboration with Bundesamt für Kultur Bern.

"How to Do Time with Art." In *Francis Alÿs: A Story of Deception*, edited by Mark Godfrey and Klaus Biesenbach, 190–92. London: Tate Publishing, 2010. © Tate 2010.

"Liberation in the Loop, Paul Chan: The 7 ~~Lights~~." *Parkett*, no. 88 (2011): 64–75.

"Scenes of Limited Subjectivity." In *Anri Sala: Answer Me*, edited by Margot Norton and Massimiliano Gioni, 130–36. New York: New Museum, 2016.

"Looking for the Great Sunday." In *Compossibilities: Olga Chernysheva*, edited by Silke Opitz, translated from the German by Christiane Court, 32–39. Ostfildern: Hatje Cantz, 2013.

"Answering a Call." In *Yael Bartana: And Europe Will Be Stunned; The Polish Trilogy*, edited by Eleanor Nairne and James Lingwood, 134–39. London: Artangel, 2012.

"Soul = Design: Althamer's Golden Humanity." In *Pawel Althamer: The Neighbors*, edited by Massimiliano Gioni and Gary Carrion-Murayari, 93–100. New York: New Museum, 2014.

"Poetics of Entropy: The Post-Suprematist Art of Mladen Stilinović." *e-flux journal*, no. 54 (April 2014). http://www.e-flux.com/journal/poetics-of-entropy-the-post-suprematist-art-of-mladen-stilinovic.

"NSK: From Hybrid Socialism to Universal State." *e-flux journal*, no. 67 (November 2015). http://www.e-flux.com/journal/nsk-from-hybrid-socialism-to-universal-state.

# Image Credits

p. 10    Wassily Kandinsky, sketch for a mural for the Juryfreie Kunstschau, Wall D, Berlin, 1922. Gouache and white chalk on brown paper mounted on cardboard, 34.8 × 57.8 cm. Courtesy of Bauhaus-Archiv Berlin.

p. 14    Vallmajor de Barcelona prison cell designed by Alphonse Laurencic during the Spanish Civil War, 1939. Photo: Brangulí. Courtesy of Arxiu Nacional de Catalunya and Fons Brangulí.

p. 16    Wassily Kandinsky, *Doppelklang—kalte Spannung der Geraden, warme Spannung der Gebogenen, Steifes zum Lockeren, Nachgeben zum Dichten* (*Double sound—cold tension of the straight lines, warm tension of the curved lines, the rigid to the loose, the yielding to the compact*), in *Punkt und Linie zu Fläche* (*Point and Line to Plane*) (Albert Langen Verlag: Munich, 1926), 182, tab. 21. Courtesy of the Bibliothèque Kandinsky, Centre Pompidou, Paris.

p. 20    Alfred Stieglitz, *Fountain by Marcel Duchamp*, 1917. Gelatin silver print, 23.5 × 17.8 cm. © Georgia O'Keeffe Museum / VG Bild-Kunst, Bonn 2016.
Marcel Duchamp, *Fountain*, 1917. © The Estate of Marcel Duchamp / VG Bild-Kunst, Bonn 2016.

p. 24    "Panama" porcelain urinal, in *Mott's Plumbing Fixtures: Catalogue "A"* (New York: J. L. Mott Iron Works, 1908), 417, plate 6585-A. Reproduced in William A. Camfield, "Marcel Duchamp's Fountain: Its History and Aesthetics in the Context of 1917," *Dada/Surrealism* 16 (1987): 70.

p. 28    "Puro" drinking fountain, in "Mott's Sanitary Drinking Fountains," supplement no. 11 (1913), in *Mott's Plumbing Fixtures: Catalogue "A"*, section 2 (New York: J. L. Mott Iron Works, 1908), 4, plate 4943-A. Reproduced in William A. Camfield, *Marcel Duchamp: Fountain* (Houston: Houston Fine Art Press, 1989), 52.

p. 32          Piero Manzoni, *Merda d'artista n. 68* (*Artist's Shit no. 68*), 1961. Tin can, printed paper, 4.8 × Ø 6 cm. Photo: Agostino Osio, Milan. © Fondazione Piero Manzoni, Milan / VG Bild-Kunst, Bonn 2016.

p. 36          Piero Manzoni, *Corpo d'aria n. 28* (*Body of Air no. 28*), 1959–60. Wooden box containing rubber balloon, mouthpiece, base. Box: 4.8 × 42.5 × 12.3 cm. Photo: Annalisa Guidetti / Giovanni Ricci, Milan. © Fondazione Piero Manzoni, Milan / VG Bild-Kunst, Bonn 2016.

p. 44          Andy Warhol, *Oxidation Painting*, 1978. Urine and metallic pigment in acrylic medium on canvas, 16 × 12 in. Image and artwork © 2016 The Andy Warhol Foundation for the Visual Arts, Inc. / Artists Rights Society (ARS), New York.

pp. 52–53      Andy Warhol, *Detail of The Last Supper*, 1986. Synthetic polymer paint and silkscreen ink on canvas, 116 × 183 in. Image and artwork © 2016 The Andy Warhol Foundation for the Visual Arts, Inc. / Artists Rights Society (ARS), New York.

pp. 62, 70–71  Peter Fischli and David Weiss, *Der Tisch* (*The Table*), 1992–93. Installation view, Museum für Gegenwartskunst, Basel. Photo: Jason Klimatsas. © Peter Fischli David Weiss, Zurich 2016. Courtesy of Sprüth Magers, Matthew Marks Gallery, and Galerie Eva Presenhuber.

p. 66          Peter Fischli and David Weiss, *Raum ohne Titel* (*Untitled Room*), 1990–92. Installation view, Hardturmstrasse, Zurich. Photo: Jason Klimatsas. © Peter Fischli David Weiss, Zurich 2016. Courtesy of Sprüth Magers, Matthew Marks Gallery, and Galerie Eva Presenhuber.

p. 74          Martin Honert, *Foto* (*Photo*), 1993. Oil and acrylic on wood and epoxy resin. Figure: 100 cm (height); table: 79 × 73 × 123 cm; overall: 100 × 100 × 123 cm. Courtesy of Matthew Marks Gallery. © Martin Honert / VG Bild-Kunst, Bonn 2016.

p. 82          Martin Honert, *Nikolaus/Santa Claus*, 2002. Wood, polyester, polystyrene, paint. Santa Claus and Ruprecht: 214 × 120 × 43 cm; sack: 53 × 50 × 25 cm. Courtesy of Matthew Marks Gallery. © Martin Honert / VG Bild-Kunst, Bonn 2016.

pp. 88–89      Martin Honert, *A Model Scenario of the Flying Classroom*, 1995. Acrylic on wood, polystyrene, epoxy resin; twelve elements: 400 × 600 × 400 cm. Courtesy of Matthew Marks Gallery. © Martin Honert / VG Bild-Kunst, Bonn 2016.

p. 94          Thomas Schütte, *E.L.S.A.*, 1989. Wood, paint, 155 × 140 × 220 cm. Photo: Dorothee Fischer. Courtesy of Thomas Schütte Studio. © VG Bild-Kunst, Bonn 2016.

pp. 102–3      Thomas Schütte, *Modell für ein Museum* (*Model for a Museum*), 1982. Plywood, photograph, Kapa cardboard, paint, fabric, approx. 31 × 90 × 16.5 cm. Photo: Nic Tenwiggenhorn. Courtesy of Thomas Schütte Studio. © VG Bild-Kunst, Bonn 2016.

p. 108         Thomas Schütte, *Großer Geist Nr. 1* (*Great Spirit No. 1*), 2003. Polished bronze, approx. 250 cm (height). Photo: Nic Tenwiggenhorn. Courtesy of Thomas Schütte Studio. © VG Bild-Kunst, Bonn 2016.

p. 112         Thomas Schütte, *United Enemies*, 1995. Fimo, fabric, wood, glass, PVC, approx. 34 cm (height). Photo: Dimitris Tamviskos. Courtesy of Thomas Schütte Studio. © VG Bild-Kunst, Bonn 2016.

pp. 118, 122, 126–27      Rebecca Horn, *Konzert für Buchenwald* (*Concert for Buchenwald*), 1999. Ash, musical instruments, wagon, lightning tubes, glass construction, electronics, motor. Part 1: Tram Depot. Permanent installation, Weimar. Photos: Attilio Maranzano. © Rebecca Horn / VG Bild-Kunst, Bonn 2016.

p. 134         Jeff Wall, *Morning Cleaning, Mies van der Rohe Foundation, Barcelona*, 1999. Transparency in light box, 187 × 351 cm. Installation view, "Jeff Wall—Tableaux Pictures Photographs 1996–2013," Kunsthaus Bregenz, 2014. Photo: Markus Tretter. © Jeff Wall and Kunsthaus Bregenz.

pp. 138–39        Jeff Wall, *Mimic*, 1982. Transparency in light box, 198 × 228.6 cm. Jeff Wall, *Milk*, 1984. Transparency in light box, 187 × 229 cm. Exhibition view, "Jeff Wall. The Crooked Path," Centro Galego de Arte Contemporánea, Santiago de Compostela, November 12, 2011–February 26, 2012. Photo: Mark Ritchie, Ourense. Courtesy of CGAC Photograph Archive, Santiago de Compostela; and the artist.

p. 144            Peter Fischli and David Weiss, *Untitled (Venice Work)*, Swiss Pavilion, 46th Venice Biennale, June 11–October 15, 1995. Installation view. Photo: Jason Klimatsas. © Peter Fischli David Weiss, Zurich 2016. Courtesy of Sprüth Magers, Matthew Marks Gallery, and Galerie Eva Presenhuber.

pp. 150–51        Peter Fischli and David Weiss, *Untitled (Venice Work)*, Swiss Pavilion, 46th Venice Biennale, June 11–October 15, 1995. Video stills. © Peter Fischli David Weiss, Zurich 2016. Courtesy of Sprüth Magers, Matthew Marks Gallery, and Galerie Eva Presenhuber.

p. 156            Francis Alÿs, *Song for Lupita*, 1998. Animation drawing, pencil on tracing paper, 35 × 29 cm. Courtesy of the artist and Galerie Peter Kilchmann, Zurich. © Francis Alÿs.

pp. 160–61        Francis Alÿs, *Bolero (Shoeshine Blues)*, 1999–2007. Animation still. 9 min. 40 sec. Courtesy of David Zwirner, New York/London.

p. 164            Paul Chan, *1st Light*, 2005. Digital video projection, 14 min. Exhibition view, "Paul Chan—Selected Works," Schaulager Basel, 2014. Photo: Tom Bisig, Basel. Courtesy of the artist and Greene Naftali, New York.

pp. 168–69        Paul Chan, *3rd Light*, 2006. Digital video projection, table, 14 min. Dimensions variable. Exhibition view, "Paul Chan—Selected Works," Schaulager Basel, 2014. Photo: Tom Bisig, Basel. Courtesy of the artist and Greene Naftali, New York.

p. 172            Anri Sala, *Long Sorrow*, 2005. Video still. Super 16 mm film transferred to single-channel HD video, stereo sound, color, 12 min. 57 sec. Courtesy of the artist and Hauser & Wirth. © Anri Sala / VG Bild-Kunst, Bonn 2016.

p. 178          Anri Sala, *Le Clash*, 2010. Video still. Single-channel HD video, 5.0 surround sound, color, 8 min. 31 sec. Courtesy of the artist and Hauser & Wirth. © Anri Sala / VG Bild-Kunst, Bonn 2016.

p. 182          Anri Sala, *The Present Moment (in D)*, 2014. Video stills. Single-channel HD video and nineteen-channel sound installation, color, 21 min. 30 sec. Courtesy of the artist and Hauser & Wirth. © Anri Sala / VG Bild-Kunst, Bonn 2016.

p. 184          Olga Chernysheva, *The Train*, 2003. Video still. Mini-DV camera, 7 min. 30 sec. Courtesy of the artist; Pace, London; Diehl, Berlin; and Foxy Production, New York.

p. 188          Olga Chernysheva, *Anonymous. Part 1 (Female Subject)*, 2004. Video still. Mini-DV camera, 8 min. Courtesy of the artist; Pace, London; Diehl, Berlin; and Foxy Production, New York.

p. 192          Olga Chernysheva, *Anabiosis. Fisherman-Plants*, 2000. One of eighteen analog color photographs, 105 × 70 cm. Courtesy of the artist; Pace, London; Diehl, Berlin; and Foxy Production, New York.

p. 196          Olga Chernysheva, *March*, 2005. Video still. Mini-DV camera, 7 min. 30 sec. Courtesy of the artist; Pace, London; Diehl, Berlin; and Foxy Production, New York.

p. 202          Yael Bartana, *Mary Koszmary (Nightmares)*, 2007. Video still. Courtesy of Annet Gelink Gallery, Amsterdam; and Foksal Gallery Foundation, Warsaw.

p. 206          Yael Bartana, *Mur i wieża (Wall and Tower)*, 2009. Video still. Courtesy of Annet Gelink Gallery, Amsterdam; and Sommer Contemporary Art, Tel Aviv.

pp. 212–13      Yael Bartana, *Zamach (Assassination)*, 2011. Video still. Courtesy of Annet Gelink Gallery, Amsterdam; and Sommer Contemporary Art, Tel Aviv.

p. 216        Paweł Althamer, *Common Task, Bródno District in Warsaw*, 2008. Courtesy of the artist; Foksal Gallery Foundation, Warsaw; neugerriemschneider, Berlin; and Open Art Projects, Warsaw.

p. 220        Paweł Althamer, *Common Task, Brussels*, 2009. Courtesy of the artist; Foksal Gallery Foundation, Warsaw; neugerriemschneider, Berlin; and Open Art Projects, Warsaw.

p. 224        Paweł Althamer, *Common Task, Munich/Sammlung Goetz*, 2012. Courtesy of the artist; Foksal Gallery Foundation, Warsaw; neugerriemschneider, Berlin; and Open Art Projects, Warsaw.

p. 228        Mladen Stilinović, *An Artist Who Cannot Speak English Is No Artist*, 1992. Acrylic on artificial silk, 139 × 198 cm. Installation view, Van Abbemuseum, Eindhoven, 2008. Photo: Boris Cvjetanovic. Courtesy of the artist, Zagreb / Collection Van Abbemuseum, Eindhoven.

pp. 232–33    Mladen Stilinović, *Subtraction of Zeros*, 1993. Fourteen parts, acrylic on canvas over cardboard, each 18.5 × 13 cm. Photo: Boris Cvjetanovic. Courtesy of the artist, Zagreb.

pp. 238–39    Mladen Stilinović, *Artist at Work*, 1978. Eight black-and-white photographs, each 30 × 40 cm. Courtesy of the artist, Zagreb.

p. 242        NSK Embassy Moscow, 1992. Setting up the flag at the building of the private apartment / art space at Leninsky Prospekt 12. Courtesy of Galerija Gregor Podnar, Berlin. © the artists.

pp. 248–49    IRWIN, *Retroavantgarde*, 1996. Mixed media, 120 × 200 cm. Courtesy of Galerija Gregor Podnar, Berlin. © the artists.

p. 256        IRWIN, *Was ist Kunst*, 2005. Installation view, 9th Istanbul Biennial, 2005. Courtesy of Galerija Gregor Podnar, Berlin. © the artists.

p. 260        NSK Passport, 1993. Courtesy of Galerija Gregor Podnar, Berlin. © the artists.

p. 264         Inga Svala Thorsdottir and Wu Shanzhuan, *Bird Before Peace 'An Appreciation'*, 1992/93. C-print, 120 × 148 cm, edition of ten. Courtesy of the artists.
Marcel Duchamp, *Fountain*, 1917. © The Estate of Marcel Duchamp / VG Bild-Kunst, Bonn 2016.

p. 272         Inga Svala Thorsdottir and Wu Shanzhuan, *Thing's Right(s)*, 1995. Article 1, A4 paper. Translation of Universal Declaration of Human Rights into Thing's Right(s) Declaration, first version. Article 1, page 1 of 30 articles, 31 pages. Courtesy of the artists.

pp. 276–77     Inga Svala Thorsdottir and Wu Shanzhuan, *Thing's Right(s) Declaration Article 4*, 2013. Lithography and screen print on Stonehenge paper, 55.5 × 73 cm, edition of 6, suite of 30. Printed at the Singapore Tyler Print Institute. Courtesy of the artists.

Colophon

Boris Groys
Particular Cases

Published by Sternberg Press

Editor:            Max Bach
Proofreading:      Mark Soo
Image research:    Louisa Nyman
Design:            Chad Kloepfer
Printing:          druckhaus köthen

ISBN 978-3-95679-221-2

© 2016 Boris Groys, Sternberg Press
All rights reserved, including the right of reproduction
in whole or in part in any form.

Sternberg Press
Caroline Schneider
Karl-Marx-Allee 78
D-10243 Berlin
www.sternberg-press.com